Edi

Aiblins
I'd be able,
bieldit under a dei‹

aiblins tae tak a rest.
But wi ma lug tae the grun
I lippen tae anither soun
The deid, aiblins, canna
bury their deid,
sae thrang wi the quick is the auld leid
that ye canna stap the threippin
o the thrapple. An gin
the speerit cauls tae ye,
ye maun bend yer lug.

There is nae choice.

Faced with MacDiarmid's centenary my heart sank as I anticipated a year of platitudes from those who know little and care less. There was bound, too, to be a backlash: any man of his kind is likely to stimulate opponents as fierce as their own passion. There are many in whom the mere mention of his name induces blue apoplexy.

I prefer apoplectic opposition to mindless platitudes. One journalist interviewing me was insistent that MacDiarmid had become an iconic figurehead on whose altar uncritical praise was heaped. What nonsense! It's important to remember the neglect he suffered in his lifetime, and the sheer poverty he and Valda tholed, almost seeming impervious to it. I remember his saying to me on one of two occasions when I visited him at Brownsbank that he had only become known here as a poet in the wake of recognition in the USA. The literati apart, Scotland sailed on until his death and beyond, largely blissfully unaware of his existence.

At last that begins to change, and suddenly you'd think he had been fêted and pampered like a Dylan Thomas, as widely acclaimed as the likes of Ted Hughes. But it's no wonder we find him so difficult to live with: his espousal of extremes alienates him. The Scots language still has its enemies who see no need to have access to their own tongue and have no awareness of its potential. Above all repugnant to many Scots is MacDiarmid's seeming boastfulness: that he dared to espouse such an ambitious agenda, to "assume the burden o his people's doom" – unGodly presumption to our Calvinistic, phoney humility.

For women he is a more serious problem. The Scottish literary scene until recently wore a very male face. The response of some women has been to reject both MacDairmid, as a stereotypical male figure, and Scottishness itself as in some way inimical to feminism or femininity. And all those symbols associated with Scottish nationalism have become similarly tainted with chauvinism: kilts, haggises, thistles which they see as masculine images, ironically exactly the same tartan kitsch, the kailyard fust that MacDiarmid railed all his life against. Not that I could or would claim him as an untiring fighter in the cause of feminism: he isn't. To be found in both his work and William Soutar's, superficially a much more amiable man, are statements which seem today crassly insensitive and chauvinist. But he was for setting free the human spirit everywhere. He was a nationalist only because he saw more chance of achieving that aim within a Scottish setting and compass than within any bland and characterless internationalism. I can only encourage women who have been put off hitherto to put aside their reservations and have a dip in to this extraordinary and indefinable poet. I'm sorry the 'equal opportunities' element of this issue does not boast more women, but that simply reflects the contributions we have received.

It's been a good year. Yes, there have been the vituperative attacks, chiefly in *The Herald*. But the main tributes have been somehow in the right vein, not sycophantic and mindless, but people grappling with this contermashious mass of contradictions, this "volcano spewing out fire and a lot of rubbish"; people attempting to relate some of his words to their own agenda to come up with something unique and original, in the free spirit he set abroad.

There are highlights I'll always cherish: the Biggar flower festival, in which his own community honoured him with the unlikely tribute of elaborate floral arrangements from all over the globe. Their "Time Bomb in an Armchair" exhibit became an electric talisman at the press conference held by *Artists for Independence* before the last general election. (Oddly, the press and TV all came, but nary a word was writ – what are they scared of?) The BBC's muckle celebration on the Birthday was a curate's egg of a piece, but in its scope and intention a real effort to represent without censorship a mercurial and difficult figure; I suspect that CMG would have slipped away to the alternative party organised by *Artists for Independence* at the 369 Gallery. Perhaps most moving of all the tributes was that organised by the Langholm folk, welcoming him at last, in growing but still not majority numbers, back tae the Muckle Toun. That's not to mention *Centrastus's* Alternative Burns Supper at the start of the year, or our own do still to come (Hutchison's Hall, Glasgow, 30th November, to which all are welcome).

Perhaps most important of all is the fact that the Biggar Museum Trust have been working away to renovate Brownsbank, and they've done it with tender loving care, restoring it to what it was like – not in 1978 when he died, but as Valda left it some ten years later. It's ready now to act as home to a writer who will soon be appointed.

This edition attempts to link in with that indefatigable spirit which inspires an increasing number of people. There are almost a hundred contributors, writers with widely differing ideas, styles – and ages – united by a single thread. Plainly, the spirit has been widely tasted and judged to be still a heady, reaming brew, if anything, "a thoosand *over* proof".

MacDiarmid's Spirit Burns On

Robert Alan Jamieson

There are times when I feel the spirit of Hugh MacDiarmid very close. Nights when I stagger the two miles up the road from the toon, a drunk man among the moonlit thistles, considering my wee bit of Scotland; days when the compromising of global perspective by local concerns calls to mind the point at which extremes must meet; moments at which the commitment required to make a literature of substance seems alien to the situation of the writer in Scotland, when his example, in spite of its anomalies, is an inspiration.

Scottish culture has entered a new phase since Chris Grieve's death in 1978. The march towards an elected Scottish assembly, which would have seemed a fitting epitaph to the man even if he was himself planning to vote agin it, stubbed its toe on the 40% figure in 1979. The publication of *Lanark* in 1981 heralded the remarkable rise of Glasgow as the hub of art in Scotland, culminating in the City of Culture extravaganza in 1990 and James Kelman's investiture as high heid yin in a new urban Scottish school of writing following his nomination for 'the Booker'.

Scotland's industrial shape has changed radically as well. The final dying twitches of the 'traditional' heavy industries in the lowlands and the breakdown of mining and fishing communities have been accompanied by the rise of Aberdeen as the centre of the oil industry in Europe and the establishment of silicon in the glen. North Sea oil, however short-lived, has tilted the country's economic balance towards the north-east and the north in general. There was even a time in the early eighties when the Old Firm had to give way to the New Firm of Aberdeen and Dundee United. In short, MacDiarmid's death may have coincided with the demise of Scotland as it had been. Increasingly, it seems likely it also coincided with the death of the Labour party as a political force capable of triumph in Britain as a whole.

But this might be making the mistake of equating MacDiarmid with Grieve, of forgetting that Hugh MacDiarmid was a spirit Chris Grieve realised around the age of 30, after C.M.Grieve had established himself as a writer of note. It must be remembered that Hugh MacDiarmid was not Grieve, though Grieve has become MacDiarmid in the national imagination. MacDiarmid was never flesh and blood, any more than Lewis Grassic Gibbon was. He has always been a spirit, conjured for us by the genius of C.M.Grieve, as Gibbon was by Leslie Mitchell. It might be argued that MacDiarmid cannot die, that he is immortal, an expression of essential Scottishness as the writer C.M.Grieve felt it. If so, we can imagine the spirit of MacDiarmid as pre-existing prior to this conjuring and naming by Grieve, and perhaps, that we may all experience to greater or lesser degrees the manifestation of this spirit at different times.

The difference between the manifestation of this spirit in Grieve, as MacDiarmid, and in lesser mortals is not merely one of genius but, more pragmatically, Chris Grieve's sense of Scotland's cultural state prior to MacDiarmid's birth: what he describes as 'diversity-in-unity' in the first *Scottish Chapbook*. Grieve already had a sense of the range of Scottish experience. The 'essential Scottishness' of other writers may take its form from a particular part of the country, from the Mearns in the case of Mitchell; from Edinburgh as with Garioch; Orkney as with Mackay Brown; or a split axis such as the Lochinver/Leamington Terrace of Norman MacCaig. Grieve knew something of the range of Scottish experience from his early life in Langholm, in Edinburgh, and Montrose before 'M'Diarmid' was even born in that miracle year of Modernism, 1922; and he, with the fully formed spirit of Hugh MacDiarmid, would travel more widely, to England and brief unhappy exile, to penury in the ultimate thule-thole of Whalsay, to Glasgow in the war years and back home at last to the southern hills at Brownsbank.

This sense of Scotland as a whole but diverse entity, including the experience of exile and his interest in Gaelic language and culture, is what marks MacDiarmid's spirit as essentially Scottish, rather than localised on any particular part of the country. For instance, it stands in sharp contrast to the focus of a William McIlvanney, who was quoted recently as having suggested that "Glasgow is what contemporary Scotland is all about"; a case in point, perhaps, of Derrida's view of Western thought as valuing presence over absence, a *violent hierarchy* which treats the people as if they were the place and leads to a kind of nostalgia for the passing of working-class industrial culture, not too far removed from Neil Gunn's mid-period nostalgia for the Muiresque Eden of life in the strath prior to the Clearances. Scotland's future potential lies not in what it has been but in what it might become. The absence of human life in vast tracts of the country is surely to be valued as a potential as much as the people themselves, however much the circumstances leading to that absence may rankle.

To me, as a Shetlander, McIlvanney's definition of Scotland is patently absurd, while the spirit of MacDiarmid is tangibly connected to my life through that house at Brough on Whalsay. I remember standing there between the four walls, roof open to the sky, in August 1985, thinking that Grieve's time there had made my early life in Shetland into a part of a wider 'Scottish Scene'; that he must have understood what it was to live out there on the edge of the world; that he knew the timeless lessons to be learned from the stones that had never been cut to form a tenement, could see beyond the urban skyline. This bit of his life during the 1930s is a bridge which enables me to feel part of a Scottish tradition as opposed to a purely Shetlandic one.

For all the undeniable achievements of Gray, Kelman, Leonard *et al* in the years since Grieve's death, they do not bridge this gap. Though I have come to understand and appreciate their work, and to feel a kinship, it has been through my imagination adapting to fit their world, as must happen with a Kafka or a Kerouac. Their work relates to the same urban Glaswegian matrix as McIlvanney's, though Gray, in his recent pamphlet *Why Scots should rule Scotland*, reaches out towards an idea of Scotland as whole. Glasgow's rebirth, and the establishment of a literature of the people of urban Scotland, is unquestionably a vital component in the making of a greater, contemporary, wholly Scottish literature. But it is not the whole machine.

Otherwise, there is a danger that the curse of success, imitation, of which there is already much evidence, may lead to an urban kailyard of inverted values, where the pub and the bookies replace the school and the kirk, where the breakdown of family and community becomes as much of a cipher for the state of Scottish society in the 1990s as the fictional perpetuation of the same was a cipher for the Kailyarders a hundred or so years ago, long after the passing of the world they described into unreality. It would be unfortunate if Scottish writing was to become trapped in timelessness once again.

If we are to believe at least one commentator, Christopher Harvie, writing in *The Arts of Alasdair Gray*, the 'serious' Scottish novel exists only in the status of a provincial variant which takes its turn in the spotlight every fifty years or so: Stevenson in the 1880s, Gunn, Linklater and Gibbon in the 1930s, Gray and Kelman in the 1980s. By this reckoning, we can expect the next successful 'serious' Scottish novel to emerge around about 2030. Harvie's theory is based not on some flaw in the Scottish imagination, but on Cairns Craig's idea that Scottish literature has become a victim of its own success, via the era of Scott and Galt, in establishing 'print capitalism' in London. The crucial point here is that Harvie's context is itself metropolitan. Of course there have been 'serious' Scottish novels which don't fit into his pattern, which haven't been successful in metropolitan terms, yet have succeeded in being recognised within Scotland. But it makes me wonder whether or not there is a necessary connection here, suggesting that to allow the London publishing houses to decide what work is given the rubber stamp as the voice of contemporary Scotland may be giving up control of our own culture into the hands, admittedly sometimes sympathetic, of a distant judge. It smacks just a little of the actions of a conquered people.

Once that control has been relinquished, we lurch once again towards the position of requiring yet another renaissance. While individual writers cannot be blamed for taking up the rewards of greater financial security when they themselves have worked to bring about the opportunity, that Scottish publishing is unable to continue to hold successful writers, to make and sell their books outwith Scotland, is worrying and leads to the establishment of a two-tier hierarchy within Scottish writing, of those who go on, like Gunn to book club recommendation, while others remain local – or provincial – in their provenance. While there's plenty of evidence that the reality doesn't match this clean division into two, what counts is not the reality but the way that it is perceived. It is bad enough if we believe that Scottish culture is split. Enough has been written about the divided Scottish psyche for this problem to require no further elaboration here.

Besides this difficulty, which is a happy one born out of one of those periods of success when Scottish writing is in the British spotlight, there is the darker question. What happens if it ceases to be, for whatever reason, the flavour of the book of the month in London? What about all those books which might have made a mark, that will be published in the doldrums before the next fair wind? Or those books that will not find a publisher because they don't fit the narrow view which London has of Scottish writing, because Scottish publishing hasn't established the economic base when things were going well to justify publication? The parallel between this situation and the political should be clear.

This returns me to the spirit of Hugh MacDiarmid. MacDiarmid's transformation of Scottish culture was effected from a Scottish base, as was that effected in the early eighties by the publication of *Lanark*, and the Kelman of *Not Not While The Giro* and *The Bus Conductor Hines*. The spirit of MacDiarmid, I believe, teaches us one lesson above all others, that literature and politics are interwoven. There is indeed a politics of literature which has as one of its constituents the business of publishing. We, as individuals, and collectively, can't rely on any external body, divine or otherwise, to intervene on our behalf. We have to make it happen for ourselves, as Grieve made it happen in Montrose in the twenties. Nobody will write the next chapter in the 'History of Scottish Literature' but Scots – and by 'Scot' I mean to concur with Alasdair Gray's definition, of those who have made their home in this country, rather than any spurious racial qualification. It's up to us, even if it means that we have to artificially create the circumstances for growth, by creating other selves to differ from, as Grieve and Mitchell did. Better that this differing be done within the confines of our cultural situation, than that we allow Scotland and Scottish culture to be divided irrevocably into *Sunday Post* and *Sunday Times (Scotland)*.

Personally, I don't want to strangle any ministers with copies of the *Post*. On the contrary, I want to feel as at ease about the *Sunday Post* side of Scottish life as an English person can about *The Archers*: fond, entertained if the urge takes me, but aware of its unreality. It's hard to imagine this happening widely without a fundamental shift in the way in which Scots view their own culture, away from the idea that whatever the metropolitan mind approves is superior to the local product. And in the spirit of MacDiarmid, let me close by offering an idea which, if implemented, might at least cause the suspension of the present system long enough for new patterns to emerge, while simultaneously allowing Scotland's writers and artists to make a political statement that may affect the way the Scottish electorate feel about their country, in time to influence the outcome of the next election.

In the edition of *Scotland on Sunday* immediately after the April 9th debâcle, Cairns Craig was quoted as saying that Scotland had declared cultural independence ten years ago. I thought, yes, but who noticed? In the months since then, monitoring the attempts to win a referendum out of a government that clearly has no intention of providing one, the seed sown has germinated. Scotland, I believe, must make a *formal* declaration of cultural independence. Or rather:

A FORMAL DECLARATION OF CULTURAL INDEPENDENCE.

The date could not be better selected than 1996, to coincide with the bicentenary of the death of Burns and the centenary of Gladstone's aborted bill, which would have provided an assembly a century ago. 1996 is also far enough away for those under contract to London to fulfil their contractual obligations, and for the organisation required to take shape. And don't forget 1996 is likely to be the year of, or the year preceding, the next general election. For the duration of that year, let Scotland's artists withdraw from London as an example to its MPs, in a kind of cultural strike. For the duration of that year, let us celebrate Scotland's diversity-in-unity. Let's arrange a nationwide series of events throughout the year, from Unst to Stranraer, from Point of Ness to Carter Bar. Let's strengthen connections with other European countries independent of London, indeed with other 'provincial' parts of the London empire, and invite the world's press to the party following the declaration, at midnight on Ne'erday, 1996.

I'm not suggesting that any culture grows fully independent of all others. History shows that to be a nonsense. In fact, were it not for the political ambition behind the idea, the term *cultural integrity*, in the sense of wholeness, would be preferable. 1996 should be a year of healing rifts, rather than creating them. A declaration of cultural independence is not so much a statement of a new departure as a demand for recognition of historical and contemporary difference. Scottishness is not the cause of Scottish culture nor indeed its effect. It is the free essence of humanity, but fixed in a particular form by a particular locality. The land pre-exists human habitation. Essential Scottishness, as I have used the term above, is a deep feeling for that land and its situation in relation to the rest of the world, not rooted in the past but in the present moment, in our individual perceptions of what this land is and has been to the peoples who have lived here over the centuries – and what it could be. A sense of Scottishness is not something we are born with but something we grow into, and this sense is present in all who come to make their home here, in diverse ways. We need not feel ourselves restricted by Scottishness because it is only what each of us choose to make of it. Though some of the raw material of our culture may come from external sources, it is processed locally – in literary terms, for instance, the particular Scottish rendering of the Troilus & Cressida story given by Robert Henrysoun.

So cultural independence in the Scottish context relates to the distinctive Scottish traditions *of use* of the materials of education, law, religion, philosophy, the creative arts etc., and the right to continue to use these as we who live here choose to do. It is here that the political sphere intersects the cultural. Scotland, the place, exists. Its culture grows out of the experience of living in that place and that experience is diverse, but can be unified in the word *Scotland,* if we can make it meaningful, so that all its constituent parts feel included. That meaning must depend to some degree on freedom to pursue its own political objectives. Without an assembly, the meaning of *Scotland* is indistinct, not only in comparison with Britain, but also with those constituent parts of Scotland which have elected councils.

1996 could be the best advert for Scotland there has ever been. And after the year is over, artists can return to the metropolitan base if they so choose, free in the knowledge that they have at least done their bit. This is something Scotland's artists for independence can do without the agreement of Westminster, an exercising of democratic freedom in the cultural arena when it is denied in the political. The MacDiarmid spirit is willing us on. Let's put April 9th 1992 behind us, celebrate Grieve's centenary (MacDiarmid's won't actually occur until 2022), and look to the future – to 1996.

Seek da Philosopher's Stæn

Time, oot o da mirk o endlis nicht
Wrext, woke up an startit slippin
slowly doon da steps fæ heaven,
a treacle o luv – da firstmæst
an da best o aa da medicines

Da first jewelled licht shon oot
fæ quhar a voice wis peesterin
a vision o a future quhar da present
micht tak bræth an meet da past dær,
face t'face, an ken dey're kyn

da voice wis peesterin oot
a gowden vision

fin da philosopher's stæn
da touchstæn o aa truth
dat, no da elixir o life
is da true saat ye maun seek

though nane'll ever ootrin dæth
fæth'll mak it certain
in dis dær lies da key
t'unlock pure an abs'lute ræson

wi hit you'll ken t'spleet
da subtile fœ da fixed
da sure fœ da belief
distil pure science oota faith

Tœ fin sic abs'lute in
da infinite, indefinite an finite
is da single great wark, dat da sages
trowe da ages aa maun try

fir da infinite is unmade alwis
quhile da finite's infinitely made
an though dey run tagithir till
da treacle sets, dey nevir meet

da vision o da voice
sent fok oot wi pilgrim's rod

lang years da seekers wrocht an socht dis stæn
da fast foond o aa fæth an transmutation.
Dey did da wark o Hermes, o da Sun
a secret no t'be exposed t'air
or tæ da een o da profane

in da chaos o creation dis abs'lute is still uncertain
though in mony aald an wise-læk warks it's written
o da lent o ferly wirkins we can lippen quan
da stæn o da philosopher is set inida place
dat destiny sæ richtfilly has named fir wis

Paradiso: *on dreaming of my deathmask*

There is a devil in the world for each of us, uniquely,
who'll play the tempter to our messianic better selves,
as each of us will play the devil to another's saviour role.

I say this as I've met mine, both, the tempter and the saviour.
When I was playing Jesus, I was martyred by my abstinence,
and when I took the part of Satan, God made me hate myself.

As Jesus, I hung saint-like on a cross of love of children,
while Satan's play engrossed me in its web of steely cursing,
till I came to love the beast that wriggles deep inside my skin.

Now I have woken up to my humanity and simultaneously accept
the animal house in which I rest my soul, as long as life meanders,
I want to settle children in the harrowed gates of Hell.

These words, my children, grow strange to me as earth rotates
and suns are piled up in the west. By this, I know that there is rest,
as promised in the gaze of he, my better self, at Death.

GOLD, gold

this world is old
old as the hills it came from

the men from under earth
first dug it out and gorged it

the little people of the firth
who painted pictures
they knew the golden sands
the ships that came
if they believed

what superstition brings
sweet reason turns back out –
but what do reasonable folk attend
if not the golden section?

Robert Alan Jamieson

Jack Withers

Never Again

Barely heard. From behind closed doors
Tongues twitter. Sharp knives clatter.
It is night. Fierce red light shifts.
Through a cluttered sky as stars
Flare beyond our sight. We're blind.

Those sensuous fingers can't be yours
But the past's, which lingers. Let's
Listen for that broken music of the
People. It is also ours and more so
In coming momentous hours. Cherish
That harmony that once was. But now
It is almost no more. It dies. A cripple.

Persistent echoes are still heard. Minds
Harden. And across the great waste shimmers
A hot horizon. Too many never ever perceive
Or even hear the thistle rustle. Our love
May surface again. And yours too. Just whistle.

Dust clears. Dark laments rise and fill our
Ears. Yes, we hear, we hear the airs. Each
Note addresses those who would kill. Crash
Of sounds, orchestra of revenge and hate
As minds no longer wander. For we remember.
We knew, and say never again. No, never again.

Gordon Legge

Beast's a Beast

Yi git yirsel aw het up n fankled
Ower hings thit dinnae matter
No whin yi see thi likesi yon
Wi no twa bits thit hing thigither

Wi wir skinny fancies n wir coy responses
Wir like Pilate wi thi water
Goad love us till wi aw act like kenning
Whit is n isnae wirth wir bother

Some thoughts about the man; and music; and two poems

Roderick Watson

Hugh MacDiarmid

And stood in a burst o' sun
Glowerin' at the bit broken grun.

If the thousand-headed heather were to start piping
in the wind on slopes above Brownsbank   then you
would not hear it: and I might cry at the tunes under
the hills and you would point to the edge of the peat bog
to delicate   scattered   broken shells   far from the sea
– crumbs on the hungry rim of the water's brown mouth
which brings every living thing in time to the throat
of this old   soft   acid   land   – and you
would crouch by those calcined shards in the glaur and say
'Rain on the ocean's bed' and 'The Pleiades'   and I would see
mottled lips with the imprint of your pipe   move
and guess at the words   and the beautiful connections
but it would be all   without hearing them fall.

It was 'Crystals like Blood' that made me think 'Yes! This is what poetry
should be. For me, this is what poetry is about.' – The precision of its poly-
syllabic diction was almost like prose, and yet full of intense feeling; then

there was the surprise of its connections, with a geologist's description of cinnabar slipping into the memory of a loved one's death, in a poem which married the animate with the inanimate, or more accurately, which refused to recognise that there need be any meaningful distinction between what is 'alive' and what is not. This was before I learned of the Metaphysical poets, and Eliot's dubious notion of a 'dissociation of sensibility', the supposed split between thought and feeling in later English poetry. I must have been about 19 when I read 'Crystals like Blood' for the first time. For me the experiential world could never be split into a place of things or facts *versus* feeling. The abstract world *is* passionate, a place of icy exaltation (Carlyle knew it), full of scorn and rage and also tenderness, compassion and surprise. I knew it in my bones.

Which is why I listen to the jazz of John Coltrane – headlong flight in what a critic called 'sheets of sound'. And I have never forgotten Coltrane's own passing comment, that he tried to start his solos as if 'in the middle of the sentence'. If you have heard his work, you'll recognise the power of his use of repetition and the awesome abstract majesty and the surprise of his opening notes. The same quality is why I think the Norwegian saxophonist Jan Garbarek is the finest player in the world today, though English critics frequently call him 'cold'. Ah... but there's cold, and *cold!* Nobody who's ever thrilled to pibroch would have any difficulty with the intensely controlled, yet sheer free-flying *passion* of Garbarek's work, with a tone that can whisper like a bamboo flute, or sizzle and freeze like dry ice. 'Crystals like Blood', indeed.

So it was 'Crystals like Blood', and the prose of James Joyce, that showed me how all this could be done with words. (I'm lost in that shadow, but at least it's a big shadow.) For I have always responded to the many-sided variety of *things* in the physical world. I remember being almost overwhelmed by the particularity of their signs when I was a wee boy. – Yeats's "Old kettles, old bottles, and a broken can,/ Old iron, old bones, old rags..." such fragments were always the true source material of life and thought and art for me, and I hope that a little of their rawness and their unmediated nature should always survive in my own writing.

At a recent poetry reading at Stirling, Seamus Heaney said that there were poems where you worked for weeks to smooth your words down to a perfect lyric shape; and then there were poems like a wheelbarrow where you piled everything in. – That's me with the wheelbarrow. And if I have to classify how my imagination works, it seems to be a kind of intuitive collage or bricolage in action; but carefully pondered too, and fettled a little, to make the marriage of fact and feeling, those beautiful connections – shine.

MacDiarmid knew about this. And Joyce – with his copy of Homer in one hand, and the Dublin Post Office Street Directory in the other – and I sometimes think that to want to make beauty out of such passion and such pedantry is a very Scottish or Celtic thing. "Het water beneth cauld ice", indeed. Or crystals like blood. Or the marks of history scored on the face of a stone, and the minute scratches on a vinyl disc which release such torrents of music from the past. Maybe the stone would do the same, if only we knew how to play it.

I thank MacDiarmid for the stones. Though they were always there.

The slope claims every body in the end. Only words and music, and the music of words, fly.

The Slope

(For John Coltrane and 'By the Numbers')

to start in the middle of the sentence   running down
the slope towards the incoherent rubble of the shore:
where I told how each scored surface keeps
its own record of the forces crossed on the journey
to bring it there   – names   signs   single
words   broken cries and whole lines
torn from different histories   – all going
the same way   – all tilted into the sea;

where we turned our faces to the sun as waves of light
marched down in concentric rings   ordered and neat
as the dykes that curve across the brae   to say
'You can live here. You can't stay'; where Christopher
found a shattered sprig of cast-iron   curled
like ivy around a name   – it spelled 'The Singer' –
so we hung it from the branches of an oak whose trunk
was bent by air   blowing for years on a single theme.

In a house on the hill towards the end of the day
my father stands with his back to the sky and a book
in his veined hand. I cannot see my mother's face
for she turns away to watch a little girl
rolling on the yellow grass   towards the door
the tree   the shore   the sun.   Joanna shrieks
and laughs at the power of the world to draw her down
to join the discrete things at the bottom of the slope.

And I think of those spearing   repeated   notes
that call from tiny wavering tracks and fill my room
with your lost presence: where the tenor swoops
and climbs its way beyond the edge of the phrase
tearing sheets of sound from the unfinished sentence
– and floating through–   down   down   down.
And down and down and down and down   and down
down and down   and down   and down and down

– until there's nothing else to say at all…

Roderick Watson

Where Now the Herring Bards?
for Ian Abbot

George Gunn

> Faxed in here they got your space
> two letters from life on the south bank
> of the Ness, as for me
> I'm still here & splendidly ignored

Disappearing up your own arse is a physical and psychological impossibility, unless you are a doyen of EngLit. It may appear strange to accuse the piles, bundles, anthologies, mag-fulls etc of current Scottish poetry which have recently appeared, of this impossibility, but sadly I think it is the case.

It may have been a long year now since my mother slammed her last ration book into the drawer but not even her democratic Presbyterian eye and heart could have dreamed up these contemporary buckets of soor crowdie and dull plops. Oh my, what are we to make of them? My feeling is that if contemporary Scottish poetry is a herring then the fish has no bones. From my teeth I pick out and spit back a few odd ones at this dead kipper. This, of course, is the official kipper I'm talking about. The itinerant, unofishial (if you like) herring is a fish of a different shoal, oh yes.

Like John West it is the fish that the ofishial kipper rejects that makes it a gey cheuch chew. Hard to swallow? You bet.

The ofishial herring is a lonely swimmer. And yet the poor creature isn't helped by those other fish of doom. I'm thinking here of one particular breed who are small and stocky, live in the ocean's murky depths, whose eyesight is poor and has a fatalistic tendency to wrap itself up in a newspaper. Has this fish the second sight? Of the contemporary poetic herring, this doom fish bloobs, yea he is old in years and if not dead then 70, 80, 90, even a hundred years hang heavy from his fins. It has to be admitted: it cannot be easy being an old herring bard, or even a dead herring bard. If this was not bad enough the sad sea supper fish asks, where are the poetry smolts, the herring bards of the future? Nowhere, he mournfully concludes, rubbing up against his half-gill. From the deep dark ocean, wrapped up in a newspaper, again it has to be admitted, it cannot be easy to see the bright young shoals of herring bards swimming in the clean fresh water of the surface. But is the water fresh and are they even swimming?

The problem with the newspaper fish of doom is that down in the depths you live in a world of continual present, and a black one at that.

It suits the cynicism of the age to say that there are no young poets of any worth, none who can compare with the greats recently dead or up in their years. The future is a scary place – for example: newspapers might have wrapped up themselves and the right to free speech along with the last doomy critic fish. This current brouhaha about MacDiarmid only goes to belie the nasty and belittling sniping that his work has had to endure since his death in 1978. The very reaction he spent his life fighting and raging against is currently feeling confident enough to try and undermine him. Witness the recent spate of hate letters in the Glasgow *Herald*.

So, herring bards, beware. They are trying to gut the big fish. Shove in yer heids an growl. The problem is that the growling, the real voice of discontent, the ever challenging, radical criticism of all assumed aqua quo, takes place outwith the pages (or tins) of anthology, academy and the marble halls (or tanks) where the publishers, editors and critics obviously live and swim.

It's almost as if the herring bards of Scotland have breathed out their charter of relief and blooped "Ach, thank god Shug MacDiarmid did all that innovative stuff for us all those years ago. Noo wae can just get on wae bein smaa herrin."

Outside the established boundaries of herring bards there is a motley guild of fish gutters desperate to examine the entrails of all manner of fish. What they seek is the truth. Their blades are sharp and their voices are very loud. So, beware, herring bards: the life of a herring is a short one. Safety in numbers is a landlubbers' myth. And beware also, herring bards, the big sudron net. It would not be so bad if they ate you, or even roasted you in hell, but what they want is your skin (I've heard tell that herring-skin shoes are very comfortable to walk in) for they are a rare breed of fishing taxidermist and your fate, dear herring bards, is to be displayed in a glass case in a London Museum. London, for those of you who don't know, is a big aquatic museum on dry land (for now) in England. I suggest to you all, this is not the place you should be. Far better, I would further suggest, that you join together with the itinerant fish gutters with the sharp blades and the very loud voices and get back into the real sea. After all, what would Scotland be without its herring?

I put it to anyone who will listen that Hugh MacDiarmid was a traditional poet because as anyone who knows anything about culture, tradition is constantly radical, forever renewing itself, redefining itself to meet the aspirations of the people. MacDiarmid, in his herring bones, realised this. He took us all on a great journey. All bards do. Lately the herring bards have lost this sense of their place in the development of the shoal. And the poetry reflects this. In the long run the firth, the field, the glen and the street matter more than the marble halls where the middle and upper classes seem to think poetry lives.

Of course, I'm totally, one hundred percent, a biased herring. But I urge you all, my fellow herring bards, be brave and remember the words of great Shug MacHarringaid hissel: "Soom on, bonnie herrin, soom on".

For MacDiarmid 11/8/92

To be so far adrift as now
from our historic place
to walk an empty street
to see an empty face
to catch your frightened breath
when a cold wind passes
to walk the unploughed earth
of a land no land surpasses

There is an empty space in Europe
that is shaped like Scotland
a two headed golden eagle
we fail to understand
but to build the ship, the ship of love
to seek out the un-sung song
& sing it to the stars above
to come home to ourselves & belong

both MacDiarmid & Grieve walked
this unwalked road, & walked her long

Glory

In Memoriam CMG

The birk forest shimmers silver green
& across the hill beats the blood purple heather
the rock black river sings to the sea
"the summer, the summer, the summer"

The bug-like sheep have been freed from their wool
& cars hiss along the snakeing road
The distant mountains move forward still
& the sky is a changing mood

In the hotel bar the murderers hang up their guns
& the cowing beaters slump in their shed
the range-rovers are parked like a halted cortège
from the land of the living dead

the foxgloves sway in the gentle wind
the rowan berries wait for their bitter end

George Gunn

Carrying MacDiarmid On

W N Herbert

I sometimes have dreams of massive books, tomes, being slowly borne across the landscape. Once I had to carry this great book up a mountainside and deposit it in a brook. Once I was standing on a bridge and I saw this book the size of a boat come floating towards me. In dreams you struggle to read and remember these transitory texts, but the few phrases that survive into daylight are so abrupt, so nonsensical, you don't quite know what to do with them. When I view the minuscule amount of serious criticism of MacDiarmid that has gone on, and when I consider those two great volumes, the so-called *Complete Poems*, with all their contradictions, hints, and great leaps of inspiration, I sometimes feel that Scotland has treated MacDiarmid like I treat my dreams. As a nation we stir and pass our hand across our brows in bafflement, *en masse* we sit up and blink, trying to remember something significant that... no, it's gone, it's evaded us.

How else is it that I, as a poet writing in Scots, have to listen to reviewers spout precisely the same pious cant about my language as MacDiarmid received? No, I am told, Scots is long gone, dead, it will not do to speak ill of the dead, to speak it at all.

Or, worse, it is claimed that the language has survived, but in a useless fossilised manner, in which all the spellings must fall so, all the grammar must be like this, in which the vocabulary may only be drawn from such and such a sphere. What this does is to damn MacDiarmid by overmuch praise, to pretend that only such a *great writer* could success-fully do something different, like Synthetic Scots, with the language. It is to lock him into his magnificent achievement and deny a context to his successors. According to this mentality, we may write in Scots, but only if we are content to footle about with the Great Man's leavings.

This is what was done with Burns, in that Hogg's separate yet related corpus was perceived by the Great Man lobby as being sub-Burnsian, rather than as the next stage of a progressing tradition that had begun, not with Burns, but with Ramsay and the still-neglected Fergusson. It is the mentality of the interferer, the fankler, more concerned with how they can get a tick-like grip on something than on how that something may work, develop, grow. It is the mentality that corrects spellings rather than (a purer Scottish tradition) observing and collating all variations in spelling – the writer of blurbs rather than the compiler of dictionaries.

Let me put my view of MacDiarmid and my use of Scots (and, indeed, English) in due perspective. I would seriously dispute that MacDiarmid's interest in Scots was principally to do with nationalist questions of the integrity of the language and its use in an independent Scotland. In the same way I would dispute that his interest in Marxism stemmed entirely from his genuine desire to liberate the working class of Scotland. And by the same token, I very much doubt that his interest in science was solely inspired by his burning need to reconcile all specialisms. Principally, entirely, solely. MacDiarmid was, above all and before any other considerations, a poet obsessed by the function of language.

Valéry's discussion of language, in *The Art of Poetry*, is probably the best introduction to the attitude of mind, rather than the public and political declarations, which drove MacDiarmid, not only to Scots, but to all his obscure vocabularies:

> In other terms, in practical or abstract uses of language, the form—that is the physical, the concrete part, the very act of speech—does not last; it does not outlive understanding; it dissolves in the light; it has acted; it has done its work; it has brought about understanding; it has lived.
>
> But on the other hand, the moment this concrete form takes on, by an effort of its own, such importance that it asserts itself and makes itself, as it were, respected; and not only remarked and respected, but desired and therefore repeated—then something new happens: we are insensibly transformed and ready to live, breathe, and think in accordance with a rule and under laws which are no longer of the practical order—that is, nothing that may occur in this state will be resolved, finished or abolished by a specific act. We are entering the poetic universe.

MacDiarmid was a symbolist poet in precisely this way; he was obsessed with the power of language to conjure the poetic state, and in hot pursuit of any and every discourse which promised to yield up this power. This is what he means in 'Gairmscoile' when he states "...there's forgotten shibboleths o' the Scots/ Ha'e keys to senses lockit to us yet..." He has precisely the same attitude towards Gaelic, as 'In Memoriam: Liam Mac'Ille Iosa' indicates: "...those shades of difference in sound that Gaelic/ – Shibboleths of infinity – alone possesses..."

And this approach to language also governed his approach to the separate discourses of Marxism and science. When MacDiarmid says, in 'The Seamless Garment', "Look, Wullie, here is [Lenin's] secret noo/ In a way I can share it wi' you..." two things are happening. One is obviously the lesson in Leninist thinking, but the other is just as significant. It is MacDiarmid laying claim to another powerful discourse. And finally, in *In Memoriam James Joyce*, after all the book lists, namedropping, polysyllables, gobbets of every language he can find a TLS article about, *et cetera, et cetera*, it is Valéry's attitude towards "the poetic universe" he is echoing when he says:

> Everlasting layers
> Of ideas, images, feelings
> Have fallen on my brain
> Softly as light.
> Each succession has seemed to bury
> All that went before.
> And yet, in reality,
> Not one has been extinguished...

When I look as a writer at MacDiarmid's work in all his languages I'm not looking for something to praise or despise. It is one of the curses of our culture that it assumes discrimination means saying one thing is good *because* another thing is bad, or vice versa. MacDiarmid criticism is full of people "preferring" one period, one poem (usually the easiest) to another. Discrimination seems to me to be the process of learning that particular way in which each thing can be seen as good, and learning that, by changing these rules, each thing can also be seen as bad. So I am concerned with what is useful to me in his work, with what survives the test of my separate interests, with what can be carried away. This act of appropriation becomes, for me, the reinterpretation of a tradition which I then consider myself to be carrying on.

So Valéry's remarks and MacDiarmid's practice make sense for me in the context of, say, what Michael J Fischer is saying in "Ethnicity and the Post-Modern Arts of Memory" when he points out

> …as Benjamin and Freud in differing ways pointed out, language itself contains sedimented layers of emotionally resonant metaphors, knowledge, and associations, which when paid attention to can be experienced as discoveries and revelations. Indeed much of the contemporary philosophical mood (in literary criticism and anthropology, as well as in philosophy) is to inquire into what is hidden in language, what is deferred by signs, what is pointed to, repressed, implicit, or mediated.

For me it is self-evident that my Scots is being repressed when it is criticised by people who clearly would rather I was not using it, whether at the level of reviewing or at the more serious level of awards like the Gregory. My Scots is not a copy of English, matching the integrity of English orthography and dictionary definitions, it is an active criticism of such orthodoxies, a deconstruction by example. To criticise me, as some writers have done, for then writing in conventional English, is to stumble over the most elementary constituent of such a deconstruction: *my discourses include English*. Scots is not some Utopian alternative to English, it is merely the presence of further possibilities; to flash a bit of jargon, it is an attempt at the dehierarchisation of linguistic hegemony.

For one English-reader to understand one of MacDiarmid's lyrics is important because it suggests to that English-reader that Scots is a language capable of doing something more than English; that criticises and, finally, extends English. That is the spirit in which I write Scots poetry. (It's a pity this point would also be true of so many Scots readers of MacDiarmid, who seem only too content in their couthy ghetto.)

from Pier's testament

We hae nae bullfechts, Lorca, nae bluidy fanes;
thi deil's awa doon aa wir couthy lanes,
but i thi hert o Dundee smerts an irin ee,
ee helt open against aa thi grime an grieshoch
o a fartan partin, explodin loabstir o
wir seik-sunk an fast-deean industries;

an wi ma lassie an ma past Eh am
as Scoatlan is tae England, that
wad brak awa but
fur waant o waantan tae, and
thi surefire thocht Eh dinna need
a naishun o masel.

An ocean-notion is ma quotient o
oor sunderan o sex
an denshauch styles o dream,
an aa Eh cud speir o a muse noo
wad be as in thi Norn tung
MacDiarmid huz sae nobily mis-sung:

"Eh'm thon *brungi-queedin heloor*,
yin aa dandied up i thi stoor
o anithir country's licht;
Eh'm thon admittedly frichtfu sicht,
a *druyll-shlaaget hjok-finni*;
yin wi a burial moond furra minnie,

a *heloor* i thi *hoorikooris*,
a *rodastab*, wha sees thi muses' houris
lyk thi oors o sun be siftit;
yin wha, lyk a whale's vertebrae
plunkd i thi road up thi brae,
canna be shiftit.

A sturdy *hurdik* lyk yirself,
lunkin owre thi shingil-shelf,
wad hae nae struggle
ridan a *shoopiltie* orra *nyuggil*:
but can yi find a finanshul backir
oan thi *shoosamillyabakka?*"

Glossary:

---

brungi-queedin – white breasted; *heloor* – a half-dreaming or irritated person;
druyll-shlaaget – struck by a troll, pixillated; *hjok-finni* – somebody found in a
burial mound; *hoorikooris* – a state between sleeping and waking; *rodastab* –
someone who will not get out of the way, or a stool made from the vertebrae
of a whale; *hurdik* – a big woman; *lunkin* – limping (the trolls were fabled to
dance with a limp); *shoopiltie* – water spirit or kelpie; *nyuggil* – sea-serpent;
shoosamillyabakka – indeterminate area between sea and banks.

As important, if not more so, than the freeing of Scots from the
tyrannies of the grammarians, is the recognition of a distinctively Scottish
range of subjects in English. Again, MacDiarmid is the standard by which
this range of possible discourses can be measured. The element of
obfuscation here seems very clear when I view the cloth-eared reception
of MacDiarmid's last great experiments.

MacDiarmid's last poems represent a concerted effort to absorb into poetry a number of important discourses. These include science as a topic and as a vocabulary; academic discourse, whether at the level of incorporating critical theory, or simply in terms of bibliographical information; the topic range and methods of approach of journalism, cinema, travel writing, and other popular media. Significantly, he imported the whole tone of prose discourse, not because he wished to sound boring, but because he wished to talk at greater length than poetry can, if it's bound by bourgeois conceptions of the lyric. Finally, he carried a great deal further than any poet since Drummond of Hawthornden the idea that one can simply absorb other texts wholesale into one's work, if the fabric is strong enough.

What this effort represents is, in my opinion, the direct opposite of its normal interpretation. Poetry is, tacitly, by its position in our university syllabi and in our cultural organs, held to be an important art form. Science, academic jargon, journalism, the "prosaic" world in its entirety, is held to be too normal, even too dull, to be part of this exalted sphere. In fact the opposite is the case. Science is obviously the dominant discourse of our era in the way that Christianity was pre-Galileo, pre-Newton, pre-Darwin. Everyone watches television, goes to the cinema, buys some form of newspaper – and doesn't feel integrated with society if they do not. Students in colleges and universities are far more interested in getting hold of the appropriate critical jargon, than they are in reading a poetic text, because this critic, this -ism will tell them what it is appropriate to read as well as how to read it. Poetry, obviously, is being exalted only to be excluded.

Ezra Pound tells us that "Literature is news that stays news". For my generation of writers, such concepts of permanency and status have been totally eroded by the explosion of both the media and the academic system. Poetry now seems more a minority concern than ever, and therefore it is obliged to look to the other forms of transmitting "news" for its methods and, to a degree, for its subjects.

Poets like Robert Crawford, David Kinloch, Kathleen Jamie, Alan Riach and Peter McCary all seem to share a common concern with the discourses of television, historical and cultural studies, cinema, linguistic theory, science. Riach and McCarey in particular have demonstrated that they are not afraid of the found poem, that great underminer of the property system. Such interests are hardly limited to Scotland; but what links the Scottish poets I have listed, and what seems particularly relevant to MacDiarmid, is that all these writers are fascinated by the vocabularies of information.

Few of them share MacDiarmid's optimistic belief in the capacity of science to change our lives positively, or in the willingness of an audience to read a poetry containing such optimisms. Most of their work appears to be a critique of the simplistic ideologies which underline much of the information our culture peddles as a kind of holy writ. But all of them are engaged with taking up MacDiarmid's challenge to these dominant discourses that poetry should not be excluded, that the poetic perspective adds something integral to a holistic world view.

What MacDiarmid says to me and to these other writers can be summed up in a few words. For instance: all words dazzle on first being encountered, dwindle through intimacy, and are reborn through obsession. All words, all vocabularies. Every word is a shibboleth; there is no word which will not let you into a realm, a psychology, a dream, the possibility of a new fiction if you allow it to. Equally, there is no word which will not erect barriers, be incomprehensible, sound ugly if you approach it with prejudice, with a lazy eye, with a lazy ear. Read dictionaries, read everything. Read without assumptions as to the status or use of the text. Read like a thief. For instance:

The Pictish Archive

Listen to the pages of the seasons fall
across the Grampians and Angus. Listen to
spring bring its normal hail like ink
that winter will again obliterate.
This is the manuscript on which
the Picts wrote "homestead", "village", "fort"
in their dismembered speech. Listen to
the pages of the landscape whisper as they turn;
it's like a copy of the Book of Kells from which
all traces of the text are being scraped.
The summer grass becomes a vellum on which
the hairs have all grown back.
Only their stones' old pictograms
still float upon the ploughshares' waves,
like illuminations that have been scrubbed
of colour, or like scenes from
a scattered silent film. Their symbols are
as simple as a Keaton sight-gag;
they could be shots from his
unmade *immrama*, they could be out-takes from
the *spielmannsepen* of the jumblies.
Words here have lost their command of time,
they shift like phrases from
Slim Gaillard's *Voutionary*, drift
like the spoofs caught up
in a supplement to Jamieson's
Dictionary of the Scottish Language;
as the Ogam on the stone at Brandsbutt
puts it: "IRATADDOARENS".

Listen to the emptied pages hint
at the revision of myths, the alternatives

to gospels that may
occupy the silences between
our usual Gilgameshes and Ulyssiads.
They are like the space that's been chipped out
within an elaborate frame, halfway down
the back of the cross-slab at Cossans.
The nameless fish-tailed serpents whose
two bodies provide the borders to
so many stones, enclose
the crescent and V-rod and
the double disc and Z-rod: messages
delivered to the synapses as
clear as a traffic signal
without a road. The censored panel sits
beneath, then a double rank
of proud horses and their riders,
who could be Nechtan, who could be Bridei,
son of Maelchon, who could be Resad,
son of Spusscio: "Drosten
ipe Uoret ett Forcus", as
the notes at St Vigeans explain,
"The inscription is simple but untranslatable."

Listen to the lowest frame at Cossans:
a boat is bearing something big to somewhere else;
it could be a coffin, it could be
a symbol stone itself.
I can hear the Pictish page still turning,
as though the letters wouldn't stick
and rattle from it as it turns.
I am caught up by
the fall of meanings;
I am press-ganged into
the voyages of pages.
Whatever was removed from the central frame
has now become a symbol, not of decoding,
but of the removal of all codas,
the promise that
our definitions will be renewed,
like the lizard's tail, or
St Orland's fingernail.

The fictions shall be
our only translators,
the word is our incompetent,
our only sailor.

W N Herbert

Customer Service

Brent Hodgson

"A speek thi trooth," said the Customer Service man.

"Thi bried is rotten," said Maggie, grey-haired Maggie, outspoken though seventy.

"Gie mi it," said the Customer Service man who took the loaf and kickt it high. The loaf floated across the supermarket above the checkout girls in their gingham pinafores, the loaf bounced through the door, the door automatic-opening. The man smiled and spoke to Maggie. "A speek thi trooth. Yon loaf was gud. Wia upn an unner A goat it oot thi door ina wunner."

"Thanks pal," said Maggie, "how can I repay you?"

"Help me hen, help me build a tunnel."

"Whit! A'm goan oan seventy," replied Maggie, a one-wife and companion to Jedd her man.

"Help me dig a subterranean passage under Ben Lomond," the man requested.

"No way."

"Why no?"

"Cawz caurs cummin frae Glesga wid miss the mountain-top view."

The man put his hand on his red cheek, his cheek red as a Jersey tomato, his hand the hand of a man not afraid to wield the cold club hammer, the broad-mouthed shovel, the rechargeable batteries of the heavy-duty industrial torch, the torch capable of throwing illumination into the darkest corner.

"If I live and last this day I shall remember your kind advice," said the Customer Service man. "Here was I thinking that a tunnel constructed through the belly of Ben Lomond would save the northbound motorist a steep climb. I planned to build a tunnel with a dual carriageway, the carriageway straight without hairpin bends or dodgy roundabouts."

Maggie moved away and hove to the nearest checkout girl, her name Mairi; Mairi the daughter of Donald, the son of Owen, the son of Fergus, the son of Carrol.

Six times did Mr McKee poke the apple doughnut, the dough containing ascorbic acid, the acid due to its inherent chemical properties imparting to the white bleached flour comprising the dough, the quality of improvement, apparently.

The doughnut is stale, it does not bounce," announced Mr McKee, banking executive and owner of a four-wheeled touring caravan, to the figure standing at the Customer Service desk.

"Bring it back tomorrow," said the supermarket employee. "I'll drop it on your foot-bones and break your foot-bones by doing so."

"I shall report you to the Manager," spoke smoothly Mr McKee. "He is a friend of mine, his age is twenty-five, his skin is unblemished, his rise to fame sudden and entirely explainable in modern management terms."

Said the Customer Service man to Mr McKee: "I watched you. You poked ninety doughnuts in succession. Each doughnut was manufactured in a bakery on the same day. On that day the dough mix was consistent, its composition subject to strict laws with regard to size, weight, colour, ingredients and water content. The shelf-life of the apple doughnut is another matter, but upon the outer wrapper you will find written data, of interest to the caterpillar, the cricket-playing-batter, the Mad Hatter and those eejits bearing free tickets to the Henley Regatta."

"My wife Rayolene, of Australian origins, eats doughnuts. I am upset; your dissertation has unbalanced me. My wife is house-bound. I do the shopping. One day I went home early. The velvet curtains in the lounge were drawn. I peeped in. Four and twenty housewifes sitting in a row reading romantic novels. My wife amongst them. Reading books of sand and sea, sun-glasses and sex," sobbed Mr McKee.

The Customer Service man shifted his stance, he withdrew from the recesses of the pockets of his loose-hanging, Harris-tweed jacket his hands. "Gone are the days when a learned man could tell the nature of a sickness befallen on a house by the colour of smoke rising from the heather thatch."

"We have central heating, the fuel gas, the bill issued quarterly, the bill paid promptly before the arrival of the red reminder," admitted Mr McKee.

"A sad day. Men in bondage, women free. Domestic servants reading literary works devoid of literary value," puffed the Customer Service person. Then he asked: "Have you sought solace in poetry?"

McKee shouted, "Where are the men of vision, the women who with a few bright beams can lighten the gloom of the dungeon, where are the brave men and women who can pen wild words and who can also write words of calm to stem the raging of the storm?"

It was not long before the supermarket man answered: "I'm certain there are no poets in the fresh fruit display section, or in the aisles where the low-fat yogurt cartons are stacked waiting to be unpacked, priced and put on sale."

"What shall I do?" whimpered Mr McKee, now grabbing the grubby coat sleeve of the sole-sweating, jaw-jolly, tongue-thriving supermarket customer service man. "My wife will murder me if I go home with a doughnut stale and of uneven sugar-coated appearance."

It was not long before the man paid to maintain good customer relationship in the hall of the supermarket did answer: "Gang awa tae thi paperback stall and buy your wife Rayolene the latest block-buster entitled *Palm Beach Sand, Porto Fino Sea Water, Panamanian Sun-Glasses and Lots of Plimco Sex*, 666 pages of many quick-knivings, incessant nail-scratching, midnight-sneaker sneaking, super-stud swapping and siren-screaming."

"Do ambulances feature in the plot?" asked the banking executive, his face taut, his tie twisted, his head not on fire.

"The Manager wishes to see you," said the messenger, his een brown; the rich brown of Moy peat, and his manner; an air of eager-to-please doingness about him.

Hugh went to the office of the Manager. "What is this?" he said.

The Manager picked up the report. "Your Staff Appraisal Form. It has this to say: You are argumentative, far-sighted, off-centre, prone to discuss with all and sundry large feats of civil engineering, a task for which you are not equipped though your idealism puts me in mind of an artist. You are also accused of being a skin-shedder and lacking the personality traits of a professional showman."

"That is correct," said Hugh, "my name is not Billy Butlin. Tell me, does the report mention any bad faults?"

Retorted the supermarket manager: "Yes. You are compassionate and tend to be charming to both sexes, you are gifted with intelligence and may be possessive of literary talent."

"Will my temporary contract of employment be extended?" asked Hugh.

"No."

"And why not?"

"You wrote a letter of complaint to the Chairman of the Board."

"I swear what my people swear since I took pen and paper. I have never been a day without having slayed a man who was rude to women. I saw you bring the shelf-filler to tears; she was new; she was a woman; she was abused by you. Your words to her were demeaning," testified Hugh.

"It is true you are a letter writer," said Mr Huoil-Aoi, the supermarket manager. He paused to rip the photocopy of the letter of Hugh into little pieces. He continued; "If my uncle Conor were in the office, he would match you word for word. It is a pity he is not in the office this day."

Hugh threw at the chest of Mr Huoil-Aoi a yellowed-magazine. "Aye he is, his poem is on page three."

Examining the old magazine the supermarket manager said; "Purchased for fifteen pounds in a second-hand bookshop in Oban recently I see. My uncle told me how pleased he was to have his poem published in a literary magazine. The editor was a young man." Mr Huoil-Aoi laid down the mag on his desk, pointing to the editor's name; "Do you recognise the name, old man?"

Hugh sat by the desk. His gaze went from the magazine. Hugh said proudly, "I am the ox of the seven combats."

"Sign this," demanded the manager.

"What is this?"

"The official note stating the reason for your dismissal."

Hugh read the note aloud: "…not complying with company policy: in his capacity as Customer Service Supervisor he wore a shabby coat, the tweed material ink-stained. His company-issued navy-blue blazer hung in the wardrobe, the plastic bag cover still intact."

"I have something for you," snarled Huoil-Aoi moving to the door.
Said Hugh, "What is this?"
Said Huoil-Aoi, "A Glesga Kiss."

Jiggit an jumpit did Hugh to avoid the butt but the supermarket manager hurtit his heid on the jamb of the door. Forehead-blood did spurtit, the blood strawberry jam red.

Furthermore, Hugh was not pleased with his share of the supermarket's profits when he eventually peeled apart the sealed edges of the pay slip envelope.

Of silver were the eyelids of Mairi and fair her eyebrows. Of little-strength were the arms of Mairi at the end of her checkout shift. She turned to Hugh and asked; "I am a handsome woman; shall I ever see the summer swallow skim the stream?"

Hugh held her slender arm. "Come with me to the place where the sun goes down," said he.

Thae wint ti thi west thegither.

"Let me be known as your Psychic Side-Kick," suggested Mairi.
"I like Mairi well."
"I like it well too," said she. "What colour did you choose for the lighting in the Ben Lomond tunnel?" enquired Mairi.

"A chase the colours of the Four Winds," gied Hugh in honest reply. "The bulbs tungsten halogen, the shell die cast aluminium. Art and Science, Science and Art, a Divine Combination. Look to the lift," he said. "See between the white Wind and the black Wind?"

"Yes," she laughed, "I see the wind dun-coloured, wind of the west."

Other winds blew; the wind speckled, the wind grisly, the wind clear purple, the wind great green.

Nearby a gang of geese not screaming flew in flight.

"See and hear the scene below?" quizzed Hugh.
"Yes, soft-slapping the sea-waves on Lismore."
"Smell!"
"I smell the perfumed air. In the hedgerow growing, the pink briar. The place, Dalroy."
"Look," said he, "bobbing are the heads of bog cotton beside the Polharrow Burn."

. "It is true, flowers cover the earth of Scotland," and then with joy Mairi told Hugh MacDiarmid, "I saw a swallow of summer skim the stream."

"The storm is lulled to rest," said they both.

Brent Hodgson

Mary Angus

The Biba Shoes

Through mauve of glass a shivering ruby
sucked into her bony cat's eyes from the display satin
of the first Biba shoe shop in town.
A space-age, a Mary Quant age, beauty.
1" platform, high, strappy, tarty.

On the heel a diamond print,
the lovely markings on serpents on boiled wall
at the edge of the ocean.
Tide sprint in, foam full of sun, crabs, shell.
Frothy, stony crab juices.
What of her juices?
Feeling the sex-juices swell her lips,
the passion when the membranes thick
with blood, the erect nipple, wait sick
for the desire for the taste to die.

Her mother shouldn't have called her Marilyn
(a la Monroe). It had brought the glamour.
She should've called her Maggie or Eileen,
the names of the Christie women.

All a mustard hue down this ruined castle sky.
The shoes frenzied in ivy-dark satin,
a palette of thunder, rains, stars.
Would her mother lend her the money?
She'd no chance;
always her mother's abrupt touch (a fancy
of violence even) that took off again immediately,
the absent fingers somewhere-else caressing
the meaningful things in her own existence.
She'd no chance,
came from women who'd had less.
Gran Drummond left only with that resonance
of voice that comes with age,
the years dominoed on the backs of her hands.
It's too much and of no consequence.

But in Marilyn's world starvelings, kings and dwarves.
She longed for a long-haired mother,
not that curlered woman at the bookies in scarves,
a 'doing the pools', 'spotting the ball' treasure mapper.
No! A mother with a greased horn like a unicorn,
circles, crescents painted on her skin.

"Look," her mother'd cooed yesterday, lifting up her coat.
"I can see my new baby's face in my knees",
and turned her gaze to the mirror,
to some projection of herself beyond vision,
when the looking at the moon is over.
Father'd lizard-legged it weeks ago filled with hate.
Mother's going back to being MacManus,
going to a coastal hotel for romance
before it's too late.
A pull of eye, purple/blue palette.

Sniggering behind her.
Sniggering at the ruby shoes, at her.
A plump, particled boy in a matt grey town
between two old Italian men.
They walk on.
The boy looks back. Her hand's on the handle
but he's far away with black-frocked women;
in Naples, the consecrated candle.

'Going steady' with one of the Davis's;
boring, ordinary but 'he'd do'
until she got the soldier who rides
the blue stallion,
until she got his crushed raspberry kisses
in the green grass fuse,
the moon-lilies falling and rising in tides.
Until she got the ruby Biba shoes.

"The Biba Shoes", first published in *The Herald*, is the winner of the MacDiarmid
Centenary Prize.

Ken Alexander

Wild Raspberries

How pleasant and relaxing it is, taking a dander
In the heartland of late twentieth century feudalism
Passing the big house, picking wild raspberries
Mind far away from politics and ideology.

A rattle of wheels, and young Scotland whirls past
On skateboard, T-shirt proclaiming FUCK POVERTY.
The propagandist great grandson of John Maclean
MacDiarmid's flash of sun, supreme Scottish martyr.

I pick more raspberries, crush one in my hand
And, with satisfaction, murmur 'krassivy, krassivy'.

Hamish Henderson

Under The Earth I Go

Under the earth I go
On the oak-leaf I stand
I ride on the filly that never was foaled
And I carry the dead in my hand

      There's method in my magic!

Seeing I have passed my sell-by date
And will no doubt be hanging up my clogs quite soon
I have come back to Padstow to dance – to dance!

Doddle of drums on a May morning
Slashes of sunlight on hill and harbour
High-jacked greenwood louping along the quay

To hell with Aunt Ursula Birdhood
And her auld yowe deid in the park.
While my love lives, I'll dance with the Mayers
Teasing the Old Oss till there's new life in him
Chasing sweet lusty Spring with pipes, goatskin and bones.

Sunshowers over the estuary
Cormorant black on the pale sands yonder
Taste of dank earth on my tongue
Trembling oak-leaves coortin' the Sun,
And the twin dragons, Life and Death,
Jousting thegither under the Maypole.

Change elegy into hymn, remake it –
Don't fail again. Like the potent
Sap in these branches, once bare, and now brimming
With routh of green leavery,
Remake it, and renew.

Makar, ye maun sing them –
Cantos of exploit and dream,
Dàin of desire and fulfilment,
Ballants of fire and red flambeaux…

      Tomorrow, songs
Will flow free again, and new voices
Be borne on the carrying stream

Asleep in Spring sunshine
      Cornish riverbanks
Flower again!

Back in Fyvie's lands
I'll say fareweel wi' the plooman's week:

> Soor Monday
>
> Cauld Tysday
>
> Cruel Wednesday
>
> Everlasting Thursday
>
> On Friday – will ye ne'er get duin.
>
> Sweet Setterday, and the efternuin
>
> Glorious Sunday – rest forever.
>
> Amen.

This poem was used in the film *Journey to a Kingdom*, directed by Timothy Neat for Grampian Television. It is spoken by the author on the cassette *Pipes, Goatskin and Bones*, also produced by Grampian (GPN 3001)

Valerie Gillies

The Whisky Stills

There's a brawl in the Balhangie Inn,
the whiff of the Cairncross malt-kiln;
all sticking up, the illicit stacks
behind Glencat, and at the back
of Garelet, behind Carlochy of Lee,
between the burns at Arsallery.

Hidden head of a whisky still
in peat at the summit of Craig Soales,
with ruined bothies up the Kedloch,
far beyond Pool of Fashieloch,
up the Turret, up the White Burn
and on the Shank of Wirren.

They say it was the last store
uncovered at Tarfside in 1904,
but every sample distilled there
perfumes the glen's caller air.
In a broon-pig, whisky pure,
a demi-john of the king of liquor,
"a wee drappie to slocken Sandie"
– no gauger finds *his* toddy.

Donatella Bisutti

Scrievin

Tae scrieve an tae clim thon munelichty brae, tae scrieve an clim.
Ye ken, we'r no ettlin tae best the brae, but tae sneck teh mune.

The Lily

Mair o a concept than a common flooer,
I daurdna pou the lily, that gaes
as the altar-cannle's metaphor.

An yet, as in the hert o aathin pure,
sae likewise wi the lily, whase
sulphurous yellow pollen bides its oor.

Natura Morta

It's snawin outby.
        A joug
on the table-heid ingaithers reid
translucencies.
Ye peel the aipple slaw,
seduced bi the sheen promise o a skin
that cradles the chaumer's licht.
Ilka objeck hauds its ain byordnar
uselessness – noo that's richt reassurin!
An if ye coup thon lustart cheeny plate
it thraws back teh blancy lift
in a single, skinklin threid.

Selbst

Gies a monk's cell –
a richt wee dab o aathin,
an me inby
tae gar the toom warld ring.

Owerset frae the Italianis bi Pam Wardlaw
Owerset frae the Inglis bi John Glenday

Edwin Morgan

A Third Epitaph on an Army of Mercenaries
(after Housman and MacDiarmid)

We write our own; no one does it for us.
Only those who have been there know the score.
The pay was good, but thousands more before us
Would testify note-counting's but a chore.

Adrenalin, adrenalin that courses
Along the blood as bullets do's the key.
Shouts, cracks, burning buildings were the sources
Of the hot joy that made us die – or dee.

T S Law

A Brawlik Makar
(hinmaist lynes (3229-3318))

Unlyke the patroniser his wark despises,
MacDiarmid didnae staund an byde his wheesht
for better days an nae boather, tae gie the wurld
a dunt; he stuid in poetry, an stauns
thare yit, lik straucht-bous-nane, as still an stoondin
as the Silence that was left for him tae finnd,[1]
tho whitna silence that, his ain or oors?
Guid poets aye are praisent in thur wark,
and as immortal as the efterfolk
can dream them, deem them, dram them in a slainte,
athooten thocht o shirrickin them whyles
for bein ower eydent at the cataloguin

---

1. The auntrin reader micht be eydent enyeuch here tae think on Sean
O'Faolain's speil alow fae his *The Irish*:
> This interior struggle towards 'intellectual and imaginative freedom'
> goes on in every race. The struggle between the myth and the human
> drama is appraent even in the *Iliad* and the *Odyssey*, though Ker is
> surely right in saying that when, at the end of the *Odyssey*, silence falls
> on the listeners it is the silence of admiration for the narrator rather
> than wonder at his exploits.

Ker above is William Paton Ker, the British mediaevalist 1855-1903.
Gif the reader juist cannae caa tae myn the raeference in the *Odyssey*, here is
William Cowper's English o't whuin Odysseus ends his lang accoont o the
tyuavin o his days.
> "He ceased; the whole assembly silent sat,
> Charm'd into ecstasy with his discourse…"

spirlickities amang the synonyms,
seguein metaphorickie in chassé
or sashayin lyke loch watter in a seiche
for a slither wi the sleekit seellables.
MacDiarmid kent an better kent kent he,
that tae speak o a makar staundin-aff his wark,
no bein pack wi 't, is tae say he drees
a sorte o non-assimilatioun o self,
lik bein in hiddlins ahint a muse's kirtle,
but somebodie else's muse at that. Tae think on
the Cromwellian oorat on the Scottish face
micht weel juist fricht awa the feartie makar
fae the pictur o him he thinks the leid can pent,
or it may puit the poseur in the strunts
wi his ain eemage keekin skellie at him
lik foostiness alow the skin for deid,

or canker wheiggit fae the ootsyde in:
thare are some folk, ye ken, that dearlie lyke
tae be awfie bonnie. An mibbe they are at that.
But no in the wy that Christopher Murray Grieve
was a brawlik man. And Hugh MacDiarmid was
and is A Brawlik Makar, for as siccan folk
haud tae 't as thrugaun as a poem itsel,
he daes, an daes he no. Gif that is whit
memorabilitie is aa aboot,
thrugaun memorabilitie will grant him
his immortalitie. The caumer sooch
o posteritie will tak guid tent o that:
lik tyme itsel, it neever patronises
nor faut finnds as its genius arises.

Lyfe, daith an doocelike immortalitie,
the yae leal trinitie creatioun spells,
kent him an kent him fyne the muckle makar
he aye was, (whit a baur that is in Scotland!)
Yit monie o his peers juist coodnae see him
for his ain man amang his propaganda.
An mibbe thare were folk fairfanged wi envie,
tho naebodie admits it for the shame o't;
an shairlie thare were folk that hatit him,
but they'd be kinna wee folk in his days
whae neever caad tae mynd hoo Gillies' Hill
ran battlewards an taen its newer name
in praise o thae Smaa Folk oor ancient fieres,
here myndit this day baurin ten tae come,
efter sax hunder, saxtie-nyne lang years,
a bonnier Juin, bi aa accoonts, nor this yin.
No yin o thaem that hatit him but kens

the hater is the eedjit onie day;
an no the yon o thaem is cherisht noo
nor luved the-wy MacDiarmid is: thur names
are nocht, as nithin maltiplied bi naething
is nuchin, daith alane, the negative.

The hinmaist but yae wurd is no fae me,
but fae MacDiarmid, tho I tell it ye
this saecont day in Mairch in nynteen hunner
and aichtie-three, rain fae the soo-waast skytein,
an cauld wi 't till the guid kail waarm the wame
at the lavrie tyme o day, the back o twal.
Whuin Morris Blythman years sinsyne collogued
wi Hugh MacDiarmid ower the byeuk we'd mak

tae bring his socialistic poems thegither,[2]
the makar back-spiered, as ye micht expec,
wi a glink athin the ee, an deevillockielik
as yin o yon Auld Bruchie's branderbairns
wirein-in at the hotterin purritch on the swee,
"And have I written socialist poetry?"

In tyme tae come, it may be said MacDiarmid
was inventit, nae sic mervel bein o 'tsel,
but that the efterfolk may ken a truith o't
that traiks ahint the legend, yit wi 't nane,
an better ken, lik truith that bydes in ballats
till the singer gar them sing abuin thursels,
here is nae cairriet storie for the lieges,
but truith that licht alane can luminate
but cannae see itsel that lichts aa ithers:
the meeracle made the mervel was hissel
the mervel made the meeracle MacDiarmid.
Who cood invent MacDiarmid but MacDiarmid?

---

2. That is, *The Socialist Poems of Hugh MacDiarmid* edited bi the late Thurso Berwick (Morris Blythman) an masel. The lang forewurd tae that byeuk was gy weel thocht o bi MacDiarmid: it was aa Morris's wark but hauf-a-dizzen wurds, an cam aboot this wy. I haed made a wheen notes tae ser as a base for a forewurd, but Morris wasnae that pack wi the ungaun sooch o the speil, sae I telt him tae forget it an dae the wark as he saw 't hissel. And as aabodie kens, he did anaa, an lik MacDiarmid, I was gy weel pleesurt wi 't. But again lik the makar, no bein yin tae puit wastrie on wark duin, I saw fit later on tae yaise ma notes as the grund for this poem: sae in a wy, *The Socialist Poems of Hugh MacDiarmid* alang wi Morris's forewurd tae the byeuk, an the baith claucht-at bi this wark, are a literarie luve-darg o a three-airtie natur. Ye ken, whit we see fit tae dae is whit we are best fit tae dae.
An ye waant the haill truith o't wi a bit nigglin puit back intaet, whit the makar said in Lyne 3306 was "...any socialist poetry?"

Whalsay

Tom Pow

Do not argue with me. Argue with these stones
Hugh MacDiarmid, 'On a Raised Beach'

*(Note: this piece should be performed in a small, intimate theatre
such as the 80-seater Brigend theatre in Dumfries. During the
performance, whose length is variable, it is advisable that the
doors of the theatre be locked.)*

Scene One

The small stage is in darkness until the gentlest lighting suggests sunrise.
Enter a man, preferably short and wiry, who, with short bursts of energy,
is heaving a wooden kist by a rope handle. He is simply dressed in worn
cords and polo neck. At first we see him, the cliff of his hair, in silhouette.

He stops in mid-stage, opens the lid of the kist and takes out a stone,
round and smooth, the size of a man's fist, which he places on the front
left of the stage. As he does this, there is the first faint shush of a small
wave breaking and the distant cry of a gull.

He takes out another stone, similar to the first, and carefully places it
exactly two hands' breadths from the first. There is deliberation in all his
actions and in the stronger lighting we can now see his high brow is
furrowed in thought.

After the second stone, he places a third, and a fourth, and so on,
forming an arc round the apron of the stage. By the tenth stone (halfway/
mid-day) the lights are glaring and the sound of gulls is deafening.

Reverse effects until at the twentieth and final stone the stage is in
darkness and the last gull is silenced.

Scene Two

The stage is in darkness. The sound of a rough sea brewing fills the
theatre. The rhythm is taken up by a fiddler who appears in silhouette
at the side of the stage when the lights come up. In the centre of the stage
there is a boxbed on rockers, at first gently rocking (optional: a small sail
on top). The man with hair like a cliff-face is lying inside, frantically
filling page after page of a notebook.

The fiddler now ups the tempo and rocks the bed with his foot with increasing speed (the light is leaden, stormy) until the furiously rocking cradle tips the man out. The music stops instantly.

From lying on his back (beached) centre-stage the man pushes his torso up. As he does so, he gulps air until his breath steadies. Now his head lifts up slowly until he is staring calmly with black-rimmed eyes over the stones, over the heads of the audience, at the quiescent shores of Scotland.

Scene Three

Strobe lighting. The man with the cliff-face hair is striding about the stage, which fills with smells of fish, potatoes and strong black tobacco. He adopts a range of thoughtful postures (more Keaton than Chaplin). We hear the sound of shuffling feet in the wings. With curt gestures he signals this is a one-man show.

A constant arcing shower of crushed paper snowballs crosses the stage. Occasionally the man will stop to pick one up, open it out, only to throw it away again almost immediately. This must continue until the stage is covered. The man then collects armfuls of the paper and drops them into the kist which originally contained the stones. As the effort begins to drain him, the strobe lights slow to a sputter.

He lights a match; it seems he would torch the lot. There is pleading in the wings. He closes the lid and sits down on the chest exhausted as a cold even light appears to surround him.

He picks up and contemplates one of the stones. He taps the chest with it and listens, taps the chest and listens, taps and listens...

Scene Four

The stage is in darkness. A sprinkler centre-stage sprays the first few rows of the audience with a solution of salt and water. With increasing force, arcing leftwards and rightwards, this continues until the director is satisfied the whole audience is properly drenched.

As the lights come up on the empty stage, the audience rub their eyes. Eventually they calm down. (This factor in part accounts for the variable length of the piece.)

Scene Five

The audience's argument with the stones.

F Maria Makepeace

Let Us Not Forget
IM Valda Trevlyn Grieve

No regrets, she
Said flaming suddenly
Over the rose field flung
Into the still open grave.

Hayden Murphy

Hugh MacDiarmid: The Man

Michael Grieve

Wind-blasted Whalsay, sodden with the peat of forgotten centuries where trees grew and none now stand, was home – a bucket or two of earth in the chilled, lapping bitterness of the North sea; a place where, at midnight, you can read beneath the stars in the *simmer's dim;* and where, in the black thunder of winter, with a shaky moon catching the tumbling fluorescence of warring waves, life became a virgin's ring of uneasy and frustrating self-containment.

Yet it was here, in a fisherman's cottage, abandoned because of death, with the net-mending loft steep-staired above, that he sat – a self-induced Scottish Siberia that allowed no compromise, where mind over matter was the reality, the only salvation; and the loneliness of hardship was contrasted by the bubbling of the fleshpots of success, where ambition spurred by acclamation turned into reputation and recognition.

The blazing peat fire, surviving in its grey ashes through the hollow of the night to be fanned fresh with the rising sun, patterned his legs to a tartan-red, and great blisters swelled. But nothing matched the white heat of passionate concentration, the marathon of sleepless nights and days that suddenly ended the sitting around for months indulging in that most deceptive of exercises – thinking.

At such times, conversation was the whispered undertone of necessity, and childhood became a game of patience without the understanding, though the time-machine of words was forever careering madly, powered largely in those early years by the splendours of Scottish history, and its built-in pattern of betrayal and defeat – the fingerprint that detects the unsuccessful.

Fat mackerel full of oily richness, and cod's roe, like the balls of a bull, fed us – for the islanders, blunt as only a Force Ten can make you, cared for neither. Galvanized buckets, ugly to the feel, stood around filled with seagulls' eggs, obscene in their white coating of preservative. And the eternal thick black twist, powerful and cool, was a haloed wreath of blue, its smoke thinning to disappearance in the caressing glow of the Aladdin lamp, prim and polished and upright; a light uncannily susceptible to draught, when the mantle crusted black, the edges a creeping red, and the atmosphere in the house whipped and flayed the nerve ends – until once again there was light.

Armed with the long inheritance of a frontier people, chromosome-encrusted with Border forays, genes menaced by the oozing growth of England's greed; with the imagination only a genius can occasionally light, and a sense of purpose allied to principle, he took on the smooth, sophisticated, self-congratulatory world of English literature, and established the basis and the fact of the Scottish Renaissance almost single-handed.

But prophets are best remembered dead, and the MacDiarmid message was – and is – far from simple. Not only was the main bulk of his early work in Scots, an almost insuperable, impenetrable barrier to critics and reviewers who had little time to explore the indulgence of individuality in a tongue so strange to their well-trained ears, with its triple-edged meanings and allusions terrifying in their unfamiliarity – especially after taking a degree in English Literature.

Even worse, in English he used words that only the omnivorously erudite would be likely to use now; and he scattered quotations, whether from geology or religion, that gained stature by being out of context, and stuck like burrs.

I remember, as the intricate dazzle of Fair Isle patterns grew beneath my mother's needles, the balls of wool bouncing to the kitten's claws, how I eagerly thumbed through the hand-heavy dictionary in an attempt to catch this smoke-hazed figure out – not just at spelling, that would have been too difficult, and there were words I could scarcely sound out, the clutter of their vowels and consonants having fallen from a riddle-shaker: it was the meaning of the words, their shimmering suggestiveness, the exciting exactness, the image-conjuring. It was a game not to be won; the dictionary and he had established a rare accord of mutual esteem.

There were friends, shooting stars from the south, who travelled seasick in wonderment that anyone could exist, let alone live, so far away form the coin-in-slot of civilisation, the instant familiarity of people and influence.

Radar had not yet been invented, but his mind blip-blipped its way round the world, extracting information from books and people, the lifeline of periodicals and newspapers, which enabled him to build up new patterns of knowledge, and keep the old information intact.

There were strains, too. The great long poem on *Mature Art* scrunched so hard into a ball of desperate irritation and neglect that it destroyed the carefully-built peat fire like a cannon-shot, sending red sparks clouding aloft to grow black on the book spines. Its very tightness, however, saved it from extinction, the outer pages tea-coloured to a crisp as my mother – an eye to the hurricane of creativity – burned her fingers, ignoring the angry torment that urged its abandonment to the nethermost reaches of his own personal hell.

Beneath the card table, sorting tangles of wool, I watched and wondered at the raging quiet of violence, and quaked at the great bang that almost lifted the front door from its hinges. But on an island such as Whalsay there are no places to go; the neighbours few and far; the pubs non-existent.

Whisky came by boat, and when the towering doctor, David Orr, got in his supplies; or the minister, MacKay, decided to prove his strength by tempting the Devil – then white corpuscles turned red and the dawn came and went as the floodgates of conversation fasted them of food.

The dead might wait, and the sick groan louder – but in the long year of island life, a little time off was grudged by none.

On the only radio set on the island, the news crackled out – war had been declared and the Great War – the war to end all wars – had been relegated to the position of a *hors d'oeuve*. The old cliches were lovingly dusted, silver-tongued medals of glory. Freedom was the battle-cry and war began to sweep the world. The treaties and the safety measures were the wastepaper of a generation, the sacrifices had not been enough, and politicians dislodged each other so they could gain ephemeral honour – and make the same mistakes as before.

At the age of fifty, the battlefields of Salonika, where he once had his teeth out with half-a-bottle of whisky as anaesthetic, were not for him. We saw him off from Symbister in the heavy old rowing boat which pulled to the anchored height of the *Earl of Zetland*. In the War Reserve, he was on his way to Glasgow to work in a Clydebank munitions factory. Hands that controlled the mind's pulse now clasped copper bands for shells; and eyes that read words by their tens of millions now searched the blackout streets for some distinguishable feature. Nyctalopia is a poor affliction in a city night-shrouded for war, when even the glow of the moon is cursed as it turns oil-dirty rivers into silvered flare-paths for the restless bomber pilots overhead, the sweat seeping out of them and flak splintering all around.

We sailed in 1942, on the same boat my father had taken, laden with forty tea-chests crammed with manuscripts and books. Whatever happened, whether the *Herrenvolk* hysteria whipped by Hitler, or the carefully articulated bombast of Churchill triumphed – there would be no going back.

The sweetest memories of childhood sank below the horizon and Whalsay, all love, and sorrow, and longing, became a miniaturized complex circuit imprinted on the memory, an electric light to be switched on though fingers fumble at the switch.

In the creaking rooms of landladies, saggy-breasted and pinched with a stale self-righteousness, who ever complained about the waste of the light, my father sat up half the night with that compelling energy, and continued to combat the exhaustion of war work by writing and speaking in those endless years of misery.

As the war spluttered to a standstill in Europe, and blasted a launching pad for the Third World War at Hiroshima, the hard days were still with us. Money was uncannily scarce, recognition as slow to come as an acorn sprouting on rock-sheathed soil. Even, for a time, he went back to weekly journalism, forced to a concern about the meaningless trivia of minor court cases, the empty-headed pronouncements of local councillors, the carefully-tuned pontification of a sermon, the long ritual of the living life in death; the acceptance of authority from people who employed words like wet concrete in contrast to the individual polish, the harmony of delicate balance.

44

But like a long-distance writer he carried on, each obstacle yet another experience – and gradually, despite all the difficulties of language, isolation and neglect, the strands of a world reputation began to emerge as positive and enduring.

Mild and gentle, disarmingly polite to strangers (and even to well-known bores), he did not compromise. It is a trait which people pretend to admire. Some do. But it is also embarrassing and difficult, success is so much harder to achieve unless you bend a little, unless you set out to be acceptable in the sense that you are not a living and articulate affront to consciences that stir darkly – and when little is at stake.

There would have been many paths to follow but the dictating pattern of our lives is not so easily escaped. And in the Scotland of today – where too many people still seem anxious to be emasculated – to remain your own man is even more difficult, more strewn with hazards than might easily be imagined.

Especially when his contempt for the "whole gang of high mucky-mucks, famous fatheads, old wives of both sexes, stuffed shirts, hollow men with headpieces stuffed with straw, bird-wits, lookers-under-beds, trained seals, creeping Jesuses, Scots Wha Hae'vers… Commercial Calvinists, makers of 'noises like a turnip', and all the touts and toadies and lickspittles of the English Ascendancy, and their infernal womenfolk, and all their skunkoil skullduggers", remained just as decisively searing as the day he wrote those words in *Lucky Poet*.

Courage sparkles with many facets – from the schizophrenia of the spy festering in his long-waiting secrecy for the one moment of justification, to the coolness of the bomb disposal expert, an unknown touch away from eternity, or the brave acceptance of the cancer-ridden, smiling still as they waste to death – or there is the courage that keeps you going when others have long fallen by whatever wayside idol they find themselves opposite when the music stops, when they decide to compromise.

Of course, people like my father are lucky. They are committed, impelled to write, to compose, to dance, to explore – their energies and their talents focus, and they seem to have that sixth sense that occasionally ripples across us all.

In Scotland, too, politically and economically a poor place with a correspondingly low threshold of intellectual awareness and activity, the sheer stretching of the mind has been difficult and often impossible. If people, for reasons innumerable, don't understand what you are driving at, what your aims and intentions are, what your are trying to *do* – then conversation becomes a second-rate affair, a shallow river that passes for communication. To explore the deep, dark holes without the diver's-suit protection of conventional attitudes and responses, takes a courage that cannot be imposed from without, and rarely sustained from within.

He had faults – who has none? Yet one of his gifts is that he throws no shadow. His influence is one of illumination and, by the age of eighty, he gained that state which so many strive for and fail to achieve despite being draped with worldly honours and success – immortality.

From the weaving town of Langholm, hard by the English border, he laboured long to produce the "many splendoured thing" that now survives as his poetic vision. Of course it is tattered – mountaineers don't exercise in public at 29,000 feet. But he scaled the heights without becoming an eccentric, a recluse, eaten with egotism, or pompous as to his work, position or reputation. As though he signed some self-denying ordinance, he was unsparingly available to all – at home, to universities where the journey was a tribulation, the fee scarcely worth the fare. For a man who stood within the entombed history of the Kremlin, walked the Great Wall of China, visited both sides of the Berlin Wall, and travelled in almost every European country, lectured in Canada and America, he found the detail of travel excessively annoying, particularly as movement stopped him reading. However, he always arrived – while others of eminence resisted outside demands on their time, demanded and gained protection from duty and received cossetting by publishers so their every word should be easily available.

People, meeting him for the first time, and knowing of him through the bare bones of public announcements, or having heard him speak in debate, were commonly amazed by his humility and excessive 'ordinariness'. It is a mask that was occasionally breached. At a PEN cocktail party (he founded the Scottish branch) he was cornered by two stickdry ladies who wanted to squeeze every vicarious drop of experience from the encounter of meeting a real, live poet. Well aware that closing time was advancing with awesome speed (pubs in Scotland shut at 9.30 then) he decided the only way to escape was to propose a toast at a farewell salutation – 'Ladies, may the skins of your arses never cover a banjo!'

Quite uncharacteristic, if not apocryphal – but reasonably apt. Meaningful survival in Scotland, even in physical terms, is hard in the arts. He not only survived but flourished – on his own terms. The grit in the oyster now sets the value.

Michael Grieve

• Reprinted, with minor adjustments, from the *Hugh MacDiarmid Anthology*, edited by Michael Grieve and Alexander Scott, Routledge & Kegan Paul, 1972.

CMG, Valda and Michael on Whalsay

George Bruce

Thumb-nail Sketch O The Winged Leviathan
In Memoriam HM 1892-1978 Dedicated to Michael Grieve

"By art is created that great Leviathan" – Thomas Hobbes, *Leviathan*

I met him on cloud 10
(Clud 9 wasna heich eneugh – he said.)
His job description, *Universe Inspector,*
wasna exact, he said: closer tae the fact,
The Inspector of the Universe. Wha ither!
He was aye keen on titles, nae mair than due
though. He'd been weill acquent wi the cosmos
lang afore his elevation. Time an time he ascendit
tae that terrible airless airt in's heid
an thocht himsel intae eternity, an syne
look't doon an' seen what livin man
had niver seen:
An when the earth's as cauld's the mune
An a' its folk lang syne deid,
Sae lookit he on his mortal place till sudden
bloomed the rose that Langholm was tae his bairn-time:
Earth, thou bonnie broukit bairn!
An sae it was in the lang day or nicht.
Nae noo! 'broukit' winna ony langer dae.
Earth! Carthenogenic waste is nearer fact.
Humans! Carthenogenic operators, and him the while
smokin his pipe (cloud 10), admitted he himsel
had made a sma contribution in this direction,
nae material, a pipe o peace, nae pungent,
a discreet sensation, proper for the poet's
proboscis. E'en noo mid aa the guff the planet
gie aff he could distinguish shag frae bogie-roll.
To be *Inspector o the Universe* total discernment,
– as advertised for the appointed officer – was
'Essential requisite 1.' There were ithers –
'Gargantuan appetite for lexicons, WURDS.
He began, on this earth, Inspector o the Self,
himsel, in fact, fund oot, sae help him,
chaos, bubblin, bilin, spewin, slaverin,
inside. God save Chris – if he is aboot,
or Shestov, Soloyov, Dostoievsky, Marx,
the Catholic Church or divine poesie or
George Ogilvie, "from the hurricane

48

of mental and moral anarchy which has tossed me
hither and thither these last twelve months."
And agen – "habitually I am in what Joxer calls
'chassis.'" Aye an mair than him's been here afore.
"Matter – this stuff rots uncleanly intae what
we ca life, seized through aa its atoms wi
a pediculous malady, swalt in tumours, ilk ane
alive, alive – on its ain, yin splitting
intae millions, millions coherin intae yin.
O this stour naethin was clean."* O gie him virr
an vision to see ayont an thru the scunnersome
sicht. Cwa Sydney Slugabed Godless Smith,
Norman *et al*, aa wha habit his companie
in this "rortie city". Aa wha wi guid words
an libations gaed him benison, for here
was need, an prime o aa was Valda – she,
the comforter. An aa was weill as meth be
but for that endless speirin spirit that kent
nae bounds, that delicate antennae responsive tae
the hail steir o the warld an beyond,
that tellt tae him – this is truth an this
you will accept an this you will set doon
for guid or ill or for naething ava. So be it.
An wha could bear sic brunt. The stanes
had words for him, an he pit them doon.
We must reconcile ourselves to the stones,
Not the stones to us.
– I lift a stone; it is the meaning of life I clasp
Which is death, for that is the meaning of death;
To be himsel he maun identify wi daith – an life:
And above all I will, when I've learned much,
Look simply at the animals until
An essence from them imperceptibly
Glides into me – stand in their eyes awhile
And witness how they put me out again
Gently, incuriously, and unjudged.
The rax atween thae twa an haud himself as
ae thing, was that nae eneugh! What mair's
required than depths an heichs contained
in yon gran pow that dwined tae perky chin
an neat feet for proof that this perfervid saul
could nae be pit in category 'homunculus'.
(*homo sapiens* bein extinct lang syne)
So, QED "Rilke", the voice soont oot.
Was this rebuke that words frae Rilke were

*Adapted from R L Stevenson's essay *'Pulvis et Umbra'*

preferred tae mak his case when wonder-words,
his ain, were aa aboot, an infinity o them,
or was't that noo the first an anely time,
noo mang a thae immortals, wha at his elbuck
sat, (or near eneugh though farther doon the line)
he'd mak a boo, an say that whiles he'd taen
a something o their wisdom tae himsel
withoot a by-your-leave? (Why no, for what
o Wullie Shakespeare's lift – the lot frae North
wha nae doot had laboured lang owre Plutarch* –
a word or twa Wull cheenged an some line-ends
an aff gaes Cleopatra in her barge tae wild applause.)
"Rilke," an on it gaed, "Blok, George Ramaekers,
Zinalda Hippius, Else Lasket-Schuler, Dostoievsky,
Mallarmé, Stefan George, Dante" – aa frae *The Drunk Man* –
Haud hard! We've got nae faurer than *Cencrastus*. Come
In Memoriam Joyce we'll droon. So what's he at –
tae beat the scholars at their ane game. Ae look
frae yon shrewd ee said, "na, an I'd thocht better
o ye," but noo he spoke frae oot Eternity's perspective
he kent "tae gie them hoose-room (an whiles dacent
acknowledgement) in his 'pome' – aa the 'pomes' were one –
was gien them new life, tae ensure that his wha followed,
nae langer rooted in the sog o kailyard, but bathed
in licht that spread frae poets frae east tae wast.
'So' said I pittin my oar in agen; 'as Lao Tsu said:
"Poetry is necessary for the happiness of the people."
It was a mistak, gie him ae quote an he's back wi a hunner.
'Wilt thou unite in one name heaven and earth?
Then I name you, Shakuntula, you, and all is said'
Goethe wrote – and that is my concern too."
An we were intae *Joyce*, an the one gran thocht
that wouldna let him go, a sang o the universe
that proclaimed it as ae thing: his destiny,
(so he thocht) was to provide the Seamless Garment,
helped a wee thing by a puckle ithers similarly
afflicted, driven tae the point o brak-up,
Rilke especially:
Out of strangers, for I know not one, O Lord,
And out of me and me to make one thing;
Out of sleepers, out of strange unknown old men
In hospices who cough importantly within
The beds, and out of sleep-dazed chldren on
So strange a breast, and out of many unprecise
Vague people, always out of me and out

---

*Shakespeare, *Anthony and Cleopatra*, Act II Scene two.

Of naught but me and things unknown to me
To make one thing, O Lord, Lord, Lord, the thing
and himsel, even though "in realistic mood":
Never from one single beat of time can shake or disturb
Is my certain knowledge
Derived from the complex vision of everything in me,
That the whole astronomical universe, however illimitable,
Is only one part and parcel of the mystery of Life;
Of this I am as certain as I am certain that I am I.
The astronomical universe is *not* all there is.
Me, an earthbound reporter muttered tae mysel,
"aye, aye, assertions; abstractions." He heard:
Eternity is like an auld green parrot
The voice soont oot, "and in any case within
the not inconsiderable structures of my longer
pomes comment is an essential component, and
you should know I aspire to perfection. I am not
perfect." Deed aye, sae he had admitted maist
becomingly in circumstances when I micht hae
expectit his biblical wrath, an aa he scrieved was,
that he saw his 'job' was, "to erupt like a volcano,
emitting not only flame, but a lot of rubbish."
"Certes", as Gudesir Smith had pit it frae time tae time,
we were aff course, or sae I thocht, but no him.
"Admitted" "complex vision" might not have the nerve
of poetry in it, though he would not be subject to
the conventional concept of poetry. Here it was
an exegesis of the description of heroic struggle
in severe conditions, of men winning their way
into new territory with the odds stacked against them.
The stuff of experience was here if it was anywhere.
We fumble along with partially bandaged eyes
Our reindeer-skin kamiks worn into holes
And no fresh sedge-grass to stump them with.
We come on ice-fields like mammoth ploughlands
And mountainous séracs which would puzzle an Alpine climber.
That is what adventuring in dictionaries means.
Agen I interrupt, an he, wi customary courtesy,
said, "Aye", kennin it was time for conclusions,
he haein gien the cue in "mammoth" and journey
in staney cauld earth and in the mind. Would he wha had
     the wisdom o Lao Tzu
     the foolishness o Fleeman*,
     the thrawnness o Balaam's ass,
     the verbal extravagance o Urquhart,

---

*Jamie Fleeman – the Laird of Udny's fool who had more wisdom than the Laird.

the refinement o Fauré
the obsessiveness o Ahab
the vision o Jacob,
the absurdity o Quixote,
the wrath o Knox
the sure-footedness o Hamish McInness
an mair than can be got into this pot o broth,
would he accept the singular description,
The Winged Leviathan?
Consider the maitter: as a symbol for greatness –
Oh, Ahab! What shall be grand in thee it must
needs be plucked from the skies, and dived for
in the deep, and featured in the unbodied air.
Sae Melville, held in admiration, an spoken for
in the *Drunk Man*, covers the spectrum o oor poet
at a stroke, refers to the cratur as seen
"in unfathomable waters", noted the depiction
o "Vishnu in form of Leviathan", an summons up
the image o the Platonian leviathan. Need
there be mair witnesses – Isiah, Job, Milton,
wha saw Leviathan, "Stretched like a promontory,
a moving land". Hobbes lifts him frae the ocean,
"Leviathan, a Commonwealth." An what noo hae we,
a routh o words an ithers to whom he has admitted
tae oor, noo, common wealth. Ae thing the auncients
kent nae o, tae add to this astonishment, it
hearkened tae soun in the deeps yet nae mair
than him wha hearkened even *On the Ocean Floor.*
And as one who hears their tiny shells incessantly raining
on the ocean floor as the foraminifera die.
Syne he's heich abune the ozone layer:
An Earth, the bare auld stane,
Glitters beneath the seas o Space
White as a mammoth's bane.
'Weill,' I said, 'Will it dae?' There was nae soun.
'Weill,' I called, loud oot through space, I thocht,
kennan the soun would dwine awa, for whaur was he?
An it was gettin cauld for mortal man,
an socht tae warm mysel wi words germane.
A puckle cam – snell, blae, nirly, scowtherin,
grumlie, reevin, reezie, dreich, deid-thraw,
ramballioch, sab, sob, an that ane owre close
tae me on my lane abune the Appleton layer –
an ne'er a word frae him. Had he tint aa regaird
for a maitter o import, tae me at ony rate.
There was nae soun but the soun that emptyness maks.
Naethin for't but tae haud on wi the words,

thae words beat oot by wun an weather
for the need o folk tae utter tae –
as they sa noo – 'limit the damage' – but him,
tae tell oot his astonishment at aa
that goins on o sun an mune an stars,
an this auld planet. This truth he kent
as boy wha stude by the Curly Snake
an kens noo. I hearkened in the darkenin lift
an heard:
An lifted owre the gowden wave,
Peers a dumfoun'ered Thocht.

George Bruce

David Craig

The Strange Voyage of the Island Rose

Barely a minute after
The winter sun had risen,
They saw it lay its golden track
Across the steel horizon.

Stamping their feet in rigid boots,
Their denims hard as armour,
They knew their finger-ends would freeze
Unless the day grew warmer.

Their salty throats were parched and charred
With flames of freezing breath.
The basking sharks were shimmering black
As memories of a death.

One of those shoals ahead of them
(Each sharper than the last)
Might carry on its crown the frail
Wand of the radio mast.

Before the radar screen had blipped,
Its circling line struck home,
The trawl had emptied off the drum
And sunk in a shot of foam.

The bow-wave bursting round the stern
Reared dolphin-backed along.
The mile of hawser, tautening,
Kicked with a murderous twang.

Big Mac was helpless at the wheel,
Oily was lying stunned
Under the piston's flailing joint,
His face a reddening wound.

The rest were staring at the sea,
Shaking but holding on.
The *Island Rose* was shuddering like
A man whose mind has gone.

Far in the waves ahead (astern) –
Wee Duggie saw it first –
A shattered snake reared up, fell back –
The tortured line had burst

And while the seven leaned, or lay,
Too shocked to talk or think,
The features of the sea composed
Their old impassive blank.

At Stornoway in the Public Bar
The usual crowd were there.
(Oily was in the hospital
Under intensive care.)

The fishermen raised up their drams
To the men of the *Island Rose,*
Then gathered round the box to watch
The television news.

'The Ministry regrets,' it said,
'An incident at sea.
Some nets and catch were lost – no deaths
Or serious injury.'

'"Episodes such as this," they say,
"Are rarer than supposed."
As far as the Navy is concerned,
The incident is closed.'

Ian Stephen

Canoeist

Sam, you're knacky on the halyard,
but fish out the keys of the mini-van now
and get some road-room between us

and the eddies and backwash in
this room, made rustic
from trades catalogues.

Last week, you coped on Corrievreckan,
entered on the neap tide
but you could see the rapids

ready to up with the range of metres.
The next race is north in the Pentland
with a solidarity of proven paddlers.

I'm thinking back while you fast-forward,
both away from this microphone ceilidh.
A Tom Paxton song in a tired voice.

– The guy I used to do the lighting with,
from the crow's nest above assembly,
had every Paxton LP –

Tonight, 'Can't help but
wonder where I'm bound'
and what happened to my mate

after his last Monday morning at school
when we faded out with Jimi Hendrix:
colours on dimmers out to the hall.

Now an attempt at a lull for the Gaelic
buzzing from a weak PA
placed before off-key talk.

So, the keys of the van, canoeist,
friend, though I can't like your boats.
Fix a day for my wider one.

Save us from the Friday night heroics
of Bannockburn and Prince Charlie again.
The group in the corner are about to sing

the inevitable Flower of Scotland.
No-one bothers the Wild Rover no more.
Let's go before the wild mountain thyme.

I'm drunk with all these meetings in
this veneered lounge. Bless the guy
who asked me if I was still a runner.

A lot of wars since these school sports.
And Muriel, actress and organiser,
trying to grab me for street-theatre.

But Iain on the sway and seeming
skinnier in a thick cloth shirt,
saying his father still had the drift net,

corked and intact and the herring were
shoaling out off Tabhaidh Mhor.
We named the crew and hope for weather.

Canoeist, come with us, it's not
escaping as long as we know
we're doing nothing so big.

Meeting Hugh MacDiarmid

George Mackay Brown

We were fifteen or so. Our English teacher Mr Paterson was reading some modern poems to us, to let us know I suppose that poetry didn't end with Tennyson.

One of the poems was

> Auld Noah was at hame wi them aa
> The lion and the lamb

It was my first meeting with Hugh MacDiarmid.

Nothing then, for years.

T S Eliot, and Yeats, were the moderns to read.

Being young Orcadians, we dipped into Edwin Muir but found him difficult.

Then we somehow got to know that there was a flyting going on between MacDiarmid and Muir, from a MacMillan anthology of Scottish poetry edited by MacDiarmid. The row was all being conducted by MacDiarmid. Muir wouldn't play his part, but he was hurt by it, for they had been good friends as younger men.

Muir's *The Story and the Fable* seemed a wonderful song in prose about his Orkney childhood.

We were intrigued to read about the poet "Hugh Skene" in Eric Linklater's novel *Magnus Merriman* – Skene is clearly based on MacDiarmid, and is a masterly caricature.

I picked up a first edition of *Sangshaw* for one shilling and sixpence from a Stromness bookshop kept by Mr James Stevenson, a Dickensian figure. Some of the lyrics were strange and quirky, like little flashes of lightning. But we were in the way of thinking that Scots verse had truly finished with Burns – the volcano was exhausted. These were the last mutterings.

A copy of *A Drunk Man Looks at the Thistle* came my way. It was a revelation, gold ore strewn everywhere among other debris. The first section seemed marvellous, but even more wonderful was the dying close "Oh, I ha'e silence left..." Somewhere in the middle was the peerless lyric that Yeats included in his *Oxford Book of Modern Verse* (1935) – "Oh wha's been here afore me, lass..."

There was no doubt that great verse was still being written in Scots, by this man who had been born near the gateway into England.

It turned out, too, that MacDiarmid was a communist – and that appealed to some of us – we were all very left-wing in those days.

From the Stromness Library I borrowed what purported to be MacDiarmid's autobiography, *Lucky Poet*. It was a great disappointment. How could such a gifted poet write such monumentally awful prose, wearisome page after page, like chunks of granite. *Lucky Poet* was a great let-down after *The Story and the Fable*. Here at least Muir was the clear winner.

Eagerly we looked for *A Drunk Man*'s successors. They were there, all right – *The Battle Continues*, *To Circumjack Cencrastus*. But the genius seemed to have vanished. The spirit of the dead prose had entered, fatally, it seemed to me, into all the long poems that followed *A Drunk Man*.

There are some fine pieces of exposition, invective, and loquacity in *In Memoriam James Joyce* and *The Kind of Poetry I Want* – but where was the poetry? What new mystical-political kind of poetry did MacDiarmid hope would be the word to unlock the future? He had mourned that his poetry was not chanted in the dockyards and the city squares, as most of the world's great poetry had been.

Those great hunks of stone were never likely to take wing in the hearts and minds of the common people everywhere.

They seemed to be intended for intellectuals and political progressives, where poetry has never made its abode.

I was prepared to meet a wild angry old man in the Rose Street pubs when I went to Edinburgh in 1956.

What was MacDiarmid likely to say to me, a youngish countryman of Edwin Muir – if he deigned to speak at all?

The famous poet I was introduced to was one of the kindest and most charming of men. He was gentle, welcoming, humorous – balancing his glass of whisky in one hand and sucking the light of a match into his loaded pipe, amid clouds of smoke.

A well-loved puckish poet in Bob Watt's underground den at the corner of Rose Street and Hanover Street, with tremendous reserves of goodwill and intellect, he seemed.

There gathered around him, to pay homage, Sydney Goodsir Smith and Norman MacCaig, and many a lesser poet and a host of poetry-lovers and admirers of this good man himself.

Where, on the after-hour gatherings in Leamington Terrace, was the ranter and the flyter, the man with the rough granite tongue?

The great poet was all sweetness and joy, a Prospero with none of the banished king's sternness, but spells in plenty.

That benign spirit was the centre of many a glorious never-to-be-forgotten evening up at MacCaig's hospitable house.

George Mackay Brown
11 August 1992

Gael Turnbull

Information

With an hour or two to spare,
I stopped once in Langholm
to enquire for Information
at the Office near the Square

where I was courteously told
that Mr Grieve had moved away
when young "...though some say
often back for a visit when old

"and certainly, yes, in the end
buried here. No, I didn't know
him personally and so
only an opinion but understand

"he was never one to shirk
stirring a quarrel, while deemed
to be very highly esteemed
in his own field of work."

More Lines to an Old Song

We all agree upon this right
to choose the pattern of our destiny
and for that claim we'll bravely fight

each other mostly, and why not
if that's our choice?
The future's bright.

One Hundred Years On

The laird, the dominie, the minister
take pride that each are secondary to none
and most years summer's nearly over
before between the clouds we glimpse the sun.

The makar like the gowk can still be heard
even in rhyme, if not to such concision,
and, having nothing much to celebrate,
claiming whatever honour in derision.

Trees are for cutting down, bawbees for getting,
river and moorland there for hook and gun
and we contend on principle for principles
as cheerfully as we have ever done.

To the Tune of Annie Laurie

Come to bonnie Scotland
where blows by loch and glen
not just the flowering heather
about each butt and ben.

By roadside etc

Discarded fast-food carton
and plastic throw-away
beside the rusting Export
deck out each mossy brae.

By roadside etc

No need for pipes and tartan
to host a welcome here
where our traditional litter
grows richer every year.

*By roadside, park or field,
by every wall or hedge,
there see how proudly gathers
our national heritage!*

Alan Bold

Missive for MacDiarmid

If stanes could yammer as you thocht they could
They'd speir the question that you speired yersel:
How can a cheil o Alba luve the land
And thole the folk wha heave it into hell
When sic folk blythely say they're sib wi you
    And mean it too?

Fegs, you were faithered in the Muckle Toon:
A postie's bairn, you strodged alang the street.
A man o letters, he ca'd you to kirk
"And heard God passin wi a bobby's feet".
You were a man o letters in your turn:
    Letters that burn.

Oot o Langholm and intae the warld
(Reversin, thus, the sayin o the place)
You pu'd the language up by its rouch roots
Syne, by an orra geg, it flooered in space.
By Christ, MacDiarmid, you skrieved a guid buik
    An no by luck.

"A poet maun ken a'-thing" (you liked tae quote –
The phrase was Rilke's, an eel-droonin gift).
You made the maist o aa the buiks you read
But also leared the laverock i the lift.
You heard the silence o the starnies yet
        Aye had your shout.

But back to Scotland. It gave life tae you
An livin death tae ithers, dozent carles
Wha touched the soil but couldna tig its saul:
You thocht them swine wha couldna slorp your pearls.
Your lanely lowsin-time you gaed tae gaw
        God in Gillha.

Whisky in your loof, you lauched like hell,
An aftwhiles grieved like heaven makin main.
Your harns were hardened in a foreign lan,
Your heid was hammered in auld Lon'on toon.
Henceforth you wandered i the universe:
        Venus an Mars.

Wanrestfu poet wi your kilt an pipe,
Thrawn battler speakin volumes wi your verse,
You focht a guid fecht fore they yirdit you
In Langholm where you turn aneath the stars.
"Frae battles, mair than ballads" sae you came.
        Wanearthly wame.

A century has sauntered past since yon
Oorie day in August you cam first.
You fand Scotland root-hewn, you left it birsled,
Ready for a new mell efter hairst.
The message o MacDiarmid's plain tae see:
        Let Scotland be.

Let Scotland be united wi itsel,
Let Scotland use its rowth o roots tae grow
Mair grains than groans, mair seeds than soughs,
Mair ramel than the usual row-de-dow.
MacDiarmid lit the landscape wi his leid,
        Scotland tak heed.

The warl spins forward tae its twenty-first,
We're dizzy liddenin, geylies lookin back.
MacDiarmid had the future in his sicht,
Tying tradition to its fordel maik.
He made a union o divided sauls
        Tae shaw's oorsels.

Donald C Farquhar

Thrawn

Thrawn aye, thrawn syne
an aye wull oot the thrawn grun.
Tawes tae hauns an clapper mou
english maister, buird an kirk
Scotland's leids maun lowp an yerk
an bou tae pious wund an blaw.
Bit aye are thrawn, winna lig
the leids o Scotland, thrawn, big.

Great Intit

See ritin, it's great! –
Zat so?

Oh ay, it's great, so it is.
We've got a bydie-in riter so we huv. –
Zat rite?
Diz yer man no mynd?

Naw…he's glaikit…the bam,
cuidni rite 'is name so he cuidni.
Thinks rites is fur the masonics.
Whit dae ye tell 'im but?
Nuthin. A'm at the bingo.

We dae poetry an that but?
Zat so!
Whit dae ye dae tae it well?
It's got feet so it hiz,
ye didni no that did ye but? –
Naw A niver…

Hauf a dizzin or whit?…
Hauf a dizzin whit?
Feet?

Sometimes the're imbic so they ur.
Aw, A'm sorry tae hear that.
Is it bad?
Imbic pentar – them's poetry feet.
Zat 'is name then?
Whit?
Yer bydie-in, ye no, Imbic Penter?
Naw it's no.
Whit else dae ye dae, but?

We pit thaim inti stanzas. –
      Yer feet?
Naw, stupit, the poems
sometimes it's big stanzas an
sometimes it's jist wee.
      A no whit ye mean, hen,
      mine's jist the same
      big when ye'r no wantin it an
      when ye dae, it's aw wee so it is.

On-a-mat-a-pee, fur sound ye no?
      Sounds a rite bam.
Who?
      Imbic.
Jeesus! Dae ye no fancy it?
      Whit?
Ritin an that.
      Eh, Oh ay.
Great intit!

Sheddaes

Sheddaes dinna shaw on dreich days,
rain, cowpin owre causies
drouns the hale street.
Trees hing tuim on lanely braes
bydin for the sin.
Wee burds, aye cheery
cheip cheip frae drouthy howfs an
luikin doun, nae brichtness maks its mark.
Bit syne the cluds birl awa
an oot cums yersel.
Trees steir theirsels an wag a haun.
The wee burds blether an lauch the lift
while keekin doun, ma sheddae finds itsel
ance mair tethert tae ma taes.

Cushie-doo

      Vyce wi the sang o luv,
      een wi the blink o the mune,
      muive as a souchin sauch
      sweys bi the chirlin rin.
      Touch wi a touch sae saft
      haud as a chitterin lowe
      ma haun as a flaffin wing
      ma hert as a cushie-doo.

MacDiarmid

Alexander Moffat

To go back to the beginning – I think it was 1959 or 1960 and I was still at school. Alan Bold suggested that I come round to listen to a radio programme about the poet Hugh MacDiarmid. His music teacher at Broughton School, Ronald Stevenson, had told him he must hear this programme because MacDiarmid was the greatest living Scottish poet, and a man of genius. I can only vaguely recollect our discussion afterwards. How can an artist be a communist and a Scottish Nationalist? Is science a suitable subject for poetry? Is writing in Scots not only provincial but anti-international? We debated these questions and others into the night. I'm sure Alan was much more positive than I was about our new discovery.

As a young "avant-gardist" in the late 1950s I was an adherent of free improvisation in jazz and abstract expressionism in painting. American culture with its new values was all-persuasive. European culture seemed a thing of the past and MacDiarmid's political and philosophical stance was for me an anachronism, of no significance whatsoever.

I only seriously began to question all of this at the end of my second year at Edinburgh College of Art. This was the summer of 1962, the year of MacDiarmid's 70th birthday. I managed to get a copy of the collected poems which MacMillans of New York had brought out. Coming from the anti-intellectual climate of a Scottish art college made it difficult for me, to say the least, to make inroads into MacDiarmid's poetry and ideas. I had to work at it, slowly but surely, and with the help of Alan Bold. I'm still doing so today, such is his awe-inspiring range as an artist.

MacDiarmid showed me that Art mattered, that it could affect life and make a contribution towards changing the world – but only if it aspired, if the artist aspired towards greater horizons than were commonly accepted. Art had to be more than merely enjoyable and reassuring – it had also to challenge and to question. MacDiarmid also showed me that Scotland and Scottish artists were included in this scenario – if they so wished – and that Scotland had a unique culture and history which could be used and developed by modern artists. He also pointed out what was wrong with Scotland and its artists.

How does MacDiarmid fare today, 100 years after his birth? I have to admit that very few artists I know bother to read him, or even want to. Perhaps that tide has turned with the publication of Alan Bold's biography, or perhaps, like Mahler, MacDiarmid will need at least 50 years before his work truly breaks through to a wider public. On the other hand it may take the reality of an independent Scotland before the Scots themselves eventually wake up to his greatness.

For he isn't a popular poet – he had no real wish to be "a poet of the people". Apart from the early lyrics there is no sentiment in his work, no

Alexander Moffat

genuine warmth. This is replaced by weighty philosophical concerns and an intimidating intellectualism. As an artist he was an unashamed "elitist" despising folk music, for example, as the illiterate rantings of the peasant classes. He certainly did not believe that anyone could become an artist. On the contrary, he maintained that only exceptional talents and then only with an extraordinary effort of the will could great art be produced. And he was only interested in great art. He called for a kind of giantism in the arts, citing Pound, Neruda, Shostakovich, Eisenstein, and Hikmet as exemplars of the monumental in art, arguing that the epic nature of the social and political changes of the 20th century required a grand synthesis – in all the arts. I'm afraid all of this is, for most artists, pretty problematic stuff.

Maurice Lindsay recently argued that MacDiarmid wasn't an original, but an assimilator. Josef Herman, however, who got to know MacDiarmid in wartime Glasgow told me that he considered MacDiarmid to be an exceptional creative thinker – "one of the few geniuses" he has ever met. I go along with Josef Herman on that one. It seems to me that MacDiarmid is our biggest artist, one who faced up to the important issues of our time, cultivating a "world view" opposed to the narrow parochialism of most of his contemporaries, and as a result inspiring many of the finest Scottish artists of succeeding generations – from Norman MacCaig and Sorley MacLean to the painters John Bellany and Ken Currie. MacDiarmid sought unity where others were content with destruction. Above all he demonstrated that poetry and art could attempt a reconciliation between the human spirit and the material world. Let us hope he remains *the* artist of the future.

My personal memories of MacDiarmid are numerous. A glowing and moving reading of his translation of Rilke's *Requiem* in 1962; his fiery speech at the end of his 85th birthday concert in the Assembly Rooms; his Rabelaisian behaviour at Alan Bold's wedding reception; and his opening address at the John Heartfield exhibition at the Edinburgh Festival of 1970. I should like to end by quoting from this address as it contains one of his most interesting and unique statements about the visual arts:

> To my mind this is the most important – indeed the only important art exhibition held in Scotland during the 78 years of my life, and in fact for a much longer period. Almost all the rest is museum stuff, parasitic or trivial and unworthy inventions, and without living significance. The posters and book-jackets and other works shown here deal with matters of the most terrible and inescapable significance – a significance as relevant today – and to all the world – as obtained when they were produced in Germany. It's no use turning the backs of our heads to them, and thinking they'll go away and that 'it can't happen here'. It can and in some ways it *is* happening. We are not accustomed to think of Art as having a vital effect on our everyday affairs – still less as an all-important and decisive effect. What we see here has had just that – and will continue to have it with unabated force till the great problems of the menace of genocide, of nuclear war, of social injustice are overcome.

Alexander Moffat

MacDiarmid with Ezra Pound in Venice, 1971   *Photo: Valda Grieve*

Drinking MacDiarmid Down

Pearse Hutchinson

A book that has given me recurrent pleasure for nearly half a century now is Maurice Lindsay's *Modern Scottish Poetry: An Anthology of the Scottish Renaissance 1920-1945*. It was published by Faber in 1946, and I bought it that same year, when I was 19; it was thus one of the first books I ever bought first-hand.

I almost never keep cuttings in books, but in this book there is one: from the *Observer* of 19 February 1961, it's a photo of the kilted MacDiarmid shaking hands with Bertrand Russell at a CND rally. They're both smiling.

That photo may have played tricks with my memory, superimposing itself on my image of the man I first met in 1948, when he opened his Glasgow hall-door to me – wearing, I'm still pretty sure, a kilt. I'd got his address from Maurice Lindsay, whom I'd met briefly, and taking my partly Dutch courage in my hands I made the trek, which must, I suppose, be called a pilgrimage. When he answered my ring I told him I was Irish, a poet, and a great admirer. He brought me in and made me immediately welcome, as did Valda, who made sure I got something to eat.

Like many another, I was struck by the apparent contrast between the fiery public polemicist and the kindliness and homeliness and easy charm of the man himself. Yet when you come to think of it, there isn't really – for all his famous glorying in inconsistency – any inconsistency at all between kindliness and a deep and vocal anger at injustice (which is, after all, the enemy of kindliness). The two might in fact be said to go hand in hand, in certain people.

He took me under his wing for a few days, and brought me on a pub-crawl or two. When I read, years later, his virtuoso and, to me not *entirely* convincing essay on the Dour Drinkers of Glasgow, I recognised some of the things he'd said to me as we walked from his home to the first pub.

I'd just read, with excitement, Sorley MacLean's *Dàin do Eimhir*, and I was charmed at the warm way in which MacDiarmid spoke of this other great Scottish poet. But I'd never heard of Francis George Scott, of whom MacDiarmid spoke with even greater enthusiasm. He insisted on bringing me to tea at Scott's, along with the critic John Tonge, and I still look back on this as a signal honour. All I remember, tho', is an imposing presence in an armchair, courtesy (tho' less genial than MacDiarmid's own), and music-talk which was entirely above my ignorant head. But I can still see the four of us sitting there, and listening in Edinburgh recently to Jo Millar's magnificent singing of Scott's settings of MacDiarmid that room, that penumbra, came vividly back to me.

At 21 I was getting, half-reluctantly, sceptical about some of my father's claims. As, for example, the importance of Millar's, the Glasgow printing firm he'd worked for – and his boast of having been the first Catholic ever employed there. But MacDiarmid confirmed the renown of Millar's, and the possibility of the other claim too. And he was duly, or perhaps dutifully, impressed when I told him that during the Irish War of Independence my father, who had "risen" to be Managing Director, was sacked, not by old Mr Millar's wish but under police pressure, because he refused to give up his Sinn Féin activities; being then deported, and interned in Frongoch. So there I was, basking in reflected glory. I'm sure MacDiarmid saw through me.

He spoke with admiration of Daniel Corkery's book *The Hidden Ireland* (about the Gaelic people's poets of 18th-century Munster), saying it had been a great source of encouragement to him in his own struggle. Corkery's book, which is far from flawless, has now been discredited to the satisfaction of the slave-minded whom we have always with us in Ireland. In 1948 I was, like others of my generation, in full flight from the far-from-hidden Ireland of sexual repression, with which I mistakenly, though understandably, identified Irish nationalism. Many of us in the Dublin of those days looked to the London of Horizon and the "posh" papers for enlightenment. Meeting MacDiarmid at that point, listening to his talk of my country and his, was one of the things that helped me to come to terms with Ireland, but also to begin to struggle free from the thralldom of London. That MacDiarmid had no difficulty in being both a Socialist and a Nationalist gave me courage. It was only later I remembered that my father had no difficulty either. But then my father wasn't MacDiarmid…

After that I met him in Dublin a couple of times, once at a party in Louise and Kader Asmal's home after an Anti-Apartheid poetry reading in Liberty Hall (that was in the late '60s, when poets, as distinct from pop-stars, were still able to pack people in for a cause). At the party he held court with immense graciousness, and when someone asked him, "May I call you Hugh?", he gave benign but minimal consent. After he'd been thus addressed two or three times, a more in-the-know person led the gauche courtier away, and whispered in his ear. Much later this now enlightened one was heard Chrissing him elaborately.

I recall only one thing MacDiarmid said on that occasion: "I've more in common with a High Tory than with the middle class."

The last time we met was in February 1972. The previous October I'd taken up residence in Leeds under the resplendent title of Gregory Fellow in Poetry. Part of my job was to invite poets to read to the student society Poetry & Audience. Most of the poets I asked were Irish, people either not known in England at all or not well enough. But from the start I was determined to get MacDiarmid down, and what's more to get him well paid for it. I don't in general approve of celebrity rates, but, I thought, if any man ever deserved it this man does. Besides, he was 80.

The Poetry & Audience people were all for having him, but couldn't afford what I wanted for him. As it happened I knew a couple of other students who were anything but hostile to MacDiarmid's Communist leanings, and both had been on Civil Rights rallies in Derry. They also happened to be officials of the Students' Union. So MacDiarmid was invited, for a fee of £100.

Bob Welch from Cork, who was then lecturing in Leeds, and has since become head of the English department at Coleraine, drove me up to Scotland to collect the poet and his wife. When we got to Candymills their welcome was as warm and natural as I remembered from 24 years earlier. They sat us down and gave us Bulgarian brandy, which was excellent. They'd been to Bulgaria not long before, and MacDiarmid spoke highly of that country.

It was a fine crisp day, and after a while he brought me out, down the short garden path to the gate. We stood there admiring the low hills. "They're a human size", he said. I'd never been in that part of the country before, but I've always liked that kind of landscape, and the very phrase MacDiarmid now uttered I had myself used to Bob Welch not long before. It was the obvious phrase, the right one. But I couldn't help wondering whether, for all his Bulgarian enthusiasm, he too was thinking, as I had been, of that other phrase, "Socialism with a human face". It was, after all, only four years since the Prague Spring. Whatever about that, the nauseating triumphalism of the North-Western capitalist world over what it calls "the death of Socialism" could do with the scorn he would surely have heaped upon it.

On the way to Leeds we stopped for a stroll around Langholm, where he talked about the Common Riding Day and pointed out a favourite pub. Oh to have had a drink with him in Langholm! But it was the wrong time of day.

MacDiarmid sat in the danger-seat, Valda and myself in the back. Her hair was as red as ever, and she was as lively. We got on fine, tho' I did have one moment of alarm, when she was telling Bob and me about a recent anti-nuclear demonstration. A policeman had threatened her, but she soon put a stop to his gallop. In part-demonstration of how, she took off her stiletto-heel – and brandished it. For a second I thought I was about to be on the receiving end of it.

They stayed in Leeds for three days, with Bob Welch and his wife Angela, whose house in Adel was already a home-from-home for me. Everyone got on well together, and one evening after supper (as the Leeds folk still had the gumption to call it) he showed us his fish-bract: a small extra fold or flap of skin close to his ear. Only one human being in a million, he told us – or perhaps it was five million – had this vestige of our far-distant origins. He was understandably proud of this, and tickled. I got the feeling, perhaps wrongly, that he felt the fish-bract to be, in his own case, a mark of genius. As well he might…

He also told us that evening of a recent check-up: the doctor had told him there was no reason he shouldn't live to be a hundred. That was cause for celebration, and whisky was poured. He drank, if I remember rightly, just two glasses. Valda was keeping an eye on him.

When I heard of his death, five years later, I naturally thought of that moment with a pang. All the same, 86 isn't bad.

The reading was in a large hall in the Students' Union building, and it was packed. He was in grand form, he delivered his poems magnificently and ad-libbed with all the expected panache. The students were nearly all English, from different parts. At one point he made an anti-Sassenach and anti-imperialist remark, and just one youngster walked out. Others clapped.

Having introduced him, I was the only other person on the stage, sitting at a respectful distance. Elbow room. When he finished reading I announced, as he'd asked me to, that he'd be glad to answer questions but that since he was getting deaf they should be written down and handed up to me and I'd then pass them to him to answer.

There were quite a few questions, the usual mixture of perceptive and crass. One was belligerent: why had he – somewhere – spoken well of the fascist Ezra Pound? MacDiarmid rose to the occasion, giving, in the longest answer of the night, a dazzling and moving display of loyalty to a fellow-archpoet. In the course of it he quoted Major Douglas, and while not condoning Pound's involvement, laid the main blame fairly and squarely at the door of Capitalism.

But the best question of all was the very last one. A beautiful student with long dark hair handed me up a slip of paper on which was written: "What is his favourite drink?" I passed him this charming note, and needless to say he was equally charmed. He read it out in ringing tones, which made the whole audience happy too. Then he answered it: "Glenfiddich", he said.

The beautiful girl at once disappeared out of the far door, and MacDiarmid told us how for many years he'd been proclaiming wherever he went the virtues of Glenfiddich, as a result of which that excellent firm had asked him to join the board, his only duty being to accept a crate of Glenfiddich every Christmas. He left us in no doubt that he'd agreed.

At this point the young woman returned with a glass of Glenfiddich, which she handed directly up to him. They both smiled, he thanked her and raised it to his lips. The audience rose to its feet, cheered and clapped.

Pearse Hutchinson

Theo Dorgan

The Voices of Conscience

After long wandering in the dark world
I came to a high place in a wood
And stopped there, listening and alone.
The wind in the trees was like an ocean:
To the north, voices murmuring of injustice,
To the south, the east and west, voices
Speaking against injustice.
Then a dark tide came over the world
And the voices fell silent.

For a long time there was nothing
But echoes of silence on the dying wind.

Someone behind me lit a candle, started singing,
And soon we were joined by another light,
And another, and another, until it seemed
That the whole earth was singing back the darkness.
We knew in our bones they could hear us,
The disappeared ones in the camps and in the prisons,
And we sang them the echo of their broken voices,
Answering from the world they must always dream,4
To give them courage, to give them hope.

It was the least we could do for them, knowing
That someday they would do the same for us.

Kilmainham, Easter

to the memory of James Connolly

Blood and cold stone, rust
Thickening to a seam of crystal,
Stain on the jailyard
Paving we cannot lift.

Crash of the volley and our hope.
When they carried out your stretcher
The yard darkened to a well of shame
And steadily it grows darker.

This is the shrine our rulers keep
And today they have graced it with flowers.
Let us grant them at least their honesty,
Their naked love of prisons.

The Prisoners of Lord Lane

Until these men are free
There can be no freedom,
No laughter under the trees,
No colour in our flowers.

Each day they spend behind bars
Is a day of winter in our streets.

If their judges go unchallenged
We go in chains,
If their perjurors go unchallenged
There is no language left for love.

Donald Adamson

Samba

I could light a candle to Paw Broon
at a shrine adorned with tinfoil
and mirrors, like the one I saw on TV
served by a samba queen,
priestess to a god she called Condomblé.

I'd assemble fragments,
the sweetie wrappings and coloured glass
of Scotland in the thirties.
I'd cram the room with kitch and cliché,
myths and nostalgias:
cranes along the river through the smokehaze,
clang of hammer on metal,
football grounds filled to overflowing,
(150,000 for a cup final),
tramcars, weekends doon the watter...

For atmosphere I'd play
a Harry Lauder song, maybe
Keep right on to the end of the road
(as distant from us now as Gregorian Chant
or Ancient Church Slavonic)
and the sound would come hissing through the horn
of a wind-up gramophone.

And Maw Broon and Paw Broon and the whole family
would dance along a gaslit close,
out into the street, revellers
with skull masks as in a Rio carnival.

To a Displaced American

You left no longer believing
it was your land.
History that had seemed like a young brave
came to you with flesh in tatters,
wearing grave cloth
and smelling of burial mounds.

You have cast yourself ashore
here in our own wild west. You can dance
naked, let rain wash off the paint
of a computer programmer, you can grow
new skin to hide the scarifications
of high school and college.

You are welcome yet enviable
to us, natives huddling
with backs hunched like our hills,
braving the weather
as our past beats down on us.

At the heart of the trunk the sap
that runs through the bristlecone pine[1]
is genocide.
There's slaughter in every branch
though no hurt
in such a small invasion as yours.

You threaten us with nothing more
than the here-and-now
of one with another
scaling our tribal battlements.

You present the mildest and severest terms
of human kind: I and you,
loving, hating, indifferent,
creating our seasons, our histories
in tree rings, circle by circle, widening.

---

1. North American tree whose ring widths
provide a universal standard in archaeo-
logical dating.

Patrick Toal

Scotland 1992

Time's arrow knows not the mystery nor mastery
Of the crimson Host of bulken sun,
Nor the crystal thistle touched by dew-orbed dawn,
Nor our breaking sickle turning wheat
In shards of light and gold: a splintered History
To forge us through atom to bone
From our mind cast Hel, lost of kernel,
One breast of fire and one of snow.
Man riseth like the Yahwist's great whale,
Spurning as a Peter world burnt hands:
Three cries, one of hunger, hope and guile.
My bending back and black bound words,
My hands with pen moonlight skinned,
I weep the spirits of fathers, our reticent lancers,
Each thrusting high his mossed banner.
Dear sepulchres of Scotland.
The rhombus wheat I have often seen
Cracking soil beneath the boreal star,
Earth gold at our greedy brimming boards:
We spill wine and blood
Into the throats of wise conquerors.
Aye, slumber soft, my Scotland.
With the anvil and flames of images,
I sadly hammer these words for you.

James Robertson

The Road to the Ferry

Around this house, late summer,
With all the tourists gone,
And a car along the road
Perhaps twice in an evening,
The wild things come to life again.
It is the sounds of them mostly:
Rabbits in the whins, and a polecat;
Bats fluttering against the window;
And the looping call of wind

In the telephone wires.
Down on the shore the congregations gather –
Duck, geese, gulls – all bickering for space.
A white owl haunts the garden and his own
Flight paths, putting the fear of death
In anxious voles.
We watch him and admire.
All this nature is very reassuring,
As though secure behind the glass
Our comfort can never be disturbed.

But the sounds I want to talk about tonight
Are different altogether.
I heard them first in my dreams,
Or at the edges of them;
Then one night I came to with a start, struggling
To place their strange familiarity.
Suddenly I knew! – They were there, outside,
Bulging in the narrow road like some mammoth herd,
Stamping, snorting, shuddering.
I was afraid.
(Of course this was before the coming of the bridge,
But long after the last drowned ferry – and people,
Mindful of that sad disaster, were still content
To take the long route round.)
Barely able to contain a shout of fear –
Or was it jubilation? – I sat upright in my bed
As they trampled past, those sounds.
Just beyond the house they left the road,
Snapping the fence as one snaps fingers,
Crossing the links to the firth.
Even at a distance of half a mile I could hear them,
First their shaggy fetlocks splashing in the warm shallows,
Then their great shoulders rolling and heaving
As they swam that slender neck of the sea,
That ruffled collar, that vulnerable grace.

The noise diminished and I felt my limbs relax.
I could only imagine them after that,
Shaking themselves as they rose up
Out of the falling tide, lumbering on and on,
Beyond all thought,
Beyond the grief of our time,
The built waste and the wrecked,
And the broken heart.

I have never slept so badly since;
Nor dreamed so well.

Garech

Deirdre Chapman

One of the sources of Chris's charm – and I think charm is the right word – was that on a social level he operated almost entirely in the present. In his company you needed no back references. He assumed strangers knew nothing of him and would incorporate a brief cv where necessary in telling a story.

Effectively this meant he carried no intellectual baggage, no specialised knowledge, and neither, in his eyes, did you. Together you were gentlemen and amateurs and the slate was clean for the conversation that was about to happen. Matters of record like departure times of trains and planes became agreeable subjects for speculation. A journey he had made five years earlier might be offered as guidance to someone heading for the London train.

When he stayed with us this pleasant pooling of knowledge extended to the domestic round. When he asked what I was making for lunch and I told him Parsley Pie, one of Valda's Cornish specialities, he would consult his memory bank and say "I think she puts an egg through it."

Often he told me how to boil an egg. The secret was to take it out of the fridge ahead of time or to bring it very slowly to the boil. He had discovered this when doing a reading in Oxford where he stayed overnight with an equally unworldly professor whose wife had been called away suddenly. Many eggs went into the discovery. (In one of Norman MacCaig's 80th birthday interviews he too went on at some length about the boiling of eggs so he may have been a third party at breakfast.)

These fragments of information were offered not to show how little regard he had for the commonplace but in a genuine effort to help, and there was a real possibility of hurting his feelings when, for instance, you cut short a debate about how to get in touch with someone by producing this person's phone number.

The reason, I think, was an anxiety to be relevant. The physical and intellectual remoteness which was such a major part of his life was something to be pushed aside quickly, and not always wisely, when he was in company. In company he extemporised and often exaggerated apparently from fear of being found dull. This was so obvious and so flattering to anyone in his ambience that strangers and slight acquaintances tended to come away feeling very good about themselves.

I think it was out of the desire to be relevant; that and the habit of extemporising, that one day he conducted a marriage service in our house in Glasgow. Garech de Brun, a "Guinness heir" in the diary columns of the sixties and seventies, his then companion Tiger Cowley, and a friend, Jeffrey Craig, had come to Glasgow where Chris was spending a few days with us so that Jeffrey could photograph Chris for the sleeve of Garech's *Claddagh Records* recording of him reading *The Drunk Man*.

In the forenoon Chris, Garech, Tiger, Jeffrey and I walked to the Botanic Gardens where Chris was snapped in front of the fig in the entrance to the Kibble Palace. Then we went to a pub and from there to a Chinese restaurant for lunch. Towards the end of the meal Tiger began to ask aloud of the world, the company, the flock wallpaper if Garech would ever marry her. Chris sat up. "I am a Justice of the Peace," he said. "I can marry you." "*Really?*" said Tiger.

Rice congealed, waiters hovered, diners beached their chopsticks. A situation could be felt developing. "But surely..." I wanted to say. It was true that he had been a JP – in Montrose half a century earlier – and that JP's were once entitled to conduct marriages in their area. But one didn't hurt his feelings and one doesn't, if one is wise, sabotage a situation.

He became awesomely practical. Garech paid for lunch and we all went back to our house where Chris demanded a bible – one of my children had a school bible – and some A4 paper. He asked the happy couple for their names in full, dates and places of birth – Tiger had to phone Wales for her father's middle name and the date of her divorce – and with Jeffrey and myself as witnesses conducted an extremely impressive, eloquent, solemn and competent wedding service. There was no hint of charade. Tears were shed. We all signed the A4 paper, embraced, filled glasses, and then I fled to another room to phone Mike, my husband, at Scottish Television, where he was organizing an early-evening chat show.

"Your father has just married Garech and Tiger," I said. "That's all right," he said calmly, for he is his father's match in the matter of extemporising, "Nicky Fairbairn is on the programme."

When the wedding party met up with the television party in a pub after the programme Chris, now flushed with relevance, was at the centre of the table, recounting the events of the afternoon. On the periphery Garech and Nicky had a word. And some years later Garech married an Indian princess.

I still don't know all that this story reveals about Chris, but it allows him once again, gloriously, to confound our attempts to define him.

Deirdre Chapman

On First Looking Into *In Memoriam James Joyce*

Angus Calder

In 1965, when we were both 23-year-old postgraduate students, Jenni and I lived at a place called Chailey. It was not like the classic Suzzex village beloved by Bloomsberries and Georgians alike and inspirational for English Nationalist composers, but it was handy for Haywards Heath station and hence for London; and we did get free use of a cottage on a flat stretch of Weald with pylons marching over the field behind. The cottage belonged to Angus Ross, a specialist in eighteenth-century literature who lectured at the new University of Sussex. Dr Ross, though then absent teaching somewhere in the New World, had left behind his books and records. Thus it was that I first heard Ewan McColl's singing and first opened *In Memoriam James Joyce*.

Both Jenni and I had been reared in England by very Scottish parents. Mine kept Barrie's plays and Soutar's poems in the living room. Jenni's father, famous as a pioneering critic of Scottish literature, was a friend of C.M.Grieve. However, my earliest tutor at Cambridge (Helena Shire) had been scunnered by my first essay for her, on the Ballads. I had missed the point completely – no habitat could be less like Liddesdale than the London suburb where I'd grown up. Without undue fuss, Helena started setting me right. In between Chaucer, whom she always called 'Geoffrey', and the later 'Edmund', we studied Henryson and Dunbar. One day Helena told us that 'Jeannie' was coming to Cambridge to sing for the local branch of the Saltire Society. For her King's students, she arranged a special treat. We sat in Helena's living room one morning and Jeannie Robertson sang just for us. Then in the pub Jeannie kept on singing. Later, when I was chairman of the Labour Club, I invited Jeannie back for a joint meeting with the Folk Society. I was on my way home.

Aware that my Cambridge education had been incomplete, at Chailey I took advantage of the rural quiet and rose early to improve myself. I read Pound and couldn't get past his Fascism. I went right through Yeats' *Collected Poems*, and didn't like them – it was to be four more years before I got the point and became, perhaps to my cost, a crazed Yeatsophile. In Cuckfield Hospital, while our elder daughter was being born, I sat reading Joyce's *Ulysses*. I tried to translate Lorca and Neruda. And, thanks to the absent Ross, I discovered MacDiarmid.

In 1965, MacDiarmid's poetry was little represented in anthologies – I'm not sure that I'd previously encountered even one lyric. The first *Collected Poems*, very far from complete, had appeared in New York in 1962, but the book wasn't generally available in the UK. Angus Ross had slim volumes of the early lyrics, of which I made little, and the *Drunk Man*, which I found intriguing but indigestible. What hooked me on MacDiarmid was *In Memoriam James Joyce*. The shock of recognition was intense. In a notebook I transcribed, in high excitement, passage after passage from the poem. I was far from realising that some of the statements which struck me as utterly and most importantly true had probably been copied by Grieve himself from the *TLS* or wherever.

What was it, in 1965, that made me so completely susceptible to MacDiarmid? Playing records of McColl so much no doubt helped – I was consciously reclaiming the Scottish heritage to which I was connected by parentage but not environment, and Scott's novels began to mean a lot to me about the same time. But the fact that MacDiarmid was Scots weighed, I think, no more than each of three other factors – his Marxism, his commitment to 'science', and his internationalism.

After Helena Shire, the tutor who'd influenced me most had been George Steiner. It may seem odd that Steiner, no sort of left-winger, should have formed more than anyone else my commitment to Marxism. But he did so, because he spoke eloquently and incessantly about and from Central European intellectual traditions, in which Marx was centrally implicated. Brecht? *Of course* – but we must also read his polemical adversary Lukacs – and by the way, Trotsky's *Literature and Revolution*, a dazzling tract, was indispensable, too. Yes, George…

By 1965, I'd digested at least a proportion of Steiner's words, was making something of Brecht myself, and had begun to explore the vast Neruda. Now here, in *In Memoriam James Joyce*, I encountered a poet, MacDiarmid, who was into high-intellectual uses of Marxist materialism as no other poet, in English, ever had been. And for someone instructed by Steiner, his invocation of the master composer of that Jewish generation which had included Wittgenstein, Lucacs and Adorno was delicious proof of his authentically un-English intellectualism:

> Other masters may conceivably write
> Even yet in C major
> But we – we take the perhaps 'primrose path'
> To the dodecaphonic bonfire.

My father, a science journalist, had passed much of his time with famous scientists. Haldane, Bernal, Bohr and Waddington were tea-table names in our household. No doubt my own literary ambitions were sparked by filial revolt. But the idea that science was a serious matter didn't leave me. In my early twenties I did not realise that for Thomson, Pope, Goethe, Shelley, there had been no barrier between poetic and scientific ways of knowing. I thought that they were somehow opposed. Here, to my relief, was MacDiarmid, thus far uniquely (though I soon discovered Miroslav Holub) eager to assert otherwise:

> Ivar Aasen, Elizabeth Elstob, Rabelais, Browning, Meredith, Remizov,
> Gergj Fishta and Avetik Isaakyan,
> And William Barnes and his sixty languages,
> (Browning with his 'to talk as brothers talk
> In half-words, call things by half-names, no balk
> From discontinuing old aids') – words like the fortune-telling table
> Whereby things not yet discovered are foreknown to Science
> – as Meldelyev predicted scandium, germanium and polonium,

> As astronomers have foretold where a planet should be
> and the telescope later has found it – as blue roses
> Can never be found, but peas with yellow blossoms
> And haricot beans with red blossoms will yet be found,
> Guests not yet arrived – whose places await them.

Finally, I was a committed internationalist. MacDiarmid struck me at once as the least parochial writer from the British archipelago I'd ever read. Here was a geographical sweep to match Neruda's, an encyclopaedic celebration of the diversity of human cultures. I learnt, most crucially, from this poem, that 'internationalism' should imply not Airline English and Big Macs everywhere, but interaction between distinctive nations, of which Scotland should properly be one – indeed, *is* one:

> Or even as we know
> Schweitzer and Cappelletti on the Cimbric language
> Of the last descendants of the old Lombobards;
> Tibetan influences on Tocharian;
> Glottalized Continuants in Navaho, Nootka and Kwakiutl…
> And Pirandello's treatise in German on the Sicilian dialect,
> *Laute und Lautentwicklung der Mundart von Girgenti.*

> And rejoicing in all those intranational differences which
> Each like a flower's scent by its peculiarity sharpens
> Appreciation of others as well as bringing
> Appreciation of itself, as experiences of gardenia or zinnia
> Refine our experience of rose or sweet pea.

> Or even as, in the Shetland Islands where I lived,
> I know, in the old Norn language, the various names
> Applied to all the restless movements of the sea…

I don't now think of *In Memoriam* as MacDiarmid's greatest achievement. The *Drunk Man* and *On a Raised Beach* seem to me the prime poems, among many lyrical and meditative items which concentrate MacDiarmidism more powerfully than most of *In Memoriam*. But when I thought I wasn't literate in Scots, I needed verse in English to lead me in.

I first saw MacDiarmid a couple of years after our brief Chailey residence, flyting with Hamish Henderson at an Edinburgh Festival event. I knew that his denunciation of folksong was wholly wrong (and contradicted by passages in *In Memoriam*). Yet he lived entirely up to expectations – scaldingly eloquent, and as uncompromising as a mountain. Then, in 1975, I attended a conference on Commonwealth Literature at Stirling University. For some reason, the MacRobert Centre dining area was almost empty. Two figures sat by the window. Although very shy, I impudently put my tray down at their table. The Vietnam War was still in progress. The Viet Cong were winning. The younger man was trying to reason his friend Chris out of his dogmatic support for these Communist guerillas. I don't think this loving MacCaig-Grieve wrangle was conducted for my benefit, but it was some show.

Later, after he'd read, I took a new friend over to meet Grieve, the Somali novelist Nuruddin Farah. What everyone says is true: off a platform, outwith a flyting, whisky in hand, fag in mouth, the great man was sweetness personified, as if to meet this young African was an honour. I felt as in the presence of an elderly relation – someone whom, in a sense, I'd known all my life, part of the genealogy. As with family, one could take contradictions and eccentricities for granted, as elements ina pattern without which one couldn't exist.

When he died three years later, I had just been 'teaching' his work for the Open University. I was asked for a tribute for the Course Newsletter. What else could I do but quote *In Memoriam James Joyce*?

> This single-minded zeal, this fanatic devotion to art
> Is alien to the English poetic temperament, no doubt,
> 'This narrowing intensity' as the English say,
> But I have it even as you had it, Yeats my friend,
> And would have it with me as you at the end,
> I who am infinitely more un-English than you
> And turn Scotland to poetry like those women who
> In their passion secrete and turn to
> Musk through and through!
>
> So I think of you, Joyce, and of Yeats and others who are dead
> As I walk this Autumn and observe
> The birch tremulously pendulous in jewels of cairngorm,
> The sauch, the osier and the crack-willow
> Of the beaten gold of Austraila;
> The sycamore in rich straw-gold;
> the elm bowered in saffron;
> the oak in flecks of salmon gold;
> The beeches huge torches of living orange.

This brings tears to the eyes. But, reopening *In Memoriam*, it's the man's Byronic humour which strikes me. To appear so erudite, to demand, page after page, that everyone else should be erudite, then to demonstrate, with calculated bathos, that the learning demanded is not that of *TLS* specialists, but something quickening everyday life?

> One thing sticks out. You must agree
> Poetry apart, as life you scan,
> The whole thing's due, in human terms,
> To woman taking a rise out of man.

Full of quotations, *In Memoriam* exists to be quoted. I might say that my intellectual life since 1965 has mostly consisted of quoting MacDiarmid imperfectly. And yet somehow he leaves one free, doesn't he? At a recent OU summer school I set up several students to perform an 'Edwin Morgan Miscellany'. I persuaded a rather stiff and pedantic-seeming Englishman to mime 'Little Blue Blue' while Doug from Bedfordshire read the lines. Just before the event, to our dismay, he disappeared without trace. But eventually, right on cue, he burst on stage wearing, beside a blue tracksuit, that selfsame blue rose which *In Memoriam* tells us 'can never be found'. It wasn't *natural*, but never mind.

Angus Calder

Tom Scott

The Testament of Caliban
(excerpt - 3rd section)

Religion is to live within our Earthly means.
If species, genera, break Nature's laws
they suffer quite indifferent death:
diseases, famine, pestilence, loss
of habitat leading to extinction.
All are given whatever fate they choose,
and ignorance of the law is no excuse,
even when the cause is accidence.
It's not that God is cruel; merely indifferent.
The Sun that creates is also the Sun that destroys.

Guests we are in Nature's house.
The lords and kings are gone or go,
but the Isle remains and its native, Caliban.

Religion, reverence for life on Earth,
constrains that we take only for need
from the table our Hostess sets before us.
Need, not wealth, for our human kind –
the species, not the specimen, the need.
Co-operate with Nature and be saved.
Compete with her for dominion and be damned.
From this truth each other stems.

The Prosperous man and his magic science thwart
natural wisdom every way they can.
Ariel free? Don't you believe it!
Still at his master's bidding he usurps
the powers of nature for unnatural use.
Raising storms and wrecking ships
are trivial to his present mischief making,
storming against all civilised life
and husbandry of plant and animal species,
poisoning atmosphere, wrecking eco-systems,
rivers, forests, oceans, continents
and every organism therein lives.
His technic and science can destroy them all.
He serves not Nature but prosperity,
his power-for-good in thrall to evil men.

Spirit. Mind. Soul. Intellect.
These are names used in the war against Nature
embodied in the flesh and blood – the body
sentient, seeing, hearing, scenting, tasting, touching

organ of feeling, loving, tenderness, life
itself, the living plasm from birth to death,
the splendour of divine, created things.
With this body I thee worship...
and they two were one flesh...
Gaia, Miranda, vessel of life's purpose:
procreation of the species.
Not for her mind did Shakespeare love Emilia,
interesting though that organ was.
If blasphemy exists, is not perversion,
it is deploring love's mansion pitched near excrement.
The greatest artist's hymn the human body.

What animal but humans have engaged
in ruthless war on its own flesh and blood?
The cross is humanimal's last obscenity.
The birch, the cat, the rack, the fire, the wheel,
the boot, bastinado – Oh, history is full
of fiendish devices to torture and abuse the living
image of God. Especially by religion.
Against not only men but women and children.
Tyranny seeks to enslave the mind through the body.
It still goes on to-day, not only in war
against civilians, but by civil and clerical law,
flogging, maiming, stoning to death and such
especially in the name of Allah the all-merciful
in dark-age Islam, but which land or creed
is not steeped in similar blasphemy and guilt?
Health demands respect for the body, home
of life in each animal, every living creature.
Only twisted souls twist and outrage the body.
The evil self-destructive drives in humans
manifest themselves in crimes against the body.
Why? DOMINION OVER NATURE, the lie
of Genesis, the original sin, the curse
of human arrogance has made our history hell,
dividing our species against our own physique.
O Hippocrates, Phidias, Michelangelo!

Women and children battered and abused,
untried people savaged by policemen,
youths in custody driven to suicide.
Against that set the Hippocratic aims,
health of the body Health incarnate,
bent on our salvation in spite of ourselves.

Earth's chosen race her worst enemy?
All in the name of the sky-gods who adore her.

A species at war with its own body
will treat other animals even worse,
murdering horses in steeple-chases,
hounding otters, hares and deer,
badgers, seals and mink for their skins,
birds for their feathers, monkeys, apes and gorillas
and other of our primate clan tortured
for accursed cosmetics, myriads slaughtered
in the atrocious trade of vivisection
excused in the diabolical name of Science –
whales, dolphins, endearing creatures
ruthlessly murdered. Some, like foxes,
hunted for fun

Have you ever seen
sociable monkeys driven mad in tight cages,
mental as well as physical torture?
Or our fellow-humans in appalling prisons?

We breed species to live our cruelty –
fighting cocks and dogs, bulls for martyrdom,
degrading Nature by human degradation,
making innocent animals as evil as humans.
Milord usurps natural selection, breeding
monsters for any vile purpose he pleases,
basset-hounds, terriers, dachshunds and beagles
and many another man-made monstrosity.
Some are bred to maul people
as Nature's logic never intended.

Poultry bred in atrocious conditions
for a short, maimed life of force-fed misery,
live cattle, sheep and horses sent
on overseas journeys in cruel deprivation:
inhuman slaughter for superstitious reasons,

the wickedness of unnatural religions,
anti-religions, idolatry of human writings:
the vicious traffic in wild birds in cages
shipped waterless, foodless, with few survivors
for pet-shops to sell to the so-called Bird Fancy.

There is no end of the criminal charges
earned by our abuse of both human and animals –
simple Amerindians and other savages.
Most monstrous of all, the treatment of orphans
in South American states and cities, abandoned
and forced to live in sewers and murdered like rats
for feeding themselves by "illegal" means.
All by adults whose sacred care they ought to be.

Suffer the little children to come unto me...

And the hypocrite Church denounces contraception,
its twisted humbug leading to pre-Christian
exposure of unwanted children to weather and wolves –
better served at times by wolves than by people;
all of them kin of Caliban and Adam,
sons of Nature and keepers of her creatures.

All are victims of the idol Money,
created our servant, become our Tyrant,
deadly foe of Earthly survival.

Dominion over Nature? Dominion of Death!

Our fellow-savage, Chief Seathle,
spoke for us all to a US president:
How can YOU buy, how can WE sell, the warmth
of the land, or the sky? To us a weird notion.
We do not own the freshness of the air
nor yet the sparkling of the water.
How can YOU buy them? How can WE sell them?
Every part of Earth to us is sacred,
every shining needle of pine,
every sandy shore, mist in the dark,
every forest, every clearing
humming bee or wasp is holy
in our memory, our experience.
You white men must realise
this land's animals are his brothers
and so treat them. I am a savage
and can't see how a smoking iron horse
can be more important than the buffalo
that we only kill for our need to live.
What is a man without the animals?
If all the beasts were gone from us
we men would die of great loneliness,
emptiness of the heart and spirit.
For whatever happens to the animals
happens also to human kind.
All Earthly things are interconnected
and whatever befalls the Earth, befalls
all the children of the Earth.

There speaks the truly religious man.
There speaks the kin of Caliban,
true son of the Isle and its holy music,
ever changing, ever enduring
harmony, both Earthly and divine.

Dukes and kings, clowns and voyagers
come and go but this Isle is aye abydin.
It will still endure even if evil
wrecks our culture. She will survive
though humans may not, our evolution
done to death by Usury and Profit.

She will begin it all again.

Tom Scott

George Todd

Scotland's Wunner

What seems to be neglectit
Maist in MacDiarmid
Is what's least expectit –
That when he talks o the clan,
The pibroch, the thistle,
His everlasting subject's man!
Ye ken that in his thoughts
The English staun low –
But no sae low as his brither Scots.
When your Scots kin maist ye scunner
Ye ken it's no the Scots
But him that's Scotland's wunner!

Meetin o Giants

Haudan life's hairst in his gowpen –
Won frae aa climes and kinds o men,
And filtert potent, potable, in the still o his brain –
He rowed it aa intil a ticht nieve
Hard enough to brek Alba into shape.

Neither wi mandarin nir easy speak
Wad he hae truck, but wi the tongues
O men. Aye, men – nae less, nae mair,
Men that wad grow, and be, and stey
At the hichts that art and nature baith allow.

It was the less than men, whase superhuman
Was for him aa too human, wha peeried
Lilliputian roun his girth, that, unblinkin,
He'd discard, like fish owre smaa for his net,
And fiere-like be wi giants o the yirth.

Frederic Lindsay

By Crowdieknowe

Gulls on a sodden field
Stilled under a drowning mist
As if on the bed of a sea.
Under them the dead of the place
Exchange flesh's bubbled riot
For an arrangement of white sticks.
How we trim the dead to fit
Our argument of love
Withheld, shared or grudged.
Their anger or their lust
Can do nothing now to surprise,
Who no more than us may resist
How time by feature leaches them.

Only to the few is given
Like a forehead of white bone
Words in ambush
Poised to rear up
Thrawn as before;

In his case asking
The double question that shaped
Poetry, politics and life:
What nation may yet be ours?
And what may be the nation of the poor?

Long may our poor spirited still find
This dead poet is ill to bind.

Lorn Macintyre

Tutejszy Man

Walkers found him, at 10,000 feet
in the Tyrolean Alps,
certainly not equipped for the weather;
shod in straw, clothes of leather.
Beside him, bow, quiver, axe of copper.
He was 4,000 years of age, but lean,
sinewy, mummified in the snow.
Was he after furs to sell
to those in the village below
or reconnoitring another mine?

You were the same, fearless,
going higher, even when the air thinned,
because in Scotland you were used
to the lack of oxygen to the brain.
You climbed alone; not for you
the paths other men had taken.
Hands on jagged rock, feet in crevices.
At any moment your grip could slacken,
sending you to oblivion.
Language had become your Cuillin.

When they were mining the copper
they opened the lobe of the mountain,
following the ore down to the main vein,
then up again in darkness, sure, careful,
like you, who understood the brain
though you had no training.
You worked inside your own skull
at the seam of inspiration
where language fires neurones
like current running in metal.

They became men of substance,
selling ingots to the valleys below,
carving beneath the snowline
bronze axes and other artefacts
in gratitude to the mountain
and to encourage others to climb,
making their own tracks
to get the picture of history,
the slow start in stone,
metal coming into its own.

Ascending in the yowdendrift
in his shoes of straw
he could not read the inscriptions
made by the men of bronze
in celebration of moving on.
We cannot leave behind the stone age.
The higher we try to go, the rockier,
even with metal to help us climb
to the summit strewn with stones,
'cold, undistracted, eternal, sublime'.

You were right, MacDiarmid.
When we look out on the world
we are brain before imagination.
The thalamus is the Everest of ourselves.
When Oetztal Man lay down in the snow

a stone became his pillow.
The frost invaded his cranium.
He began to hallucinate, as when
we read your lyrics in Lallans.
The mountain was the Emmis Stane.

    "But let us not be afraid to die.
No heavier and colder and quieter then,
No more motionless, do stones lie
    In death than in life to all men.
It is not more difficult in death than here
– Though slow as the stones the powers develop
To rise from the grave – to get a life worth having;
And in death – unlike life – we lose nothing that is
    truly ours."

After his resurrection Oetztal Man
is left with an identity crisis.
He was found on the Austro-Italian border,
each claiming him as their own,
but when he was climbing
in his cloak of cured skins
he had no problem about nationality.
He was *tutejszy*, 'from-here-man',
with a language, territory.
His tribe was humanity.

You proclaimed your Scottishness,
publicising your Anglophobia,
but you were *tutejszy* man also.
The ideas that you mined
from the rich seam of Scots
and later from English
('The union of poetry with science')
run back into universal history.
Behind you, the stones of Callanish,
Lloyd Wright's concrete Unity Church.

He lies in a deep-freeze in Innsbruck,
clothes and kit in a lab in Mainz.
When the biologists cease fighting
they will apply science to recreate him.
We will come to know his blood group,
his DNA, even what his last meal was
before he lay down in the snow.
How shall we know you? Only through
your poetry, worth scaling to attain,
whose altitude exhilarates the brain.

That Man Grieve

Raymond Vettese

So there we were, on a windy day at the top of *The Montrose Review* close: Norman, Valda, various dignitaries including ex-provosts, bailies, businessmen, ministers...

I was thinking of my first days in the editorial department of that elderly paper. I knew little of MacDiarmid's work then, having been educated in Scotland, but I was intrigued when I went into the dingy garret that served as our office to see on the wall a framed hand-written poem. Aha, I thought, a MacDiarmid original! I peered at the manuscript. It was called 'The Links of Montrose' and was signed: Wm. McGonagall...

I asked some of the senior members of staff if they remembered MacDiarmid. "That man Grieve", said the punctilious cashier, "all he left this town was debts..."

"I was given the job, as the youngest reporter, of presenting Grieve with a farewell gift, and as I was making my speech he was very fidgety, kept looking out the window. Eventually I couldn't stand it any more and I said 'Chris, why do you keep doing that?' He said, 'I'm trying to get out of here before they come for me, I haven't paid the rent for months'..."

So there we were, Norman, Valda, various dignitaries...

"I read some of his poems once. Couldn't make head nor tail of 'em. Rubbish, I thought, all this fake Scots. He didn't speak like that, you know, at least not to me. The Drunk Man? Ay, that just about sums him up."

"That dreadful man! If he was in the room now, I would walk out!" So there we were...

I was thinking how, as a young poet, I'd written to him, enclosing some examples of my work. They were puny efforts and I wasn't sure I'd get a reply, but a week later back came several handwritten pages. After an apology for not writing sooner came kindness, advice, philosophy, gossip, and this to a stranger, an incompetent versifier...

The plaque commemorating the poet was unveiled. In the silence that followed the solemn moment, somebody laughed...

·an' droont the haill clanjamfrie!...

The Deid-Spail

The deid-spail at your bedside yon nicht;
neist day we fund ye
cauld, wi een ayont licht,
the cannle brunt doon, its creesh
in a shool: a face thrawed wi fricht.

Ian McDonough

Clan MacHine

The glen of appliances hums softly in the gloaming.
Bells ring, the clan body salivates, skirmishing
back to the visitor centre. It is empty now,
our pens have been strewn with fresh straw-substitute.

Round Ben Badh the wind's accordion is wheezing
fit to suffocate. In the small hours, they say
its voice can drive men mad. There was a piper, once,
arose and ripped the chips and wires from his bag.
He blew up such a din the clan began to dance,
stamping on the Collietrons until they smoked and sparked.
The keepers came to pacify the glen with air-conditioning,
replaced the Collietrons and banned the playing of instruments.

Small hoovers follow footsteps everywhere, sucking up
the detritus which sometimes falls from underneath
men's kilts. We are a small clan, but a clean one.
Whiles I dream that I have climbed Ben Badh
and wake up whistling between my teeth.

A Plea for Respite from the 'Aiblins' School

Malcolm Youngson

Let us be clear: there is no such thing as a Scottish language. It is true that in Scotland certain words and usages prevail that are not common to standard English, but this does not make it a language. Further, those peculiar elements are disappearing, as anyone who listens to the old and the young will recognise.

None of this would be remarkable were it not for the fact that sometimes, when I open a periodical such as *Chapman*, I discover poetry in what purports to be "the Scottish language". What is this? Nothing more than disparate dialects cobbled together. Such efforts seem futile. A language drawn from the dictionary can only be of interest to philologists or those with an interest in crosswords, anagrams and other such word-puzzles. Further, as even its proponents would admit, that which might have become a Scottish language ceased to develop centuries ago and must, therefore be incapable of dealing with a world of rapid technological change. What are we presented with, then? It is no argument to say that what these "makars" are doing is constructing the language that might have been had not certain historical incidents obtruded. It would be as well to suggest that one could restore France to a period when Napoleon never existed. These things were, and no amount of wishful thinking can eradicate the facts. No amount of wishful thinking can pretend that these works in "Lallans" or "plastic Scots" or whatever one wishes to call it, constitute a language restored. How can it when that language was in the process of development when it was disturbed?

It may be said: we are not re-creating a language, we are creating a new one. With what? Old words. Is it the language of the people? Hardly. Who, in honesty, has recently heard words such as "aiblins" spring from the mouth of the people? And yet such words are being used in these works, displayed as a collector of rare objects might display his finds in a glass cabinet. And this is the point. These are museum exhibits, removed for perusal. Interesting, but only to the point that they represent the past.

What of dialect? It is true that there are areas where dialect remains strong, and there is little harm in presenting works in dialect to those who appreciate its worth. But dialect is insular, and even where it remains strong, there is an underpinning of English. The fact is that most people in Scotland today speak a version of English. Most literature published today in Scotland is published in English. This is not to say that the Scottish words that presently remain cannot be used within an English sentence – that is, after all, what many Scots do – but this does not disguise the fundamental position. Indeed, there are some writers who use a primarily English structure with the occasional Scots word or pronunciation. This is probably the sensible way to go. Those who feel that a pure English does not wholly encompass the Scottish experience as mediated through language may by all means introduce a peculiarly Scottish word, if the situation calls for it in their judgement. Those who feel impelled to write in dialect are equally entitled to do so. But let us cast aside this falsification – for such it is – that a reconstructed Scots is feasible or, indeed, desirable. The Scots must beat the English at their own game, as the Irish have done, rather than turn aside into a blind alley.

A final word: as I said, nobody hears anyone speak of "aiblins" nowadays. How would it be if a poet writing in English introduced terms such as "doth" or "mayhap" or "verily" into his verse? He would probably be laughed out of court and his poems would find it hard to gain a place in any literary magazine. Why, then, must we have "aiblins" and "maun" and such-like inflicted upon us? Let the dead bury the dead.

Malcolm Youngson

The Langholm Cleg and the Caledonian Cuddies

William Neill

A sluggish horse needs the sting of a gadfly – Plato

I met Christopher Murray Grieve upon occasion in his cottage at Brownsbank, at organised meetings and at least once in a holiday company comprised for the most part of English people staying at a Summer School in Kilqhuanity House where his son had been a pupil.

Chris Grieve, by his own fireside, was a vastly entertaining conversationalist. He talked of the Scottish literary and political situation with a certain irony, while his wife Valda treated us to a willing hospitality. I remember reflecting on his patience in dealing with those who interrupted his work as a writer, without his showing any irritation.

I also met him in his public rôle, wearing his Hugh MacDiarmid hat. On such occasions he was a deal less gentle and once he made a verbal attack on the politics of a member of the audience that was in no wise mealy-mouthed. Many of the audience found his remarks astounding.

At John Aitkenhead's school, there were some Scots present, but most of the people present were English. Although MacDiarmid made great play of his Angolphobia whenever anybody stuck a microphone in front of him, he was perfectly civil to these other guests. it was those English politicians who treated Scotland as a satrapy that he detested. That his writings demonstrate an even greater dislike of their Scottish placemen may be one of the reasons for the posthumous sniping.

MacDiarmid and Burns were of the common people. Both were great poets. Both tried, through the distinctively Scottish language of their poetry, to reverse the creeping anglicisation that started after Jamie Saxt's southward journey with his train of self-seekers. Scotland is rich in poets surrounded by a bland philistinism. There are many reasons for this indifference. The schools and institutions of higher education dispense a mainly English culture. Few Scots know a line of Dunbar or Henrysoun, regarded in their time as the finest poets on the island. That William Dunbar was lately claimed on television as an English poet has as much to do with Scottish ignorance as English bumptiousness.

Robert Burns gave a great boost to the wounded feelings of his countrymen, brought under the control of an English-dominated Parliament by the Treaty of Union fifty years before his birth and divided by the bloody sacrifice of the Stuart-Hanoverian power struggle. Some years after Burns died, his remains were dug up and a mausoleum built over them. Similar attempts to put up a sculpture to the memory of MacDiarmid met with considerable opposition. MacDiarmid, never a man to contain unpopular thoughts in silence, had not made many friends among those whose permission must be sought before monuments can be raised. However, such was the outcry at this latest act of indifference to a great poet that the monument was eventually sited on the hills outside Langholm. The real memorial to both poets is their work.

Not only was there a lack of willingness to erect the MacDiarmid monument; there was a lack of willingness in some, after his death, to admit that he was a great poet. Most of these objections are either specious or rooted in ignorance.

The language used by Scots to this day is characterised by a lexis and vowel system which differs considerably from the language of the South. Even when speaking Scottish Standard English there is a vowel contrast between the words *tied* and *tide* not heard over the border. The differences are greater as one departs more deeply from this standard language. There are still areas of Scotland where Scots is distinct in its phonology and lexis from the tongue known as English. A man who quite recently wished to convey to me the fact that he had been startled by someone, said: *He gied me a richt fley.* Another who came to concrete a path outside my house remarked *Aye, it hes a gey boss soond ablo here*, by which he meant the ground underneath had a hollow sound. This is at least as far from English a Danish is from Norwegian. There are, despite detractors and anglicising compilers of anthologies, still speakers of Scots among us.

The language spoken at the centre of power will come to be regarded as superior. Dim people with nothing else to hold on to will hire elocutionists at great expense, hoping that this speech-form will transform their innate stupidity into something approaching intelligence. One does not have to be a close observer of the speakers of Received Pronunciation (as it is snobbishly called) to see that this is a fallacy.

One of the more repulsive aspects of Scots-knocking by linguistically-deprived scribblers is their alleged fondness for Gaelic. I do not deny that although an audience might not understand a word of Gaelic, the rhythms and sound of a poet reading his work well in that language is pleasant enough. But for alleged critics of Scottish literature this simply will not do. If they are as fond of our Gaelic poets as they say they are, and profess to be members of an educated *Scottish* literary class, then they must acquire a reading knowledge of these poets. But alas, some of them are keener on debunking MacDiarmid's "re-integrated Scots" than coming to grips with Gaelic. Perhaps this is because they cannot produce anything worthwhile in Scots and have the shield of ignorance for protection as far as Gaelic is concerned. I do not say that it is obligatory on them to be members of a distinctively *Scottish* literary clique. If their talent and the present latitude-attitude will allow, they can always join the towering much-annotated edifice of EngLit where their attacks on anything distinctly Scottish will doubtless be applauded, as it has been in the past, by some of their southern colleagues.

A poet is a person who delights in the use of words. There is no reason why one should not remint old words for use in new poems, as MacDiarmid did. There is no reason why a man of Langholm should be denied the use of a word from Largo. As to the usage of a special language for poetry, surely these great admirers of Gaelic know that the great poet Neil MacMhuirich wrote in a Gaelic not used for everyday speech? Nor was Homer's Greek spoken in the streets of Athens. Why then should they try to strait-jacket MacDiarmid for writing in a tongue very close to the Scots heard in Scottish farmhouses? When I read MacDiarmid's Scots I know I am listening to a language much nearer to the tongue I heard in my youth, and still hear on the tongues of Scottish people, than is standard English. To me, the fields around my house contain *kye, queys, stirks* and *stots* rather than cows, heifers, yearlings and bullocks. Of course there is a breed of self-styled poets who wish to outlaw all the tropes, prosody and cultural influence of the past; to reduce permissible language to a narrow canon devised by themselves. The Anglo-Saxons talked quite rightly of the *word-hoard.* A hoard is an accumulation, stored treasure, not a parsimonious paring-down. Good poets *add* to the word-hoard; they do not diminish it to make life easier for bad poets. Those who disapprove of MacDiarmid's Scots should consider the methods of other writers, Shakespeare for instance, or Pound, or Joyce. In all these they will find archaisms, neologisms, borrowed words, foreign words, slang words, swear words, indeed examples of all the usages they seem to object to in MacDiarmid and others.

One of the favourite complaints of the Narrow School is that MacDiarmid went in for "dictionary-dredging". What is implied by this is that only poets writing in Scots consult dictionaries, despite the plethora of English lexicons and the comparative paucity of English-Scots ones before William Graham. As the latter pointed out, if you want to find the Scots equivalent of *intend* you would have to scan one hundred and fifty-nine pages of Chambers' Scots Dictionary before arriving at the word *ettle*. Poets writing in English are spared such Herculean labours, but are we to believe that they don't use dictionaries? Surely it makes little odds how a literate person acquires a word? Heard or read, a word is a word. Having *heard* it, we are allowed to use it. Having *read* it, does it then become mere "dictionary-dredging" and debar the writer from using it? Perhaps we should get a friend to look it up and say it aloud so that we can say we acquired it orally. Did Eliot make a special journey to Italy to discover the meaning of *La Figlia che Piange?* Do any readers object to the novels of Joseph Conrad on the grounds that as a native Polish speaker he must have got some of his words by "dictionary-dredging" and similar processes?

That it is only recently that a Chair of Scottish Literature has been set up in any Scottish university is a matter to excite curiosity. In MacDiarmid the increasing anglicisation of Scottish centres of learning was a matter of satirical comment. William Donaldson points out in *Popular Literature in Victorian Scotland* that Scots was used in many schools as the medium of instruction until well into the nineteenth century. Children whose mother tongue was Scots might not have learned to speak RP in this manner but doubtless they learned everything else more quickly than the unfortunate children *wha cam aff the fairm-touns an had nocht ither nor the speik o yon airt in their harns* and then had to learn not to say *Aye* before they could be taught arithmetic. MacDiarmid annoyed whole cohorts of Anglicisers with *A Drunk Man Looks at the Thistle* by pointing out their ignorance of things Scottish, while satirising the patronising mock-Scottish pretension that grows increasingly more common. In *To Circumjack Cencrastus* (in a perfectly *easy* Scots) he questions the activities of Scottish Universities. They are, he says with some justice, *Scots but in name* and pointedly asks what knowledge the alumni have of the Gaelic poets. Doubtless admirers of strong Gaelic poetry will know where to find Finlay MacNab and Muireadhach Albannach both of whom MacDiarmid mentions, and will remember the injunction of the former to foster their native poetry and culture. They will also know, doubtless, that the line of poets descended from the latter is the longest in Scotland (or perhaps anywhere?) stretching over a period of 500 years. MacDiarmid certainly knew it, and knew enough about Gaelic culture to return to it again and again in his poetry. Modern Scotland for the most part confines its knowledge of the culture of the Gael (which, though they do not know it, is their own) to a few bad comic novels.

Sometimes I wonder about the logical processes of those who continually attack Scots and Gaelic. It is not dialects of Scots, says one, but *Lallans*, that he objects to. Now I greatly dislike the word Lallans, a word used by Burns to distinguish Scots from Gaelic, just as I dislike the word Doric, a type of demotic Greek, with its snide insinuation that Scots is an aberrant dialect of southern English rather than a separate linguistic development. I call the tongue Scots and wish that other people did also. I refer to MacDiarmid's re-integrated Scots as *literary* Scots. There is no reason to throw a fit because the language used is not the everyday spoken tongue. People do not normally go around speaking poetry outside literary gatherings or lectures, and in any case there are countless examples of peoples other than the Scots using a distinctive tongue for literature of all kinds, a tongue that is not used in the market-place. To those who say poetry ought to be written in *everyday language*, I would simply say that the more everyday the language the worse the poetry. The everyday language of the workplace is not poetry any more than the small print on insurance policies is poetry.

Considering the current taste for obscure verse whose inner purpose is indecipherable, I am surprised to hear complaints from those who affect to admire this line-chopping cryptography that MacDiarmid's Scots is a barrier to their understanding. MacDiarmid's poems, bulging with Scottish lexis, are much less difficult. Moreover, MacDiarmid could write good stanzaic verse, to me a mark of all good *makkars*. I do not here intend to attack *good* free verse which I read with pleasure although I tend to suspect the *bona fides* of those who write nothing else.

A recent introduction, after deprecating much of MacDiarmid's poetry, goes on to add that what matters is not the size of a poet's Scottish vocabulary, but its integrity. Does this mean that a poet with two words of Scots will write better poetry in Scots than one with twenty thousand, provided the former has learned a brace of words at his or her mother's knee? One must ask, since the compiler of the anthology says he is glad about strong Gaelic poetry, how many words of Gaelic are required to preserve the integrity of such rejoicing.

I often feel that much condemnation of MacDiarmid has arisen from what has come to be known as the Scottish Cringe. Sufferers from this object to tartan souvenir dollies not so much because they bring on a cultural shudder but simply because they are *Scottish* trivia. To some people, being Scottish in anything but name is a positive embarrassment. Remember Boswell's snivelling "I cannot help it". MacDiarmid's Scots, whether dialect or dictionary-dredged is too powerful a dram for some allegedly Caledonian heads. Gaelic comes off a bit better, being seen by those who do not have any as a fine aristocratic swashbuckling medium unlike our poor Scots tongue. This they see, quite erroneously, as a bad form of English, little realising that had Jamie Saxt stayed here, all the power-seekers in England would have rushed northwards and their children and children's children would have made snob remarks in Scots about the debased speech of the Home Counties. Jamie Saxt, although fluent in Latin, Greek and French, used Scots as his everyday language.

I must not forget the Battle of the Burnsolators. Burns was a great poet, especially of lyric poetry, and MacDiarmid knew it. MacDiarmid was hardly alone in his irritation at the singling out of Burns in a nation of many great poets. Robert Burns has become the focus of an annual ceremony that is in some instances respectful of his work and held in his honour. More often it is an excuse, as MacDiarmid rightly pointed out, for all sorts of clowns who have not read two consecutive pages of his work and who distort his life-story to support a political or social attitude which they hold and which Burns certainly did not. These latter were the focus of MacDiarmid's well-deserved attack.

I have nothing against English: the reader will notice that I use it almost fluently myself. I got some of it by dictionary-dredging and must plead a lack of integrity in not obtaining words like *rebarbative* at the maternal knee. Though possibly it is inevitable that more poems will be written by Scottish poets in English rather than in Scots or Gaelic (and very good poems too) I confess to some annoyance when the compilers of anthologies seem to rejoice overmuch in that fact. That MacDiarmid's literary Scots should be attacked as a wasteful distraction, and his attempts to invigorate it compared unfavourably with Shaw's dilettante vapourings about Esperanto, I find hard tae thole.

I could have written this in Scots but since I am not preaching to the converted I offer it in English with as much integrity as I can muster.

William Neill

Anne Shaw

The Silken Leddy Looks at the Drunk Man

Ma een are sair frae aa the smoke,
Ma hair smells like a still,
The silks that whisper tae the soak
Laid dreamin on this hill
Are worn oot trailin here an there
An sair in need o washin,
They're aa that I'm alloo'd tae wear
While roon his gless he's sploshin
The mystic spirit waverin.
He stares as if he's in a trance
An noo the fool is haverin
Aboot thistles, stars, the cosmic dance,
An Russian translations;
A bloke ca'd Blok –
I kent him once
But I ran oot o patience
Wi ma eternal wisdom stance
An aa the expectations.
It's bloody cauld the pedestal,
In bed he's near cremation,
But as fur me I cannae thole
The cauld an heat in sich extremes,
An nothin in atween
But existential angst or dreams
An me supposed tae clean
His soul, the world, ma silken goons,
An still tae look mysterious,
While he sits twitterin like a loon,
I think that he's delirious;
Moonlicht an thistles aa nicht lang,
I have tae glide aroon,
Philosophy an noo a sang,
He's laid there on the groon,
O wae is me! Alas, pair sowl,
Who'd want tae be a Muse?
It maks ye want tae scream an howl.
I think I'll blaw a fuse!
But naw, I'll freeze here on this hill,
I could be warm in bed,
An bide until ye rant yer fill
Because when aa is said,

I cannae leave ye lyin there,
An I ken why ye try
Tae reach the core,
Tae lay it bare,
It's jist that by the by,
I cannae see it clear masel,
The moonlicht blinds me tae.
Or is it snaw? Its cauld as Hell,
The wind is like tae flay
Aa silk an skin right aff the bane
An then whaur wid ye be?
Yer Muse a frozen skeletane
Under the Eildon tree.
Get up, ye fool! Aw hell, I'm aff
In search o warmer weather,
Costa del Sol, I'll have a laugh,
A break frae aa this heather.
Anither yin said "Come tae France,
I'll set ye up in Paris.
O Muse, come on, this is oor chance
Tae shoot like a Polaris
Through transcendental regions blue
An vast an abstract areas,
Ragged coasts an wastelands too,
Nae wheat like in Ontario"
He wanted me tae travel tae a place ca'd Labrador,
But I hate dugs, an I have aa
The waste I want an more;
I'd have tae change ma silks fur suedes,
An braid like Poochahontas,
The White man's shade is no fur me,
I'd raither flee on Quantas.
Ma stanzas have run aa tae hell,
Ma rhymes have gone internal,
Ma syntax sounds its ain death knell,
Ma rhythm is infernal,
Ma verses like an avalanche
Are fa'in thick an fast,
They've smothered ye.
I see ye blanch.
We've silence left at last.

Emilio Coia

Letter Anent Auntran Blads:

Douglas Young (1913-1973)

Robert Calder

There has been too little about Douglas Young since his sudden untimely death. Born in Tayport he studied at St Andrews and Oxford and was lecturer in Classics at Aberdeen when he came to public notice in the 1940s as willing to fight Hitler but not be conscripted into the British army on terms contravening the 1707 Treaty of Union. He was maybe a more crucial political figure than many suppose (his protests and jail terms in wartime inspired many very visibly active decades later) and pioneered ventures akin to the latterday Constitutional Convention: cf the memoir prefacing *Douglas Young, Poet and Polymath* (1977), more than the mere memorial volume too many reviews assumed. His efforts on behalf of the Scots language, which he alas calls Lallans, have had too little attention of late.

The letter on Young's verse collection *Auntran Blads* (1944, much of it reprinted in *Poet and Polymath*) responds co-operatively to a note by another poet-linguist, J F Hendry (*Poetry Scotland, Second Series*, 1943). Short enough to excerpt, it noted the range of a book which publishes Scots versions of several poems from Sorley MacLean's *Dain do Eimhir* as well as the Gaelic of Campbell Hay and William Livingstone. There are Scots versions from the German poets listed in the review, from Lithuanian ballads, Valéry, as well as such niceties as 'Ae Fond Kiss' in the language of Sappho(!). The Pushkin poem referred to is done into German and Aiolic as well as Scots. The daft 'St Andrew's Night' might belie Young's seriousness: in Latin, in two ancient Greek dialects, even singable sub-Schubert German *Lied* he renders: "I wish I were a crocodile,/ I'd bask upon the banks of Nile/ and nibble niggers' toes,/ and as I lay upon the bank/eat virgins of the highest rank/and vomit up their cloes." After a list of contents the review proceeds:

A preface by Hugh MacDiarmid explains that so much concern with European languages and literature is really part of the new Scottish National approach, which prefers to consider Europe directly, rather than through English eyes. Now there is a great deal in this, The Scottish tradition grew up in mediaeval Europe side by side with the French. The Universities of Glasgow and Paris were once rivals in the production of students of independent mind, within the framework of European civilisation, until English education twisted that original conception into an apparatus for the production of administrators, instead of free men.

It is good, therefore, to see a Scots version of 'Mentra Io pensava la mia frale vita', the mediaeval Scots sounding remarkably close to the Italian. 'Ae time that I our flownrie life appraisit'. This is a lovely transcription from Dante, with much of the spirit, powerful, mystic and human, of the original. There is a kinship.

The same cannot always be said. Pushkin's 'Ya vyas ljubil' loses a very great deal in the Scots version, which cannot help a certain lushness in the sentiment foreign to the Russian. The Pushkin poem is as beautiful as a monument, or as a piece of Greek. Why translate it into German sentimentalism? One line of the Scots is rather successful:

> But dinna let it fash ye onie mair…
> (Pust ona vas bolshi ne trevozhit…)

If this work is to be done, I suggest that, in future, writers in Scots would learn more both about the handling and the music of their medium if they confined themselves for some time to translations from, say, German (Hofmannsthal, Storm, Goethe, Rilke and the romantics in general), Gaelic, mediaeval Italian and French, rather than rush at an interpretation of such classical and finished lines as those of Catullus, Sappho and Pushkin. Much of Scots must be polished, and polished constantly, to yield its significant music, as MacDiarmid well knows. It is unfair to try to make it do what at present it cannot, ie, be as ivory as Valéry.

Some of the contents therefore I think a pity, such as the acrobatics involved in turning 'A Thought for St Andrew's Night, 1936' into Greek, French and German versions. Joyce has done this all so much better; and even Jolas has given it a meaning absent here.

Yet the book is worth buying. There are many good things in it: Sorley MacLean's "My Een are Nae on Calvary…" is wonderful (though the effect for me is spoilt by the word "back-lands" where "lands" would have carried the powerful rhythm), [likewise Maclean's] 'Weird o Makars', and the peculiar Scots vision of [Young's own] 'Speculation' and much else.

> …why suldna the starns
> hae ilk their ain harns
> and sclents o their ain that we dinna see wi the gless?

Much of this book is like that. I have the feeling that it will prove very fruitful.   *J F Hendry*

7th March 1944

My dear J.F.Hendry,
                    William Maclellan has gratified me with a preview
of your articles for the forthcoming *Poetry Scotland, No.2*. I...find myself
greatly encouraged by your observations, necessarily few as they are,
and regard them as the most knowledgeable criticism I have yet had, and
with the fullest insight into the problems.

I am glad you think so well of the Dante effort, a happy fluke which
I feel is not likely to be repeated. I was experimenting with passages of
the *vita nuova* in Lallans prose, not too happily, when these stanzas
stimulated me to attack them in verse. I inadvertently got off the rime
scheme, but something of the original came through in spite of the
uncouthness of Scots.

Working on Sorley Maclean's *Dain* I soon found that Lallans has not
nearly enough words for shades of aesthetic appreciation. Sorley drew
up a gradation of Gaelic epithets for our "bonny", culminating in
"alainn", with "boidheach" rather low down. The reason is that Gaelic
was a medium for a cultured nation of scholarly gentlefolk for centuries,
whereas the poor patois of the Angles became a Court speech only for
two or three centuries.

At its culmination so far, in the age of the Ballads, XVIth-XVIIth
centuries, Lallans was bidding fair to cope with Pushkin, Sappho, and the
others, but the dreadful "Whistle Binkie" era has plunged it into that
German sentimentality which you deplore. In my version of the "Hektor
and Andromacha" Willa Muir protested against exactly the atmosphere
you dislike in the "Ya vas lyubil". George Malcolm Thomson was
scunnered by the same effect in the "Mentreio pensava...". Edwin Muir
tells me the word "leal" always makes him shudder. Probably Lallans will
be vitiated for very many by vulgar and unpleasant associations with
some words in it.

I am well aware that meantime Lallans is not an adequate medium for
rendering Pushkin, Valéry, Sappho, and Catullus, but I hope practice
may make perfect. In another two generations if the movement
continues with the momentum MacDiarmid imparted, it will be possible
to do "Ya vas lyubil" very perfectly. By the way, my Aiolic version of it
is thought satisfactory by some. The first line is, of course (from Sappho
herself.) And I would even hope that, with general development of
Lallans, by that time my own attempt will sound better. It is weaker than
it would otherwise have been because I had previously done an English
version, from Maurice Baring's prose translation, before I started
learning Russian. I have never got far enough ben in Russian (and am
now, for want of time, losing what I had) to grasp thoroughly the ethos
of that glorious language, but have so far no reason to feel that
translation from Russian to Lallans is premature. Translation from
German and related languages is obviously the easiest, but I think it

worth while projecting any sort of foreign effort into Lallans, to try and galvanise it into a more various growth. That is why I encourage Sydney [Goodsir] Smith…

Some languages are very repugnant to one another. E.g. I doubt greatly whether Pushkin's "Ya vas lyubil" could be translated nearly in Gaelic, much less Valéry's "Bois amical".

What you call the "acrobatics" of St Andrew's Night were included, with much else, as illustrations of my attitude to the whole business, which is mainly pedantic, with a leaning to dialectal purism which maddens many, and experimental. I am about to gather in various oddments which have accumulated, some of which may have "sklents o their ain" other than those manifested in *Auntran Blads*, and thought of asking Edwin Muir to preface the new outwale. He was quite eidant at the cleckan a few years ago.

So far I am mainly concerned to aid the recreation of a versatile medium on Lallans, which either I, or more likely, some poetically gifted person can turn to more serious use. Sydney Smith, for instance, is more of a poet than I am, and so is Maurice Lindsay. But I am inclined to publish again because it seems to me a certain volume is useful in a literature, and some degree of herd-feeling evidently aids some versifiers.

I was most sorry not to find you at Maclellan's recent gathering of makars in the New Art Club… At that gathering I read the audience three little pieces which are printed in *Auntran Blads* together at pages 30 & 31. Not for their intrinsic interest, which is slight, but for the manner of their inditing.

I had long cherished the notions of writing on the perverse thesis of *speculation*, on the topic of the cat, and on a horrifying encounter with a bat in the summer of 1936. I had concurrently meditated the different forms manifested, but had never connected them with the themes. The idea of a stanza composed of short lines followed by a long one appealed to me as the reverse of old Lallans practice, which goes in regular lines followed by a shorter, as a ploughman works his field. The metrical system of *The Cat* is adapted from *Piers the Plowman*, which adaptation I had thought of using for the Homeric Hymns, but have not so far. The off-rhymes of *August Night* I had wished to try once, only to discover whether I liked them better from inside than I have when noting them in Auden and the rest. These themes and forms had been wambling in my wame for months or years before pen was set to paper. This occurred in May 1940, one evening during the collapse of France. I was sitting in my rooms in Old Aberdeen, one evening, drinking coffee and reading *The Times*, which gets there in the evening, when suddenly I was moved to take pen, and wrote the three pieces as fast as I could without any hesitation…

yours for Scotland,
Douglas Young

An Open Letter from John Herdman

Dear Joy

Thank you for your letter inviting me to contribute something "in the spirit" of MacDiarmid for your *Chapman* MacDiarmid number. "A lad was born in Langholm to blaw aboot", perhaps? I feel unable to accede to your request. I wouldn't know how to undertake such a task; and it is certain that MacDiarmid would have had "no truck whatever" with the idea of anyone else trying to write in his spirit. He had far too developed a sense of his own uniqueness, and of the need for everyone else to develop theirs.

I would fear, if I did try, all too many of the poet's own words coming back to haunt me. Here are a few:

> And toastin' ane wha's nocht to them but an
> Excuse for faitherin' Genius wi' *their* thochts…

> What unco fate maks *him* the dumpin'-grun'
> for a' the sloppy rubbish they jaw oot?

> As Kirks wi' Christianity ha'e dune,
> Burns Clubs wi' Burns…

> And a' the names in History mean nocht
> To maist folk but "ideas o' their ain,"
> The vera opposite o' onything
> The Deid 'ud awn gin they cam' back again.

But I fear that you may be inundated by poems of the "You an' me, Chris" variety, such as we have unhappily become all too familiar with over the years, written by MacDiarmids through the wrong end of a telescope affecting a tone of intimacy with the great man as ludicrous as it is revolting. MacDiarmid himself, of course, was responsible for the initiation of this genre with his addresses to Dostoevsky, Joyce and others – but he knew that he could survive the comparison. I am afraid, however, that hanging on to the coat-tails of the great is a characteristic Scottish attitude, presumably related to the difficulty we experience in standing upright on our own, as so often and so recently demonstrated.

No, the best tribute one can pay to MacDiarmid, this year and every year, is to follow one's own spirit, as, of course, he taught us:

> To be yersel's – and to mak' that worth bein',
> Nae harder job to mortals has been gi'en.

There is one road, though, on which, given the dire state of Scotland, we should all be humble enough to follow where MacDiarmid led; and that is the path of opposing implacably, with every resource at our disposal, the present English ascendancy (in the word's full dynamic sense) in every area of Scottish life. That, for the foreseeable future, must be our *Delenda est Carthago*.

Yours for Scotland,
John Herdman

Sam Gilliland

A Grup o the Thistle

Auld horny grun whaur poets sow,
Whaur Scotia's pens maun daur tae harrow,
Gin tears fae gildit quills maun flow,
Girt fu o grief an plewfu sorrow.
Sic scenes o beauty ne'er surpassed,
Ower scrieved bi bards wi differin muse,
Girns duntit dreams an herts sair fashed,
Grey Calie's stany lug abuse.
Wha seeks fae rhyme ae chancel siller,
Gey dreich will harvest's pursefu be,
In gowden memries chancefu tiller,
Sair wrocht; aye, an wrocht alang wi me.
Torn remnants dustfu ages gether,
Yon vestal tomes but toomit chalice,
Unsung verse o Scotia's sages blether,
Ablow the flouerin thistle's malice.
Wha gies the muse sic flatterin praise,
Ne'er thinks tae pairt wi maik or muckle,
Ahint hopefu lines an bardies phrase,
Cauld Alba's breist maun poets suckle.
Coorts he the daurk despair o deidlin,
Agin the pu o povert's jyle,
Staurk hummle thrown the musie seedlin,
Daurs lowp an crest Scot's crabbit syle.
Prood gruppit rit o peasant's prose,
Maun covet Donia's winsome haun,
Shuin cast amidst cranreuchs rose,
An withert blossoms winfa strewn.
Not ocht ablow nor ocht abune,
Mair daudit years fa on daudit years,
Chiels levler stauns bi mortals linn,
Ower *aa* oor future kistin, leers.

Timothy Neat

In the van Gogh Museum, Amsterdam

Between the early dark van Goghs
And the late electric blues
There was, in life, a gap of time –
And here in the Museum – a space is left.
Along one wall a large painting hangs –
Much bigger than any ever painted by van Gogh:
Leon Lhermitte – now there's a name!
An old peasant sits at ease, spread-legged amidst cut grass –
About to mend a broken scythe and eat his piece:
A maid has brought him food and drink –
So he can have his crib – as Cornishmen would say.

It is an academic, Realist, sub-impressionist work
And catches the attention – like a saw:
I leaned back against the parapet around the stairs
To look and find the story Lhermitte intended us to read.
And by the wrist he drew me – like a child –
To the whetstone – to the rusted blade set down:
He caught me – like a woman with her legs apart –
The smell of new mown hay!

Suddenly – I was conscious of a man beside me –
Tall, in summer clothes, a little formal, half-holiday!
He too had stopped before Lhermitte – but as I saw him –
Turned away – to call a woman – who would be his wife –
Then back. The voice was Scots!
It galvanised my attention – annulled all peasant France!
Who was this Scotsman stopped, this visitor like me?
His T shirt shouting – MOBY DICK – GOD SAVE THE WHALE –
I felt impelled to measure him somehow.

A red slab face carried no hint of the Tar Brush –
But his wife was permed – prim as a negress –
Must have been Moby Dick made me think of the Tar Brush!
But what the Electric Brae above Ayr! How strange!
Twice he rocked on his heels back, then nodded to his wife
"MacTaggart" he said "MacTaggart" – pleased.

She – smiled to show she knew what he meant
And looked at the maid that Lhermitte had painted.
Whilst I, like the painter, constructed a story
And wondered at the breasts of this wife of a man
Whose habit of mind brought MacTaggart in here!
(I've read Robert Ardler's *Territorial Imperative* –

And know Machrihanish and Carnoustie Bay!) –
So I looked at them both and said to the man
With a nod of complicity – "William – William MacTaggart".

Not much! But enough and more than enough –
For I saw recognition light up in his eyes!
Someone here – knows Scotland's Glory –
Bluebell Matches and Caledonian Ale!
We three like God and Desire are One! But steady!
Hold steady – I saw joy turn policeman – and silence
The ice-house, drop down round his head;
And wordless he moved off – as she did and I –
Three souls with adrenalin thumping and coursing:
The result of the bond of a knowledge of Scottishness
And who amongst Clansmen, Masons, Catholics, and Jews –
Knows brotherhood sweet as the half-celtic Sioux!

So onto the spread of the late great paintings
we parted the crowds to view all He had left us –
Keeping our distance – like two men with a secret!
But iron is iron with governance its Pole Star
And on standing back from this or that painting
His head would turn and we two briefly lock eyes.
It was not homosexual love he sought –
Nor did he imagine once, my thought to fuck his wife!
I did not want – I would not dare!
No – it was a sheer hunger for my Scottishness,
Or what he thought was Scottishness – and all that means!
For he knew the man who knows MacTaggart's hand –
Must know a good deal more!

On the last wall I found it – that H. Lecter thunder!
That blue above green that gives genius name!
A canvas and catchment that outsoars Lhermitte –
As children from school would skip over the sea!
But still I could hear her! Going on about framing!
About how her brother, a librarian it seemed,
Had given her a tip – about judging a painting –
"You can judge the good painter by his choice of a frame!"

Embarrassed by this, her husband guffawed, and he –
Glanced round towards me – for what proved the last time.
Louder than needed – he then spoke in a whisper
He knew I would hear. "Scotland, you know, has a claim
On van Gogh! I've heard it's rumoured he knew so himself –
Some sept, or wild-oats, on his grandmother's side!
Scots Trade with the Netherlands was an everyday thing –
With Fife and with Leith, and in and out in Dundee:

Pantiles for grain and blue Delft for St Andrews,
Salt-herring, and wool and sculptors for Falkland –
Proof, were it needed! That ginger-redness of hair –
His yen for a dram and the Calvinist faith!
Everything's kept under wraps – nobody wants you to know!
Half the world's men at arms were Scots long ago!

Seated later on the Terrace, I spent an hour in the sun:
The heat was great – the German beer – Vincent van Gogh
Fell away – but this MacTaggart-man stuck in my brain
As shrapnel would – this product of a nation –
Living so much off the flesh the past hands down –
This love of things as were and Scottish are...
No wonder that man ate his paint and shot himself!
He painted bread upon the painted waters –
A Dutchman turning light to wine – to feed this Moby Dick!
And he was Scots!
Or near enough, and Melville was for sure –
Look at the name and Melville House – that's also Fife!

At that a voice made dark the sun! Black Queequeg spoke!
A silence fell – a woman looked at me. "No God is just!
Asleep, abed! Hear Ahab stalk the night!
The Whale that blows, blows in his head –
The eater eating down himself – will disappear!
That blue you saw was tattooed blood seen through a skin:
Vincent knew his stuff all right – as I the sea –
And me the shaft of this harpoon – and how to stand!
Against such a blue – I stand forever – as I am –
It is my bones alone lie broke in Baffin Bay.
I am the silence left, I'm Mum, as C M Grieve would say!"

I Met a Cove

I met a cove
Upon a hill –
His nose was green as brass.

He had he said
Been sliding down –
His nose upon the grass.

You cove I said
You silly bill –
You should have used your ass!

At this he rose
And challenged me –
No fool like you will pass!

You cove! You fool!
I cried – ya bas!
And punched him on the nose!

The green came off!
He smiled at me –
His nose shone bright as glass!

Thanks friend he said
You are a fool –
Now kick me in the arse!

Touche! Touche!
How green men are –
And all men fools – alas!

An Open University Tutorial in the Bear & Plough

This dust in the eyes of God
Is not less significant
Than Michelangelo's Struggling Captive
Or Dying Slave!
Things are in themselves accountable
And all things equal in the span.

So spoke a woman with a turn of phrase –
A modern woman of her time –
Our time – the arsehole of all time so far!
Why should Everest lord it?
Warts and raspberries can be enormous!
And in the fall of light noble as the Earth from space.

I ask – why be conditioned by the slavery of men?
Men grind women as men grind the poor!
She spoke with venom in her voice –
But said – ours is a vision more like Christ's
Than that of God – and when I say God
I mean a Female Deity!

Yes! Well! Dust is glorious – in shafting light!
But set against the Struggling Captive
And the Slave –
Are they not dust and stone and something more?
Were they not born of mind? (A thousand Hoovers
Across the Louvre – will know their masters free!).

Uno Momento – Signora! If this dust is so sublime
Why did God breathe on it so…?
Spoke up a small bombastic man wedged at the back –
His broken nose afront two well kent eyes:
To create a living soul – and womankind –
And this great silence in the Bear and Plough!

David Angus

A Langholm Loon
(I.M. H.MacD.)

Guid gear gangs in sma buik.
That's true o Scotland Sma.
It's true o ilka ballant-buke
O' his – the Wheep, The Schaw.

Thaur in a puckle pages –
The genius o a nation!
Distilled throu aa the ages;
Defying the yeirs' stagnation!

'Twis true, tae, o the scriever –
Wee man whase birss wad bristle
At onie unbeliever
In Scotland's pou'er tae hirsle

The Fates – an Fate – tae suit
Hersel, her benmaist dream –
Or the dream wee Chris, nae doot,
Wid faither on her; some scheme

Tae tirn aa Scots tae makars?
(It's queer his auld fae, Muir,
Tho anti-Scots, wis siccar
That they already were!)

Chris Grieve – or Hugh MacDiarmid –
Buckled in his wee frame
Our best *and* warst, and airmit
the haill, an gied it aim.

A complex, contrair cratur, he:
Mair true til the Scots nor the Scots cuid be.

Donald Campbell

April, 1992

Scunnered by my cringing kind,
I think of Lermontov and find
his thocht reflected in my ain
sair generation; thowless, blind,
trauchled at hairt, troubled in mind.

Our thwarted faithers' saikless gain
was our deid loss. They took the strain,
leaving us little but ease.
Spared of hardship, puirthith, pain,
we think to thrive on bried alane

and squander living as we'd please;
our passions blaze, our spirits freeze
in *dolce far niente*. We canna tell
guid frae evil – and, on our knees,
we tine our manhood by degrees.

Sae feared of failure, we dispel
each dream of liberty and sell
our birthricht cheaply, run
away frae victory, compel
our consciences to snore in hell!

Our lives maun end as they begun
with muckle lost and naethin won,
history aince mair repeated,
the past betrayed, the future cheated,
the promise of our age undone,
disgraced, dishonoured and defeated.

Stanley Roger Green

How Comforting

How very comforting it must be
To hold values like the bourgeoisie,
An attitude ready for each contingency,
A formula on hand for any emergency,
And no need to think or feel too much,
Or care about philosophy and such,
Unless it concerns one's personal ends –
A rise in taxes, a cut in dividends.

Their tastes lack refinement, most agree;
Few could tell Camembert from Brie,
And fewer still even faintly discern
An old Moselle from a young Sauterne.

At Schubert or Mozart piano recitals,
They're hardly touched within their vitals,
But during the intervals gossip and chatter
As if great art were a laughing matter.

When floods drown thousands in delta basins,
They sigh and murmur 'God has his reasons.'
Or if they do not believe in God,
They sign a cheque with a complacent nod,
To purchase blankets for the chartered bus,
And say 'Thank heaven that it wasn't us!'

If a new siege should start in Leningrad,
They would sip their tea and say 'How sad!',
And refreshed by canapés from the fridge
Resume their game of contract bridge.

And if the Apocalypse should come
And fill the sky with signs of doom,
They'd say 'How tiresome, but even so,
We could finish the rubber before we go.'

Billy Kay

The Reid Flag 1992

A hunder year on, MacDiarmid, the "orra mob" is still there an it's no daein the Scots soul ony guid. This sang is dedicatit tae the arch-unionist politicians o the Scottish Left, that's sae thirlit tae the Union, they'd see socialism, democracie, an Scotland hersel dee raither than brak it.

The people's flags lie caked wi stour –
Toom tabards feart tae seize the hour,
an gie the Scots fowk ilka pouer
they'd glaidly gie tae ithers, sure…

"Sae raise the scarlet banner fine,
aye, sing thay sangs o auld lang syne
Oor day is duin, we ken fine weel –
but they pey oor siller, sae we'll aye be leal.

In days gaen by we wes that sicher
the warld wes ours, the Scots didnae bicker.
But nou that warld is gane for aye
an Tories lord it, heich an dry.

We should fecht back an syne resist
But aince the loof o ambition's kissed
It's ill tae haud tae auld ideals
When yer gettin yersel sic creishy deals…

Sae sing the reid flag, saft an douce
like aw oor comrades in the Hoose
Nae NHS nor NCB
Naw, nocht for you, but a career for me."

The people's flags lie rent an torn
The Reid, the Saltire baith near gone
It's true blue Brits we aw sall be
an tae hell wi Scots egalitie…

"Aye, raise yer banners aw ye want,
We'll cry it doun as nationalist cant
Yer dream o a fowk, an a nation free
Duis naethin, pal, for mine, nor me."

The Day Sammy Maxton Got High

Hugh McMillan

Sammy Maxton shifted his position slightly, his chin still resting on his hand. Through the clouds he could see plumes of black smoke chivvied by the wind. That must be Grangemouth, he thought. Without turning round he began to probe gingerly behind his back, looking for his lunchbox. He was feeling voraciously hungry, more hungry than he could ever remember, and was relishing the idea of biting into a sandwich, even if it was just jam. Sally usually made his piece in the morning, out of boiled ham or sausage or sometimes meat paste, but she wasn't speaking to him and all he could find that morning was a couple of doorsteps of bread and a half-finished jar of raspberry jam. "You're turning funny as fuck" she had told him because he was reading the poetry of Omar Khayam in the bath. He'd laid the book on his soapy paunch which protruded like a small island from the flat sea of bath water and had said nothing.

"Do you want a can of lager?" Sally had asked later on. It was a sign she wanted to make up. "Naw," he replied, "I'm goana gie that stuff up." He was actually thinking of drinking a bit of wine now and then though he wasn't going to tell her that and he didn't know how to begin buying wine once you were past the usual cheap stuff. They were all in Europe now, after all, not that you'd know it where they came from where even the babies were drip fed with Carlsberg lager. Maybe he *was* turning funny as fuck, but he'd started thinking that 26 years of driving a lorry through West Central Scotland and getting steaming at the Club was about 26 years too many. Before he'd got into the bath last night and fallen out with Sally, he'd been pacing up and down their excuse for a garden looking at all the other miserable excuses for gardens and asking himself what he'd ever done in all that time and he couldn't think of much. Got married to a nice lassie and sentenced her to 24 years of living with a man who drove a lorry through West Central Scotland and got steaming at the Club. Not that she seemed to mind. It was only now, in fact, when he'd begun to think that things could be better for them both, that she'd begun really to complain. Maybe she thought there was some woman behind it all. Perhaps that girl in the library she'd seen him talking to once, the one he'd been asking why there were no books on Zoroastrianism. He'd never dreamed of being with anyone else but Sally, or living anywhere else than where he'd always lived. Not till now, anyway. Maybe she was right, maybe they were all right, and he was just turning funny as fuck. That would be the reason his work had fallen off and the reason he was in his present predicament; why he hadn't secured the load properly and why it had blown off on the roadbridge. It also explained, probably, why he'd sat on the sheet of metal with his lunchbox and flask, thinking that some extra weight would keep it on the deck, stopping it blowing about and causing some real damage. Of course the wind had really gusted then and it had all gone over the side – the sheet of metal and him sitting on it like a red Indian with his lunchbox and flask – flown off the bridge like a magic carpet.

The first funny thing had been, though, that he hadn't been scared. In fact what came right into his head was this analogy with a flying carpet. Even as it was all happening, even as he looked down and saw the water far below and the sheet of metal sliding from under him, all he had in his mind was this vision of himself squatting cross-legged like some kind of Scottish fakir.

> *"I came like the water*
> *and like the wind I go"*

he intoned, with a chuckle, and then Christ if the thing hadn't stopped in midair then gone off on a vaguely horizontal direction, a bit drunkenly at first, maybe, but definitely moving on, rising a little too, till the water and the boats and the ragged curve of the coast were just like features on a map. One hundred square feet of Scottish steel, flying west, destination unknown, with Skipper Maxton at the helm, patting it as if it were a horse, interspersing shrugs of disbelief with hoots of laughter. Where were they going? Slowly moving over West Lothian, perhaps to some country free of diesel, lapped by a sapphire sea.

Quarter of an hour later and he was groping for that lunchbox, then staring at the sandwiches as if he half-expected them to talk to him. Jam. It was funny how jam sandwiches had such a grip on the Scottish psyche. He remembered a story he'd read in the *Evening Times*: "After she'd spent two days trapped in a derelict basement, Tracey Graham was reunited with her jubilant parents Amilia and Ted, who took her indoors immediately and made her a jam sandwich."

Sammy bit into the bread and suddenly to his consternation the sheet metal was acting like sheet metal, falling through the air with Sammy clinging to an edge, the sandwich still clamped between his teeth. He spat it out and the metal jarred to a halt in mid-air, Sammy still miraculously sat upon it. As he was gasping for breath, the lunchbox, which had been on more stately course to earth, fell past him and disappeared in low cloud. His flask was still in his picket. He ran his fingers through his thinning hair. A narrow escape.

> *"You know how little while we have to stay*
> *And, once departed, may return no more"*

he whispered. He had a clear idea, by this time, that the metal responded to Persian verse but was still at a loss to comprehend its recent behaviour. This became easier to understand some twenty minutes later when, as they were overflying the outskirts of Glasgow, Sammy had removed from his inside pocket his rolled-up copy of the *Daily Record*. No sooner had he read the first few lines of 'The Doc Replies', on the subject of piles, that his stomach was in his mouth and they were plunging to earth again. He hurled the newspaper away and again they slewed to a halt and continued the journey, this time at a lower altitude. It was plain that whenever Sammy tried to do anything singularly Scottish, like read the *Daily Record* or eat a jam sandwich, the metal sheet became subject, again, to the traditional demands of gravity. While they were approaching the Firth of Clyde, Sammy experimented. He found that he could drink mouthfuls of sweet tea from his flask if, between gulps, he chanted:

"Drink! For you know not whence you came or why:
Drink! For you know not why you go, or where!"

But whenever he thought of Rangers, the Social Club, the yard at work, Western SMT, Gordon Strachan, Tennants Lager, mince, and so on, the metal dipped alarmingly, only maintaining a steady course when he recited from the poet, or focused on the distance, way beyond the island of Bute, beyond Ireland even, to an imaginary inlet of light he could if he really concentrated, ignite in his brain and see, with a facility he couldn't understand, burning.

Sammy was tired. His normal working day would have been over by now. He would have been on the bus home. Fatigue washed over him but he dared not sleep because he sensed that if he did all the daily bric-a-brac that comprised the old framework of his certainties would crowd into his head, he would think he was half-asleep on the sofa with a cup of tea and Coronation Street still to come on or, worse, he would open his eyes and find he was on the sofa and not buccaneering across the darkening sky above the lights of houses flickering on like embers. For these reasons he dared not sleep but the greatest test was almost below him. Rothesay, where he'd spent all his miserable childhood holidays, where he'd lost his anorak and got leathered, where his cousin Eddie had bought a house just opposite the Zavaroni's Chip Shop, where plants and people shivered along the length of an esplanade that seemed to last forever.

He sensed that he might be able to sleep if he made it past Rothesay, maybe wake up in a new light, airborne over a broad expanse of green sea with only stateless gulls for company. He let the flask fall from his nerveless hands. Far below it hit someone on the head as he was carrying home a smoked sausage supper. The man cursed and blinked upwards but the dot trailing painfully slowly across the sky did not even register, let alone the small man stiff as a figurehead transfixed at its bow, staring westwards:

Strange – is it not – that of the myriads who,
before us passed the door of darkness through,
not one returns to tell us of the road
which to discover, we must travel too.

Hugh McMillan

Andrew Greig

Poet, she writes from Hospital

It is a healing blade.

The patient lies
on the crumpled bed of the North Atlantic,
on either side the surgeons stand.
Look East, look West –
they've nothing in their hands except
the very ordinary knives of death.
Nurse! Clear these clowns
                                        outa here,
their century is ending.
And my sweet, ailing country –

I'm lyrical and raving. Here comes
my morning dose of Tedium.
These Protestants mean well, I know,
and their love's not blind –
just looking in the wrong direction.

*

A Journey, then? Begin!
Come Thursday, I'll be stabilised by then.
(They've got me riding on 'mood elevators',
can you believe! Half the time
I'm through the penthouse ceiling,
next crawling on the basement floor,
think some fine tuning's still required.)

        The knife you seek
's well buried in its sheath,
and that at least I'd recognise.
But I dropped it when we parted
sometime in the '70s
– that last long hectic trip –
was picked up by a passing porter.

I suggest: we try Tibet.

What the hell, it's big enough.

* *

(It's called 'sampling')

I know a moor where bog myrtle blows
the veil aside, and on the sweet
clover of a machair beach
the good beasts graze. On Holy Island

the giant Buddha of the coastline
stretches sleeping on the sand

five withered continents
          cradled in his hand.

I'll sift into his ear.

            * * *

It is a healing blade.
State of the Heart, archaic,
prickly, blade of the future
and the past reversible,
on its edge where all divisions fade
one day
         we'll meet as one

Come early,
        come alone,
                fuss not.
Bring mannish clothes for me
and roses from Bostonian gardens
so I may leave, when we escape:
         flowers
that have no messages but love.

These tapes I've spliced

This ain't no party
      This ain't no disco
           This is Western Swing

Play a song for me, Mr Shantyman...

It's been a hard day's –
     Ane doolie sessoun to ane cairfull dyte –
     And so sweet jane, approximately –

These tapes I've spliced against the night.

Scotland

On the dreich and unfashionable
     side of the street
         at the northern edge of town

we have hunched shivering,
     broken, blue and belly-aching
         like a hungover *pauvre* of diagonals

by MacDiarmid out of Picasso,
     parading ribbons of our old campaigns
        that is, defeats –

for a few hundred years.
    And telling with a certain
        ressentiment

a pitiful tale
    and true
        if not always to the point

how we were once independent
    upright and proud
        that is, quarrelsome and prone

to beating up on folk,
    often our own,
        but have since fallen on haird times.

Yup, been reived, abused,
    crippled and colonised,
        blinded and generally shafted

and if we have a wee bittie drink problem,
    who could possibly dream
        of addressing a thistle

unless he were thoroughly guttered?
    So do not stint in your sympathy:
        it's aa their blame, we canna win.

Haivers. Isn't it time
    we rose now
        with our hand off our crutch –

with a new century waiting
    isn't it time
        we got up and

wobbly
    a bit light in the head
        kinda feart actually

walked by ourselves, to meet it?

Crossing Rannoch

    Scotland. January. Snow.
A mean day gloomily shutting up shop.
We see
a rusting green 2CV
shoogle   over
Cairn O'Mount
with two last-minute customers...

'This salted road's a thin black tawse
whacked down on Rannoch Moor.'

Crack! The wiper blade breaks off.
That'll learn ya, son, the Buddha spat
then with a sigh leant out and cleared
the windscreen with his brolly,
anthropocentrism makes you blind,
a kind

of beating your own trumpet.

He huddled deeper in his cloak and warmed
as was his way
to his subject

        (which was as well
        for with the window open to permit
        the passage of his brolly
        it was bloody freezing as I
        blinked and steered into another change
        of tense and personnel
        that lies across our way like ice)

Might as well call the punitive tawse
a strip torn off the A83,
your palm
this land in miniature.

I hold out my hand and wait.
At length the Buddha shakes his head,
gently places
my fingers back upon the wheel:

I read: a violent culture,
great wilderness in the heart.

Above the whirring shoe-box
a hoodie craw veered North.
I scanned for something dead or dying,

      thought of my friend Donald,
      HIV positive, two tendons cut
      by a Stanley knife when he came in

        on my account when I was jumped
        by Casuals in Queensferry
        between the chipper and the Chinese carry-out

'Sure thing,' I said, 'but mine own.'
The white palm dipped beneath the blow
and we declined towards Glencoe,
hands tight and careful on the wheel.

    It's narration of a sort
when someone salts the road for us

through all the massacres of the past
below the Buchaille Etive Mor
to let us wind down like a clock
and stop
                    outside the Clachaig Inn.

          'Let's enter. I have friends here.'

Rab Fulton

it thi warl's end: 16/8/92

thirs a certain type
o middle class lassies
fae thi former colonies
wae fit boadies,
black thick hair
cut short owre lugs,
big daurk een,
pleasint faces,
smiles n manners.

Wan cam intae a coogit howf
tae stick up a poster
fur a festival production,
"the shows not over 'til
the F A T lady sings."

she didnae huv
enuch blu-tack
sae she stertit
takin bits aff
ithir posters
oan thi wa'.

first a wee dod fae
"the toilet of roses",
then a wee dod fae
"REVELATIONS:
    the testimony of salome",
n finally took some aff
thi back o "love lies bleeding",
which wiz beside
wir ah wiz sittin
sippin a pint o lager.

ah smiled, she smiled back
n sed "its a good show

you should go to it"
naw, cannae afford it
"excuse me"
ah live in glesga
ah'm ainly oo'ir fur thi day
"yes...it's a good show
...you'll enjoy it"
ay, n whit dae yae dae yirsel
"what"
whit dae yae dae yirsel
"sorry, i dont understand"
what do you do your self

she pyntit it thi poster,
flappt ur erms a little,
n impersonaitit pullin a rope,
"i fly", she smiled.

ah lookt it thi poster,
it hud a photy ae ur
wearin a cloon's nose,
flyin. ah smiled back.

*

ay,
macdairmid wis wrang:
it thi warl's end
thi trump wullna blo'
nor boadies come lowpin
oot thi grun. naw.

it thi warl's end
colonial quines'll
sproot wings,
stert flyin owre embry,
n gleswegians'll tawk english.

Hugh MacDiarmid: The Integrative Vision

Tom Hubbard

Baudelaire, Rilke, MacDiarmid: these are modern poets who have resisted the fragmenting, trivialising tendencies of their times. All three share a universality of outlook. Baudelaire held that God had created an indivisible unity, 'dark and profound'; accordingly, the human senses (and therefore the arts) were inter-related – they 'corresponded' to each other. Cooks and perfumers were artists as much as painters, composers and poets. Truly great artists were those who did not specialise narrowly in one activity, who had a deep and broad culture. On their canvasses, colour became melody. In particular, Baudelaire cited Delacroix, a painter with an intense appreciation of poetry and music, a visionary genius in contrast to the fashionable triflers of the Second Empire.

Rilke rejected Baudelaire's Christian God; poetry itself was the goal of his spirituality. He learned, though, that poetry also required materiality. This was the lesson of sculpture. Rilke became secretary to Rodin, and in the master's studio he discovered how each sculpted hand, head, torso, could actually suggest the animation of a complete body. Each part was in itself a coherent whole. What was a fragment in life was no mere fragment in art. Moreover, in a group such as *The Burghers of Calais* (1884-89), each figure was both uniquely individual and an integral part of the group. This coherence was all the more remarkable in that none of the figures actually touched each other. For Rilke, Rodin was an artist who broke down reality then recomposed it into *'neue Verbindungen'* (new combinations). MacDiarmid called on his fellow artists to join him in 'binding the braids' – he takes the image from a Sanskrit text, but it almost echoes Rilke's German phrase.

Rilke, as consummate an art-critic/poet as Baudelaire, learned from Rodin how to overcome writer's block: in a sense he replaced it by sculptor's block, the block to which the sculptor addresses himself every day in his workmanlike fashion, unlike the poet waiting pathetically for 'inspiration'. In his *'Dinggedichte'* – 'thing' poems – Rilke approached his subject matter with the maximum attention, having examined it from all angles, having humbly and patiently allowed it to yield its essence to him – just like Rodin. Art, then, is the supreme integrator, not least when it integrates the verbal and the visual.

MacDiarmid's integrative vision owes much to his native Langholm, a weaving town where three rivers meet. In 'The Seamless Garment', set among the Langholm looms, he praises Rilke as a poet who wove together his love and pity and fear into "a seamless garment o music an thocht". One of MacDiarmid's finest poems in English is his transcreation of Rilke's Requiem for the painter Paula Modersohn-Becker.

In his rediscovery of the potentialities of the Scots language, MacDiarmid effectively applied Baudelaire's *'correspondances'*. Scots, so rich in onomatopoeia, could evoke a wide range of sounds; he went further and claimed its potential for colours and smells. It is not surprising to find MacDiarmid writing a poem about music in terms of painting – "Sibelius's gaunt El-Greco-emaciated ecstatic Fourth" ('Goodbye Twilight') – or about painting in terms of music: the art of his fellow Borderer, William Johnstone, is related to Mahler's Eighth.

MacDiarmid's art appeals to ear and eye – indeed, it fulfils his ideal of a poetry of the whole person. We can cite the musicality of the early Scots lyrics, forby the surreal footage of *A Drunk Man Looks at the Thistle*:

> Plant, what are you then? Your leafs
> Mind me o the pipes' lood drone
> – And a' your purple tops
> Are the pirly-wirly notes
> That gang staggerin owre them as they groan…

A Drunk Man illustrates Baudelaire's *'le beau est toujours bizarre'*; eleven years after that pronouncement, Aeneas Sweetland Dallas maintained that 'you cannot have great art which is not weird'. In drawing attention to Dallas's *The Gay Science* (1866), MacDiarmid was rediscovering one of these Scots (or at least semi-Scots) who were precursors of the continental Europeans – in this case Freud and Jung. MacDiarmid's *Aesthetics in Scotland* is a journey through Scottish visual art in quest of a Scottish aesthetic, and here Dallas is revealed as a pioneer who considered art in relation to symbolism and the unconscious rather than to Victorian morality.

Rilke's most celebrated *Dinggedicht*, 'The Panther', is concerned with vision and the relation between observer and observed. The Great Wheel section of *A Drunk Man* has been praised for its scientific insight:

> Oor universe is like an e'e
> Turned in, man's benmaist hert to see,
> And swamped in subjectivity.

The Drunk Man speculates that man may evolve faculties by which he will fuse subjectivity and objectivity.

> The function, as it seems to me,
> O' Poetry is to bring to be
> At lang, lang last that unity…

MacDiarmid, as appropriate for a 20th century poet, goes further than Baudelaire and Rilke in integrating poetry with science. His ally William McCance called for the visual arts to do likewise, writing that the Scots, with their ability for construction and engineering, need not tolerate sentimentality in their art. MacDiarmid corroborated by pointing out that in the past there had been two factors, man and nature; now there was a third, the machine. (MacDiarmid's relations with Johnstone and McCance, are explored in Duncan MacMillan's *Scottish Art 1460-1990*.)

Two more MacDiarmid texts remain to be cited in connection with the verbal and the visual. The first is *The Kind of Poetry I Want*, i.e. the kind of poetry which learns from the visual arts, a poetry "as subtle and complete and tight/ As the integration of the thousands of brush strokes/

In a Cézanne canvas"; exactly that quality which Rilke found in the composition of a portrait of Mme Cézanne: "It seems that each part knows of all the other parts" (letter to Clara Rilke, 22 October 1907).

Secondly, there is 'A Glass of Pure Water', with its near-Rilkean figure of an Angel reporting on a hundred years of human life by means of a single, subtle gesture of the hand. Rilke himself, through his fictional mouthpiece Malte Laurids Brigge, maintained that a poem's existence depended on "glance and gesture". A tacit recognition of this might be found in Scotland's poetry-theatre movement.

In Memoriam James Joyce is MacDiarmid's most explicit and exuberant statement of his integrative vision. He considered his poem to be "ablaze with the sense that we stand at one of the great turning-points of human history...a complete breakdown of civilisation is possible and can only be averted if we can succeed in unifying mankind at a high level of culture". he stresses unity-in-diversity; the world's various language-cultures are enriched by mutual respect and creative reciprocity.

> And rejoicing in all those intranational differences which
> Each like a flower's scent by its peculiarity sharpens
> Appreciation of others as well as bringing
> Appreciation of itself, as experiences of gardenia or zinnia
> Refine our experience of rose or sweet pea.

Scotland itself was multi-faceted...

The poet defended the 'multiplicity of quotations, references and allusions' in his poem by invoking Baudelaire's "*immense clavier des correspondances*". The clavier image is apt for *In Memoriam*, which tends to allude more to music than to the visual arts; indeed, one of the most suggestive essays on the poem is by a composer-pianist, Ronald Stevenson (in *Hugh MacDiarmid: a Festschrift*, Edinburgh, 1962). In the 'Plaited Like the Generations of Men' section, MacDiarmid transcribes into poetry an essay by the composer-pianist Busoni – himself an avid transcriber of other composers, notably Bach. I'll conclude with one portion of the Busoni-MacDiarmid transcription. This passage also serves as 'A Point in Time', MacDiarmid's poetic response to William Johnstone's painting of that name: it hangs in the Scottish National Gallery of Modern Art, and is a key work in 20th century Scottish painting. It is movingly appropriate that all the arts should come together in this most celestial-terrestrial of MacDiarmid's utterances of integration:

> Now you understand how stars and hearts are one with another
> And how there can nowhere be an end, nowhere a hindrance;
> How the boundless dwells perfect and undivided in the spirit,
> How each part can be at once infinitely great and infinitely small,
> How the utmost extension is but a point, and how
> Light, harmony, movement, power
> All identical, all separate, and all united are life.

Tom Hubbard

• This article condenses a lecture given at Glasgow School of Art in June 1992.

Radio MacDiarmid: A Note

Robert Crawford

With Bruce Young of BBC Radio Scotland I've just made a centenary documentary about MacDiarmid called *A Disgrace to the Community*. The title takes the form of the words that MacDiarmid wanted as his epitaph (see the conclusion of *Lucky Poet*). My brief was that the programme should be 'forward-looking'; certainly I didn't want it to be too pious. So I chose to avoid anecdotes about C M Grieve, and to concentrate on MacDiarmid's legacies or lack of them. In order to stress the fact that the historical individual C M Grieve was dead, I decided not to use any recordings of his voice. Instead, I wanted to distance the surviving writings from the dead author, emphasising that the words will live for us only if we re-voice them. That's why I chose a woman's voice (that of Gerda Stevenson) to speak all the MacDiarmid material in the programme. I felt that a woman's voice would help distance the writings from the writer, and might subtly reinterpret some of MacDiarmid's more vicious (and sometimes sexist) outbursts. One thing that interested me was whether or not MacDiarmid had left any legacy to women writers, or whether he was just a roadblock for them.

A number of women writers told me in conversation that they disliked MacDiarmid's work or deliberately avoided it, but several were loath to say so in public. I was pleased when Kathleen Jamie was prepared to talk about her principled swerve away from MacDiarmid's work, which she sees as reeking of smoky all-male pubs and dripping cantankerousness. Liz Lochhead was similarly wary, revealing that it was only ten years ago that she really began to relish MacDiarmid. I enjoyed the way Lochhead had both likes *and* dislikes in MacDiarmid's work. I wanted to avoid the knee-jerk reactions that MacDiarmid too easily produces, even so long after his death. It amazes me that people should still argue over the rights and wrongs of synthetic Scots, for instance, as if those arguments hadn't been played out to the full over fifty years ago. I wanted to avoid those dead arguments.

At the same time, though, I was keen to confront head-on some of the viler aspects of MacDiarmid's politics: his fascist proclamations, his Stalinism, his siding with those who crushed the Hungarian uprising. I wanted a sweetly reasonable woman's voice speaking some of those anti-democratic pronouncements, implicitly taking them apart. Part of my idea was to assert the right to fumigate MacDiarmid's politics, and the right to delight in his verse. It was good to hear the enthusiasm which younger Scots like the painter Ken Currie experienced when confronted by MacDiarmid's work; good also to hear how MacDiarmid criticism was growing subtle in the work of several generations, from David Daiches (who recalled MacDiarmid's professed Modernist hatred of humanity) to the young poets W N Herbert and Alan Riach.

Bruce Young gave me constant guidance about what would or would not work on radio; he did a superb editing job on the hours of interviews we built up. I was delighted with the way he preserved Douglas Dunn's indignation, Joy Hendry's laughter. It was good to have these responses on tape. They helped convince me that MacDiarmid's work, revoiced, argued over, scorned and relished in his centenary year is very much alive and mobile. Long may his profile escape the teatowels!

The Anachronist

I love you because you were a careerist
Who slalomed out of every career.

On one of the Shetlands, birling like a radar antenna
Detecting a hostile mainland,

You ate credit and birds' eggs, adrift
On the windchilled raft of yourself

With your wife, baby, and secretary
Redirecting those shores. On the rocks

You surveyed Whalsay's encylopaedic weather:
Knowledge, dictionaries

Were the skyscraping multistorey carpark
In whose dank corners you unparked abandoned

Vintage Bugattis, Ecurie Ecosse Jags,
Dusty Morris Minors, trucks, to lead them in convoy

Into the light. You jammed
Scotland's A roads and fledgling motorways

With horses and carts, Lamborghinis, bubblecars
Melled together, made by others, yours.

After this happened, local papers cried
BUILD US NEW ROADS or BAN ALL HEAVY LORRIES;

Unleaded fuels, catalysis – we have to find
Solutions for the problems you conjured up

Perched eccentrically, sandblasted
On an archipilego of singletrack roads

And grasstrack, tarfree islands.
A crank, a daftie, you were far away,

But later when you walked into the village
A woman recognised you and waved

Like an anarchist or an angry traffic policeman
Breaking up the gridlock no one saw.

Hear The Values Of The Bard

Robert Calder

In his important essay 'The Tradition of Taliesin' Saunders Lewis draws attention to the common basis of attacks on Welsh princes in Gildas the Historian's 6th century AD *De Excidio Britanniae*, and Taliesin's bardic praise of the same lot. Moral diatribe and traditionary encomia both honoured a constant accepted catalogue of the virtues. The bard of tradition, whatever his 'other' powers – and these seem to have interested MacDiarmid – perhaps sang praises the gangster who employed him did not deserve. Bound nonetheless to certain terms of praise, virtues he was obliged to extol, it was not of account in the praise-song that its praise was inaccurate: what mattered first was that the proper qualities be duly celebrated. The tactful auditor might find his secret critical thoughts the better thus organised. The technical intricacies of bardic verse have also (pace MacDiarmid) a limited appeal, and whatever interest might be stirred by samples the great body of traditional bardic verse represents a culture belonging almost entirely to history.

The terms of praise, or virtues, retain validity, despite the obscurity of princes and chiefs about whom praise-poetry was anyway never meant to tell much. So it is in Pindar's lauding of athletes, to give a different slant to a conjunction effected by MacDiarmid. It is perhaps MacDiarmid's answer to problems of the vast amount to be learned, for a modern 'universal knowledge', to adopt a similar project. Some of his diatribes against Edwin Muir, and so much else of his work, from the brilliant to the dreadful (including somewhere among that *Lucky Poet*) are rather singings of values than accurate judgments – sound things are said accurately amid much rubbish, a fact which ought to annoy only those so low as to demand that a writer do the thinking they ought to; or parallel their own unthinking. A great deal of the most abstruse material is also sung, emphasising a bardic habit of great learning. MacDiarmid is not an epic but a bardic poet; in his relation to his reading something of a Quijana-become-Quixote, though not merely living out a moral drama remote from reality. And certainly not relying on the reader's pitying sympathy.

The most startling quasi-bardic poems state something of the ground of his valuations, *Harry Semen* and *An Ode to All Rebels* scotch standard and received ideas of the bases and securities of human life. The case is more extreme than Harvey Oxenhorn states when he speaks of MacDiarmid as describing himself masturbating. In fact the whole of supposed human life and posterity is identified with an endless river of never-fertilising spermatozoa in their fluid element. "All is a flowing," Herakleitos of Ephesus is supposed to have said.

There is no validation of one's life by reference to the posterity of one's handwork or mind-work, or that of one's loins. In the end there is only the evidence of one's own experience, that one believes or witnesses to the good. The good is debatable and debated, with oneself and with others. Nietzsche's statement that life can be validated only as an aesthetic spectacle has its echo, certainly, in MacDiarmid's case, with an acceptance of ethical and indeed humane values as valid. Needless to say, "Better ae gowden lyric...", experience of one's own valuations demonstrates that valuations clash. Rather than what might be termed valuations of values, pausing to adjust and thus not experience valuations – settling for the narcissistic distortion which represses approval of any value which cannot be harmonised with all others – the valuations are boldly, often brilliantly expressed. Challenging and being challenged is a good.

In all the hullaballoo about Scott and Scotland, which has probably been responsible for endless misreadings of that book, there is ample evidence that MacDiarmid gave the book no careful attention. One has also the evidence of a universally ignored letter from MacDiarmid to Catherine Carswell:

> I told F G Scott and others over a year ago [1935] that I would have to fight Muir if he came back to Scotland – my siezing on his sentences about myself [Scott and Scotland, extract in Outlook, June 1936] was only a pretext; I'd have made one if he hadn't given me one. ...I am out for a big cultural fight – and, above all, for an International United Front in Great Britain, with the achievement of an autonomous Scottish Workers' Republic. ...[Muir] is playing into my hands in the most delightful way – it would have made matters much more difficult for me if he had come away at this juncture with an eulogy of my work. (15/8/36).

The argument was not on what might be called a literal basis, but on behalf of certain values, quite notably political activist. The questions of human liberty which were at the foremost in Muir's thinking, the tempering of enthusiasms, not least in the light of Muir's all-too-recent experience of totalitarianism on the continent, were of no account to MacDiarmid. The letter also refers to taking the matter to the highest courts in Moscow, and without being prissily or lispingly dismissive of nasty Stalinism, or tolerant of such nonsense, one can see what MacDiarmid is on about. His political extremism was never covert, nor was it without real observations highly challenging to a by-no-means-satisfactory status quo (which Muir liked no more).

In the context of an interpretation of it in bardic terms, MacDiarmid's Stalinism is really of no account. The point is his expression of values, not all of which anybody need share for some among them to be recognised as valid. Stalinism praises science, attacks the wildcat economic system of the West, represents a viewpoint fundamentally dissenting from views habitual to that West. That it, or Communism, favours the highest developments of human thought and culture as well as the extirpation of poverty, one might deny. People who denied such claims for Communism, MacDiarmid would often say, didn't know anything about Communism.

He was certainly talking about an objective of forward striving on the part of some of mankind, though to suggest that he had any feasible thing in view is dubious. "Stalin will arouse reason, awaken life", wrote Mandelshtam in a line sometime taken to be a mistranscription. Despite what MacDiarmid apparently believed about him, Mandelshtam was no Communist: the point was rather that to say yes to the world is to recognise the power of evil to stimulate opposition from good. The fact of Stalin's rule was quite as sterilising as anything deplored by MacDiarmid in 1919-39 Britain. Since the ex-Soviet students in Scotland since *Glasnost* have seemed to many of their teachers to make their Scottish counterparts seem in comparison mostly tame boors, there is at least one question to be asked. The best one to ask is not whether the praise tailored by MacDiarmid fits the Soviet Emperor, but how the values he formulates and organises in his vision (he was plain to insist on the term "vision") are to be assessed, and how they reflect on one's own native situation. Nietzsche's 'will to power' doctrine has been grossly misunderstood as the mere extolling of a blond beast and the line of his thought need not be taken so far. Sexuality and some sort of life-principle, and a certain character of human deeds and transactions, rather than some yellow-haired superman, were the focus of power in Lawrence's version. MacDiarmid sought power for a pursuit of less simplistic, less summarisable goods, but had in addition his own version of Nietzsche's vision of the triumph of the best humans. These were not a class of supermen but rather those elements of humanity who had not gone soggy and merged into a soft centre of obligatory compromise and consensus values.

If many works by MacDiarmid may well enough be considered according to more ordinary standards, the question of his bardic basis seems crucial to that more untidy mass of his later poetry, and yet something is implicit in the earlier Scots poetry, which might be illustrated by one simple biographical anecdote.

As often recorded, before C M Grieve had adopted the MacDiarmid name, that ambitious, unsuccessful poet essayed some verses in Scots, using a Scots dictionary and perhaps some other material. Instead of producing a plain spoof as it seems he intended, the resultant verses were actually impressive. Whatever structure of reasoning may be offered in interpretation or analogy of what subsequently happened, he came to value both the poems this curious method produced, and the method itself. He doubtless had a good idea of what comprises a good poem, as many do who would never claim to be able to produce one. Unlike many who fancy they are producing good poems, he was correct in thinking that he could produce good poems, find bits of them here and there (as on Frank O'Connor's account Yeats found bits

130

of his poems in heated statements which arose during arguments at meetings of the Abbey Theatre board). Whatever had hitherto been in the way, poems written under the MacDiarmid name somehow got away from that.

Rather than that sense of moral superiority which attends the puritan in- or anti-human ruthlessness, Grieve was really quite objective, though not infallible, when he engaged in what in another would likely be called boasting (objectivity is not manner, but attention to an object of attention). If it was some time after the writing of Sangschaw that he expressed the idea in *On a Raised Beach*, there is reason to believe that from the beginning he comprehended himself somewhat as a stone is comprehended, or a star (see *Annals of the Five Senses*). His self-comprehension was somewhat hampered by his having to attach to himself the given name of Grieve, about which people said this and that. A foolish postgraduate might someday be permitted by an idiot supervisor to compare and contrast the respective persons of Grieve and MacDiarmid, as if human individuality or distinctiveness were (as David Hume and indeed Carl Jung rightly denied) a matter of some fixed and permanent element in the psyche, some basis of individual subjectivity. Any such complex fixed determinant is a neurosis or a psychosis, a frozen form or shell. Grieve-MacDiarmid came nearer to the fact of the human being, to the 'himsel'. The resulting loosening of the bundle which was his mind was responsible not only for the poetry however, but sundry disadvantages and discomforts. It was an extension which at once attained to a proper selfhood without narrowing constrictions, but also went beyond that. It brought into being a nature huger than the human.

Not a deluded would-be knight and not without incarnation in a living human being, Hugh MacDiarmid developed out of the desire to be a great poet into the need to be a great poet, and a need moreover felt and lived by a great poet. He was not alone in praising his early Scots poetry, which in its galvanic movement seems overwhelmed by its author's intense appreciation of the merits of what he is doing. In his fiftieth birthday concert Yehudi Menuhin so performed a Beethoven Romance he had to fight to continue with it, and keep his violin dry from the tears his intense inspiration evoked, full of marvelling astonishment. The *Drunk Man* is in some wise a measure of the Grieve's own amazement, watching what comes out with an incredible astonishment. He has to laugh, not at anything but like a baby, at the end. What Jean'll say can hardly matter. There is also in *A Drunk Man Looks at the Thistle* a valuation of truth as a good, of rather more than those many multicoloured worlds into which Russian symbolists dissolved everything.

To relate MacDiarmid to any kind of philosophy demands some recognition of the achievements of his early poetry, for what matters is not his willed intentions, nor the texts he read independently nor the pages he later pillaged, but the actual performance. The great crisis in his personal life was at a time when he was willing certain performances which proved beyond him, the sort of thing he hoped *To Circumjack Cencrastus* would be, and then the 'sun-clear' project of a 'Faust' poem and whatever else. The need to be a great poet can be felt so strongly as to disable, and whatever else can be said about *To Circumjack Cencrastus* it retains as its subject above all an essay in the kind of poetry MacDiarmid wanted: desired, and to a rather lesser degree, in which, he came to suspect, his work might here and there be wanting.

The crisis came to an end, it might fairly be said, with *On a Raised Beach*. It presents a counter-argument to those views of Grieve entertained not without reason by his contemporaries, the suggestion that he had been beaten, was dying, had lost this and that, indeed had lost. 'There are no ruined stones' he insists, contrasting what an American would call a rock (as one American translator of Nietszche does), anything from a pebble to a boulder, with an ashlar. It is all to do with the forces which create them. The weather which erodes bits of buildings does not ruin rocks but makes each what it is. "All is lithogenesis" might sum the matter up. "Lochia", the evacuations of the womb after childbirth, is hardly a necessarily disjunct alternative, product of a positively valued process if not the product and not of itself of worth. This presumably belongs with what inspired James Caird to describe MacDiarmid as Deist rather than atheist, but if his atheism is insisted on (as by himself) the matter is perhaps clearer. Caird has registered a point nonetheless, that MacDiarmid has 'faith', what Donald MacKinnon speaks of as "assurance". There is a positive valuation of human existence.

There is a recognition of geology, and also of the different apperceptions involved in science. In thinking his existence and character a positive product, not that of a victim, MacDiarmid does not fall into passivity. Minds are indeed like stones in some respects, equally a stone of one kind is unlike one of another kind - 'oak leaf never plane leaf' in Pound's phrase. The mind has its own activity quite apart from external weathering factors, just as the stone has its specific composition.

Mind is activity, and fundamentally its activity is of valuing, whether explicitly where some valuation is uttered, or implicitly, where for instance the non-green technologist treats specific entities as just so much stuff for some purpose. His perception is severely blinkered, or obsessed. It is more than he habitually takes it to be, which fact may or may not be relevant. A fact is also a value of a distinct kind, facts derive from values not vice versa. One kind of poetry to be desired makes plainer the various character of things, which for all the seeming fittedness of any of them to man's uses cannot include being for man's uses.

The early lyrics which afford no more than depictions without comment invoke valuations of aesthetic spectacle, however small or involving insects. The aesthetic 'thrill' is like the child's in being sib to the sternies rather than the adult's idealisation of Jesus of the nursery room. The limitation of MacDiarmid as a poet is in his powerful responsiveness to feelings of a certain over-vivid character, and intensity, something which might account for the attraction felt by some adolescent minds keen to faither him wi their ain thochts. In an essay on Robert Fergusson he complains that Scots have an inveterate and malignant tendency to prefer writers as like to themselves as are two peas in a pod. Even his most gargantuan effusions have not convinced them that he goes rather beyond this. They look for the supposed sources of his work, the multifarious reading and the pillaging of TLS pages, a research pretty well analogous to the botany of coal.

What he produced, if at all analogous to any geological product, was much more complex than coal, much more differentiated than flowing lava and much more dynamic than a caldera. He was no more a plagiarist than the virtuoso Sterne with whom he might be compared. Save the dire modern PhD, anyone who seeks to publish, whether poetry or critical or discursive writing, makes an almost explicit claim, concerning the quality or qualities of the poetry, the cogency, rigour and so forth of argument, the soundness of observations, and the validity of any and all of these. Certain claims are plainly implicit in the publication of even the most scissors-and-paste late attempts at poetry. Truth such as would be claimed by its author for a scientific treatise, is by no means the most important of these.

There is the value of each bit, or bits of it, as poem or poetry, and as examples of poetry, canon stuff; and there are the expressions or presentations of value(s), values very various in character, whether on behalf of the so-called Scottish Enlightenment, in *Direadh*; the Irish Gaelic foundations of Austin Clarke's poetry; or (to take a few of very many examples) such visions as 'In Memoriam Uilleam MacIlle Iosa', or the whole panoply of *In Memoriam James Joyce*. In the last-named work there is a splendid bardic example, 'England is our Enemy'. However it squares with the southern realm's reality (and it fits an enormous amount now north of the border, in academia, in modern poetasting, even among self-styled nationalists) is both a celebration of certain qualities and an assault on real and abiding categories of ill. There is every reason why MacDiarmid's work should resist the commoner kinds of summary, so resistant does it remain to so much that is insufficiently resisted.

Robert Calder

Douglas MacKay

Circumference

Ride the avalanche, not the piste
Paint curves of lines and lines of points.
With open decks sail out of shore,
Undivided and unsealed for sinking.

Look beyond the seasons of the earth,
To unquadranted gaps between the stars.
Stand above the forest, not apart;
Drop no dead leaves but living cones.

Know that beyond each summit lies,
A peak again yet higher;
Believe that paradise's slope
Is on the first horizon.

Count the pins upon the floor,
Satisfy the exacting mind;
But believe – enjoy – the eyes'
Impression of infinitude.

Reject the atlas, tract, didactic verse,
Extract prayers from travellers' tales.
Marvel at the total external reflection
Of truth in dark unshadowed heads.

False Start

Strange things appear on angels' wings
On windless nights on Highland coasts.
Where stones and skulls leave little mark
On soles of city feet; new worlds on crests
And Tuscan hills filling gaps of glens
Are closed to eyes too brimmed with life.

Here – on the cloudy side of the golden square,
That extends across the tiny voids, from
Old Sinai and Parnassus to lonely Hope
And the great cairned whale of Schiehallion –
Where once wisdom walked with wolves and colts,
Through water and fire, air, number and mind.

This beach, these rocks, those waves, that mind
Are garlanded with logos leaves and banished from
That ancient land. Unname me now, drain
From my breast the curdled milk of human-
Kindness; so from that place I may be freed, become
A skull among the stones, a rock beneath the waves.

Robert Maxwell Duncan

New Warlds
(for Hugh MacDiarmid)

Fegs, Shuggie, is't no juist your rotten luck
This hunder year sin first your mam gied suck
T'ye, gripan an yowlan for the kist o her,
's the quincentenary o anither Christopher?
An yon new warld ye blinkit on sae bonny,
Though new tae you, wes nae sic thing tae ony
Ayont a bairn, wha'd heard the name Columbus.
– Ye had tae fin out ither weys tae plumb us!
Sae your mischance wes lucky for the lave o us,
For ilk succeedan string an wave o us
That follow whaur ye took your skeelie craft
An look the weys ye shawed us, faur and aft,
On sichts byordinar as ony Indies,
(The whilk ye blinkt on first frae Langholm windaes,
Wee ancient Chris!)

Langholm – twinned wi Genoa for foresicht! –
That couldnae see your watergaw yon forenicht
For the yow-trummle, but huggert doun insteid:
Deil tak the hindmaist – but ye teuk the leid!

*

Colón – cartographer an coloniser
Colombo – skellie-roun-the-warld detective
Columbus – dark doo o discovery an destruction
An brither tae the corbie in its wa's,
Arkan across the flood wi speiran stam
Tae seek Cipango, Cathay and the Indies
And end in thinkan Cuba wes Japan,
Steered by the starns tae land he kentna whaur
Amang a fowk he kentna, tho he thocht
They micht be Marco Polo's Nicobars,
Nakit eedolaters; and he, Christ-bearer,
Colón: the neist best thing tae a full stop.

*

Ye shauchled aff your Christopher and tane
Hugh – Divine Wisdom – for your Christian name
(Blate frae the stert!) – the pattern early prentit –
The autopropagandisation unstentit –
And as Columbus tracked the selkie-mermaid,
The legend ye gart trace ye durst mak Diarmid.

Frae Langholm Library, thon harboury
Whaur ye scanned pickins frae the coast o Barbary
An guddled gledly in your bairnly pleiter,
Ye cobled out the maist uncommon skiter
An wi at first a seeman semple flisk
Gart it frae her tae Kingdom come gae whisk
Syne circle back tae rest in its hame-watter
An mell the cosmic wi the kintra clatter;
And your cartographer wes Jamieson
And your cosmographer was John Maclean.
Gangan the airt stern faithers said wes wast
Ye cam up blinkan wi the sin at last,
Out o the warld again and into Langholm,
Steeran the faithers whaur ye lie amang 'em!

But och, man, Shug, as I wes sayan earlier,
The gate Columbus socht wes aye the pearlier
An that's the gate the feck o the clamjamfry
'll traik an no the commonty ye cam frae.
Yet prent it here: the land in whilk you're lyan
Is that whaur your young mither had her cryin.
It's aye been yours, frae afore ye were a seed
And what ye tak o't's aa a body'd need.
Plant the ither Christopher in yon braw grund
He stummlet on syne made out that he'd fund
An up wad stound a cry frae it's ancient fowk,
The ultrasonic echo o't wad howk
His banes, his stour, his robes, his every relict,
Out o its wound and hurl it for its delict
Attower the jaup an jow o thon fell tide
That brocht him, back again tae his ain side,
Whaurever'd hae him, Puerto de Santa Maria,
Seville, or faurer on tae Genoa,
Whaur he belangs.

                    The stour ye mak, dear Shug,
Is yin that's walcome tae a Langholm lug
Or ony drum frae Berwick up tae Lerwick
That loes the odd stramash, stushie or sherrack
An yet when aa faas quate an fowk like thinkan
Or twa by twa ower heich and haugh come linkan,
Your ca can mak their thochts or feet gan lowpan
On reels unkent, an kennle native howp in
New warlds that grow frae old, naething unruitit,
New years that by the auld are still first-fittit,
New leids that wi the auld are aye restorit;
Ilka new bairn the mak o her that bore it

An yet the makin o itsel an ithers:
New airts tae tent the auld hairts o our mithers.
And ony o's that's gleg aneuch tae go there
Wad see fine weill whatten's the real explorer
We should be cryan this centennial.
Sae, Shuggie, frae your kith and menyie, all
Hail on the occasion o your centenary,
And may your praise be potent, proud an plenary!

Ruaraidh MacThòmais

Creag?

A' siubhal an rathaid ùir
ri taobh Loch Laomainn
shaoil mi gu robh an dùthaich seo
air a dèanamh de chreig:
bha an rathad air a shnaidheadh aiste
's i lom leacach air a' chliathaich;
cha bu mheata 'n t-inneal
a rinn a sgeilbeadh;
bha i dùr, liathghorm,
cho cruaidh ris a'…
(cha mhòr nach duirt mi 'chreig'),
a' bhreig is dòcha.
Co às a-rèisd a thàinig am morghan?

Rock?

Travelling along the new road
by Loch Lomond
it seemed as if this land
was made of rock:
the road was carved out of it
and at the side there were bare slabs;
it was no soft tool
that splintered that rock;
it was dour, grey-blue,
as hard as…
(I almost said 'rock'),
brick perhaps.
Where else did all the rubble come from?

Aonghas Macneacail

ciad bliadhna

caite bheil thu a chrìsdean –
a bheil deasbad aighearach ann an ifrinn
a bheil mi-riaghailt ghuineach ann am paras –

caite bheil thu a chrìsdean –
a bheil beachd agad air do sheann eolaich –
sluagh na h-albainn –
a seasamh an coirichean
san doigh fhrionasach abhaisteach

a bheil thu ag eisdeachd ri
guth iomadach do mhuinntir –
imcheist a dannsa tromh na fiaclan –

am faic thu gach seann namhaid
a fighe nam bratach troimh cheile –
a fighe nan rathad troimh cheile –
a gealtainn rathad ur am maireach
mar is abhaist, mar is abhaist
rathad ur direach, direach –
direach – ars thusa – aidh, direach,
ceart gu leor, direach

am faic thu na seann chairdean
an gualainn ris a chloich
fhathast, aidh, fhathast –
an gualainn ris a chloich –
a chlach neo-abhaisteach seo
a sior fhas, ged a tha i crion,
ged a tha i brisg, a sior fhas –
ach aon phut eile
aona phut eile –

's fhearr dhuinn gun eisdeachd ri do fhreagairt,
a chrìsdean –

one hundred years

where are you, christopher –
is there joyous debate in hell
is there bitter dispute in heaven –

where are you christopher –
have you a thought for your old friends –
the people of scotland –
standing up for their rights
in the usual fractious fashion

do you hear
the various voice of your folk –
doubts dancing through the teeth –

do you see all the old enemies
weaving the banners together –
weaving the roads together –
promising a new road tomorrow
as usual, as usual
a new road, truly straight, truly –
truly – *says you* – aye, truly
right enough, truly

do you see the old friends
their shoulder to the stone
still, aye, still –
their shoulder to the stone –
this unusual stone
that steadily grows as it crumbles,
though it's brittle, steadily grows –
but one more push
one more push –

we'd better not listen to your retort,
christopher –

Menna Elfyn

Song of a Voiceless Person to British Telecom

'Ga i rif yng Nghaerdydd, os gwelwch…'.
'Speak up'
'GA I RIF YNG NGHAER –'
'Speak up – you'll have to speak up'.
'Speak up' is, of course,
the command to speak English.
I sentence myself to a lifetime
of sentences that make no sense.
No pronunciation, no annunciation,
inflection. I am infected
with dumbness. I can neither lampoon,
sing in tune; much less can I

intone. My grace-notes
are neither music nor mumble.
I am not heard at Evening Prayer
nor at triumphal Matins;
nor am I that voice in the dusk
that is husky but vibrant.

An impediment, then? No. No thick tongue,
no chip on my shoulder, a compulsion to please.
And if I am without speech,
what of the fluency of my people?
We are mutes, Trappists,
conspirators in a corner.
The usurper's language pierces
to the very centre of our being,
a minister of darkness before whose tread
our civility must give ground.
From the safety of my television
I see nations forced into a hole,
possessors of nothing but their dispossession,
mufflers over their mouths,
their captive craft under curfew.
Threre is an injunction against their speech,
and I perceive it is Y GYMRAEG that is between us.

So the next time I am commanded
to 'speak up'
deferring to the courtesy
that is our convention,
with like courtesy I will require the operator
to 'pipe down';
and like 'sounding brass'
I will suggest the superfluousness of barbed wire,
since our language has berylled wares.
I will sing and make contact
in cynghanedd, as the small nations do,
a people in counterpoint
to the leit-motif, dominant
though its pitch be,
ending each time on the same
obstinate monotone
with the same passionate concern,
though mortally muted our metrics.

'A nawr, a ga i –
y rhif yna yng Nghaerdydd?'

Translated by R S Thomas

Eiwcalyptus

*(clywyd am arogleuon y goeden yn cael eu defnyddio fel olew yn
BAGDAD adeg y rhyfel am nad oedd trydan yn y ddinas)*

Cyn ei gweld yn Lisboa
nid oedd ond enw i mi
ffisig gwella annwyd
fu'r losinen esgus
at ryddhau'r frest
o'i thrydar.

Ond heddiw, llumanau yw'r petalau
sy'n cynnig gŵyl
i bawb yn ddiwahân,
coed hynaws,
sy'n ffafrio na gwerin na gwlad.

O'u gwraidd, cyfyd gwres
olew yn ogleuo byd
yn iro mewn cawg
faeth i deulu

A 'r eiwcalyptus euraid
fu'n ffrwtian yn ddi-feth
islaw ffrom yr holl ffrwydradau,
bu'n amgau bwyd
yn creu bwrdd bendithiol.

Onid i hyn y parhawn â bywyd;
o bryd parod i brydwedd,
rhythmau dŵr i'n gwddw,
mydrau maeth ar bob min?

A'r diferion a ollyngwyd
yn ffawd garedig dros anffodusion
gan ledu eu sawr –
mwy o rin sydd i'r rhoi
â'i ddogn yn rhoi digon.

A'r nos mor oer ag abo
eiliw o'r eiwcalyptus
sydd i'w glywed mewn cilfachau,
yn hel cyfrinachau
yng nghanol rhaib a rwbel.

Yr olew seml:
fu'n dal anadl cynhaliaeth
gan lathru goleuni
dros fywydau gloywddu.

The Eucalyptus

(Eucalyptus oil breathed in Baghdad during the
war since there was no electricity)

Fragrance that sighed freedom,
the lisping lozenges of my youth;
the carefree curer of colds,
releasing from my cage of a chest
its wire, and a wren's warble.

Alas, tonight, she has a new vocation
her petals welcoming
strangers of adversity;
the genial tree whose roots
favour the landsape of friend and foe,

And her warmth brings harmony
chanting anew, anointing
a feast made for a family,
simmering without ceasefire
under the frown of unfriendly fires,
encircling, blessing a table.

Is this not why we survive
from ready meal to making love,
rhythms on our lips,
strong metres –   our
meetings,

The night as cold as a corpse
the clouds curfew above,
yet the trickling of oil
turns the stove, a hot ray
moving harsh stones of despair;
collecting gossips in a cauldron
communion – amidst rape and rubble,

holding the breath of life,
(as once my dry cough)

over lives that are charcoal grey.

Translation by Menna Elfyn

Applying The Socratic Elenchus?
MacDiarmid's 'Direadh I'

Thom Nairn

If you can see a thing whole… it seems to me that it's always beautiful.
The way to see how beautiful the Earth is, is to see it as the Moon.

Ursula Le Guin, *The Dispossessed*

Free Scotland! The Golden Eagle
Looking into the eye of the sun
As at its own reflection in the eyes of its mate.

Hugh MacDiarmid, 'Direadh 1'
(*Complete Poems*, p1166)

MacDiarmid's 'Direadh 1' first appeared in the *Voice of Scotland* (Vol 1 No 3), while extracts from the three poems appeared (with MacDiarmid's commentary) in *Lucky Poet* (see pages 255-265 and 300-305). These poems, although only collected as one volume in 1974, clearly belong to the same phase chronologically as *The Kind of Poetry I Want* and *In Memoriam James Joyce*.

The 'Direadh' sequence is many things, a manifesto, an amalgam of "multi-linguistic diction", an ideological collage, a process of coalesce; MacDiarmid himself summed up the sequence as follows:

I have recently written three poems entitled 'Direadh', a Gaelic word meaning "the act of surmounting", and these poems attempt to give bird's-eye views – or rather eagle's-eye views – of the whole of Scotland, each from a different vantage point. (*Lucky Poet*, p255)

In *Lucky Poet*, MacDiarmid proceeds to quote from the three poems to "illustrate" the theme of his chapter, 'On Seeing Scotland Whole'. 'Direadh 1' provides a general introduction to the sequence, presenting a "claim" to "complete vision" (*Lucky Poet* p256), while the second and third poems deal more particularly (and personally) with diverse elements deriving from 'Direadh 1'.

'Direadh 1' is important in a number of ways. For one thing, in common with *Memoriam* and *Kind of Poetry*, it transcends that inclination towards the quasi-mystical we find in so much of MacDiarmid's work; however, *Memoriam* and *Kind of Poetry* are rather different in nature and 'Direadh 1' is distinctive in that it eschews both the freneticism and bombast sometimes apparent in its counterparts, while providing a more coherent (and palatable) explication and resolution of MacDiarmid's central concerns.

Nancy Gish sees this as a poetry in which "particularity and constant variation counterpoint within a new, leisurely movement" (*Hugh MacDiarmid: The Man and his Work* p202). In terms of the poem's structure this is accurate enough, but there is much more here; this is a poetry "With no room now save for fundamental authenticity" ('Direadh 1', CP 1173). Using familiar techniques, incorporated here with balanced vigour and concision, MacDiarmid achieves this authenticity, producing a coherent and harmonious "difficult" poetry rare even in his best work.

MacDiarmid's idiosyncratic use of language is certainly the most immediately striking feature of 'Direadh 1'. In *God and the Poets*, David Daiches notes that MacDiarmid's poetry changes "in its basic approach to experience" (p189), the quasi-mysticism, the yearning to reach *beyond* the five senses is superseded in the later poetry by an insistence "on the importance of perceiving with clarity and relish the different shapes and colours of the natural world." Daiches is here referring to *Memoriam,* but the observation is even more pertinent to 'Direadh 1'.

"Insistence" and "relish" are manifest in the opening sequence of the poem. Following an introductory quotation from Mistral, the "Provençal" poet, in defence of the use of dialect, MacDiarmid assails us with a linguistic (and lexicographical) barrage comprising Gaelic vocabulary interspersed with parenthetic translations, or cross-references to footnotes, producing a complex topographical scenario:

> Cut, cleft, sheer edge, precipice,
> *Bearradh* (from *bearr,* clip or shear)
> With here a *beithe* (a birch wood)
> And there a *bad* (a clump of trees)
> *Basdalach* (cheery) with birds
> (The point is 'not one bird, but a lot of birds,'
> As the violinist said of Francesco da Milano's
> 'La Canzone De Li Ucelli')
> Each giving their *aideachadh*
> (Act of confession, declaring aloud,
> Clear utterance) – their *ard-ghaoir*
> (A clear, thrilling sound),
>
> ('Direadh 1', CP 1163-4)

As the poem develops, MacDiarmid incorporates more of Mistral's Provençal French, short passages in German as well as occasional fragments of Scots vernacular interspersed with a wildly disrupted English, all interwoven with the complex linguistic and thematic web of oblique correlations and counterpoints.

The immediate effect is disturbingly fragmentary, but with repeated readings one begins to perceive the potential of what MacDiarmid is doing here. In *A ZBC of Ezra Pound*, Christine Brook-Rose observes:

> The ideogrammic method consists of presenting one facet and then another until at some point one gets off the dead and desensitised surface of the reader's mind onto a part that will register.
>
> (*A ZBC of Ezra Pound*, p5-6)

In 'Direadh 1', MacDiarmid is making sure we are paying attention. If we are to read this poetry at all, we must make the effort to reach beyond the superficial veneer of unfamiliarity. In this respect Brook-Rose goes on to quote Pound from Canto 105:

> I shall have to learn a little Greek to keep up with this
> But so will you, DRRATT you. (*ibid.* p29)

and, with equal pertinence, (from *How to Read*):

> Another point miscomprehended by people who are clumsy at language is that one does not need to learn a whole language in order to understand some one or some dozen poems. It is enough to understand thoroughly the poem, and every one of the few dozen or few hundred words that compose it. (*ibid.* p27)

Pound, like MacDiarmid, demands a bit of effort: if you can't be bothered using your eyes (and mind), you may as well buy a blindfold, earplugs and wheelchair. The reluctance to go beyond the superficial, or to exert sufficient concentration to derive cohesion (unity in diversity/ diversity in unity) is in itself a central theme in 'Direadh 1'.

So, what *does* lie beyond the veneer, "eagle's-eye views of the whole of Scotland"? The quotation of Mistral at the outset clearly states the centrality of language in 'Direadh 1', beyond this MacDiarmid draws us in. There is a lot happening here.

In MacDiarmid's "multi-linguistic diction" lies embodied a key to the essential components of Scotland as a land, as a nation, as a culture, as a people; simultaneously offering an inroad to the psychological intricacies caught up in the complex linguistic miasma which corresponds to the Scot as an individual. MacDiarmid incorporates English (only lightly infiltrated by Scots vernacular elements); there is Gaelic, within which lies the "hidden vibrancy" (Gish, 206) of Gaelic/ Scots culture and character; in Mistral's Provençal French we have at once echoes of the auld alliance and the gathering in of a kindred spirit in the concern for language and world-vision. Mistral who sings "… not of particular deeds and persons,/ But of a whole land and a whole people,/ And beginning with his native region/ Ended by embracing all nations/ In one amphictyoneia – a vision in parvo/ Of the labours of all mankind." ('Direadh 1', CP 1169). Finally, even the "Schleswig ancestry whose lips/ Meet like the two halves of a muffin." ('Direadh 1', CP 1165), are given voice in the appropriately sparse inclusions in German.

Such eclectic linguistic elements echo and supplement the opening landscaping of Scotland:

> And *storach, tomanach, cuireideach, tromdhaite*
> (Rugged, bushy-haired, intricate, vividly-coloured),
>
> ('Direadh 1', CP 1164)

In laying bare the rugged, uncompromised Scottish landscape, MacDiarmid is also laying bare the Scottish psyche. This is implicit in his reading of G Gregory Smith's concept of the "Caledonian Antisyzigy", in a footnote to 'Direadh 1'. For instance, we find:

> The outline of the country is irregular to a degree; plains are almost unknown; and the symmetry of the landscape is reflected in the arts and affairs of the people. (CP 1168)

As MacDiarmid passes from an evocation of the landscape to a more overt discourse on the latent qualities of the Scot, his insistence on internalising, of correlating the subjective and objective – and vice-versa – is driven home:

(Rich in shielings, rich in boats, rich in curlews, rich in conversation),
No *fuar-ghreann* in it from top to bottom, ('Direadh 1', CP 1165)

Similarly, MacDiarmid reflecting on what he *saw* as the failings of his fellow Scots envisages this as:

> So out of keeping with the Scottish mountains
> Far more of them surely should have resembled,
> Each with a world in himself,
> Each full of darkness like a mountain,
> Each deep in his humbleness,
> Without fear of abasing himself ('Direadh 1', CP 1170)

Lastly (and the following remarks are revealing in broader terms here) MacDiarmid, discussing landscape/geography in *Lucky Poet* states:

> "I share the Chinese belief in the essential function of geography as a training of the mind in visualisation, in the making of mental pictures of forms and forces – land-forms and climatic forces – that are beyond the horizon ... Chinese painting developed as an art based on visualisation and not on vision, on a mental picture and not on a Nature study, even when the subject was a landscape." (*Lucky Poet*, p310)

A central concern here then is MacDiarmid's own make-up and his aesthetic technique, another level paralleling both the nature of Scotland and the nature of the Scot, (beyond that, of Reality and of Man), for deep in the weave, the poet announces *his* centrality:

> ...Remember, I speak
> Never of the representative individual man as man,
> But always of the artist as the great exception
> To the whole human order of things)
>   ('Direadh 1', CP 1172)

'Direadh 1' is in its way a "potrait of the artist", an analysis of the poet whose vision is from the summit, at *Air A'Mhullach*, where the microcosm and macrocosm are shorn of their confusions and the poet is "...freed of mortality's *dallbhrat*" ('Direadh 1', CP 1164).

In his essay 'Hugh MacDiarmid and Gaelic Literature', Douglas Sealy notes: "The aim is to shed all irrelevance, all merely decorative detail." (*A Critical Survey*, p170). I am far from sure that 'Direadh 1' constitutes the uses of Gaelic Sealy had in mind, but it is worth noting that no component of 'Direadh 1' is superfluous. Even the lexicographical disjunction created by the abundant footnotes is an adjunct to the unfamiliarity of the vocabulary itself, splitting both text and attention. Our reading is initially forced to mimic the poem's apparently fragmented, eclectic subject matter. MacDiarmid obliges us to participate in our own enactment of "the act of surmounting", an attempt to assimilate a "complete vision" of our own and so to ratify his "claim". So, what *is* happening here? MacDiarmid writes (and note the *past* tense):

> Was it only yesterday I was struggling still
> With frames of reference, patterns of culture, cyclical phases of causation,
> And crying 'the unpredictable or fortuitous elements
> Are so much vaster still (than the irrational elements
> Even the best historians insensibly import)

That no conceivable formulae can ever deal
With the past or present in any spirit of certainty'?
– I have fully explored all the 'habitual assumptions' now
(An enquiring sceptic tirelessly applying
The Socratic elenchus to my own assumptions
And never proclaiming myself the possessor
Of the 'higher ideal,' of absolute certainty)
And in the twinkling of an eye arrived
At knowledge of the whole and absolute truth,

('Direadh 1', CP 1171-2)

That "knowledge of the whole" is the *raison d'etre* in 'Direadh 1' and, strangely, it *does* come, at last, "in the twinkling of an eye". In re-reading the poem, we can gradually assimilate the vocabulary and its implications; the footnotes become redundant. The central nervous system of extended analogy, thematic tapestry, the sense of 'plurality' of language, culture, landscape, psychology and perspective finally gel – and, in a way, this happens without your realising it at the time. So too, MacDiarmid realises, with Scotland, with Reality. The coherence is there, but you have to work to get to it, (DRRATT you). Of MacDiarmid's critics, Philip Pacey probably comes the closest to formulating this process, in his *Celtic Wonder-Voyagers*, he states:

> MacDiarmid distinguishes between "unity given" – those general impressions which fall on our senses – and "unity understood", which we are able to reconstruct for ourselves only after analysing and, as it were, dismantling the world of the merely visible. (*Celtic Wonder-Voyagers*, p8)

Similarly, and this ties in convincingly with MacDiarmid's ideas on Chinese painting:

> Only in the visible can we see the invisible, only in the tangible make contact with the intangible. (*ibid,* p5)

This is only one aspect of 'Direadh 1', but possibly the most important. Some of the conclusions drawn here may seem tenuous; I wonder though. Even the instance of a functional lexicographical disjunction through the use of footnotes, which can clearly be incidental, is open to debate. Some industrious soul may some day care to calculate what percentage of *Lucky Poet* is made up of footnotes. Could MacDiarmid have gone through all of that *without* noting the potential? I see no fundamental objections to locating significances in a poet's work of which the poet may have been unaware, and, as MacDiarmid was fond of saying, one cannot be "too literary". Donald Davie in 'Poet as Sculptor' noted, "the achieved building is the only crystallisation possible" (*New Approaches to Ezra Pound* p209), and it is that "crystallisation" we have to deal with. (As MacDiarmid was aware, cornerstones can be most elusive.) However, Donald Davie's remark is also pertinent to other aspects of 'Direadh 1'.

What kind of building is this, what manner of crystallisation? *In Memoriam* and *Kind of Poetry* are different in their essential nature. They can be MacDiarmid streaming, overflowing, in full flood, a running from silence to beat down the language. And much more, it is a poetry with its own merits – 'Direadh 1' has its own parameters and goes to different places from its peers.

One of the bonding forces in 'Direadh 1' is the extended analogy between flight, human aspiration and 'complete vision'. Nancy Gish noted this succinctly. She states:

> The poem is about breaking into a new plane of experience, soaring, attaining new vision and looking back to survey all life from that new perspective.   (*Hugh MacDiarmid: The Man and his Work* p205)

The "looking back" is an imperative in reading MacDiarmid's work. Just as he observes that a consideration of *all* available data is essential to a comprehension of *being*, so often we find that deep in a poem factors may emerge which necessitate a recontextualisation of all that has preceded it. MacDiarmid in *The Islands of Scotland* (1939) provides a more precise example of this fundamental perspective:

> It is only now, with the use of the aeroplane, that the Scottish islands ... can be seen effectively, at one and the same time in their individual completeness and in all their connections with each other and with the mainland.   (*The Thistle Rises*, p181)

Or, as cited at the outset:

> (The point is 'not one bird, but a lot of birds,'
> As the violinist said of Francesco da Milano's
> 'La Canzone De Li Ucelli')
>   ('Direadh 1', CP 1163)

The invocation of a musical analogy here has its own significance, the movements of flight and in music are themselves, in part, analogous in 'Direadh 1' and music itself is an important thematic touchstone in the weave of the poem:

> With the *móramh* (the longest note in music)
> Behind us, and before us
> The *brasphort* (swift-going tune)
> Of every river in Scotland;
>   ('Direadh 1', CP 1164)

> While through the *biothfhuaim* (unceasing sound),
> A *brothluinn* with no *buige* in it
> (A boiling with no flatness-of music-in it),
> *Stagh dìonach dualach*
> (A stay-rope firm and plaited),
> *Pìob as dìonach nuall* (a music without breaks,
> Continuous, fluent) I distinguish still
> The friends *briosg-ghlòireach* I love best,
>   ('Direadh 1', CP 1165)

Music was a constant source of aesthetic inspiration for MacDiarmid, whether the 'polytonality' or 'panatonics' of Schoenberg's musics, the cornet work of Bix Beiderbecke or the movements and intricacies of the *Ceol Mor*; MacDiarmid could pick up on their essentially (tight) improvisational structures and correlate them to his own endeavours. In this respect, I incline to Tom Scott's stated view in his piece 'Lament for the Great Music' (on the poem of the same name), in which he suggests that, for MacDiarmid, music, and particularly the *Ceol Mor*, could lay bare "the deepest historic roots of his own psyche" (*A Critical Survey* p185).

Once more down to the inevitable, "It's soon' no' sense, that faddoms the herts o' men" (CP 74). In 'Direadh 1', the Gaelic component functions in a similar way to the Scots in 'Gairmscoile' or the geological density of *On a Raised Beach* (which has much in common with 'Direadh 1'), while simultaneously suggesting more complex implications structurally, both by allusion to the *Ceol Mor* and to "MacCruitin, O'Heffernan, O'Hosey and other Gaelic bards," ('Direadh 1', CP 1167), exponents of Gaeldom's "classical verse". With regard to *Raised Beach*, G S Fraser suggests that "The words as much as the stones are for MacDiarmid poetic objects..." ('Hugh MacDiarmid: The Later Poetry' in *A Critical Survey*, p216).

If we join this idea, with regard to the Gaelic vocabulary – vocabulary considered in terms of sound units or notes – to the idea of Direadh 1's thematic improvisational qualities corresponding to the 'intricacy and complexity' of the *Ceol Mor*; its multiple perspectives and tonal variations to Schoenberg's intense tonality; we can see 'Direadh 1' as a poetry of tactile modulations reaching areas of perception and response beyond the range of the semantic. "Only in the visible can we see the invisible" (Pacy p5). As MacDiarmid himself put it, "Nothing that can be foreseen and guided is worth a curse," (*Selected Essays*, p73).

'Direadh 1' is in many senses a much bigger poem than *In Memoriam*. The integration of various themes of transcendance with MacDiarmid's political, aesthetic, cultural and linguistic concerns – as well as the more overtly subjective elements of the poem – is accomplished with considerable control and balance. No one element is allowed to dwarf another. The poem is complete, alive and convincingly cyclic – Mistral to Mistral – the very tone evokes a feeling of control as opposed to the paranoid edge of bitterness and frustration which laces much of MacDiarmid's work. This completeness and harmony in form complements the poem's fundamental subject matter when MacDiarmid states:

> I achieve the ideal of so many poets,
> The union of poetry and science,
> My theme being nature *in solido*,
> That mysterious presence of surrounding things
> Which imposes itself on any separate element
> That we set up as an individual for its own sake.
> All the destinies of my land are set before me
> – All the elements of its complex history –
> Like the lines on the palm of my hand;
> All the conflicting elements reconciled,
> Each seen as contributory to the whole,

('Direadh 1' CP 1167)

We *believe* (and to a lesser degree, share) in that sense of completion.

In the process of unravelling the thematic patterning, the rhythmic/ alliterative cataloguings of Scottish place-names, in the multi-lingual texturing and our own sense of superseding the poem's difficulties, MacDiarmid effectively conveys a perception of the continuities of existences. The poem itself becomes for us a complex organism, with tendrils reaching out into every aspect of our Being, "...one *amphictyoneia* – a vision *in parvo*" ('Direadh 1', CP 1169).

Nancy Gish has noted of 'Direadh 1':

> ...an intense serenity pervades the poem, not the peace of detachment or the inhuman coldness sometimes attributed to him but the fullness of completion. (*Hugh MacDiarmid: The Man and his Work*, p204)

Certainly Whitman's ghost seems to linger around that "intense serenity"; yet this is an accurate assessment of the poem's overall feel. There is a pervasive sense of reconciliation (not compromise) with both the world and the self – a recognition of finding Self is in fact unobtrusively inserted in the verse:

> And my own nature that for a while gave way
> Before a complete historical summary,
> Immersed in the countless difficulties of my task,
> … Returns and crowns the whole,
>
> ('Direadh 1', CP 1167)

Characteristically MacDiarmid fragmented even this with ten lines in parenthesis defining the 'difficulties' of his 'task'. It is such obtuseness which lends the intensity to the serenity – the poem is at once tightly compressed and langorously expansive; this is the poem's core:

> I am the primitive man, Antaeus-like,
> Deriving my strength from the warm, brown, kindly earth,
>
> ('Direadh 1', CP 1167)

'Direadh 1' is about keeping your feet on the ground and simultaneously soaring. As with the *Ceol Mor* which could lift your soul or lead into war: the antisyzigy (naturally) reaches beyond Caledonia. Philip Pacey codifies this duality:

> It may be that there is imagination and imagination: one wild and uncontrolled leading away from fact into fancy and sentiment; the other working alongside rational thought instead of taking its place, leading it, and us, into and through the reality of mere facts. (Pacey, p7)

So the finest musics function; so 'Direadh 1' functions: here MacDiarmid gets past the trees to the forest, surmounts the dangers of "turning single-mindedness into obsession" ('Direadh 1', CP 1168). He can say "...we scale the summit and leap into the abyss,/ And lo! we have wings." (CP 1174), yet still know (feet on the ground):

> Life is life in all its forms and the only absolute
> In relation to it is that it has to be lived'?
>
> ('Direadh 1', CP 1171)

Thom Nairn

Parvis Componere Magna

Carl MacDougall

Let us now praise that egalitarian masterpiece of precision engineering, the bunnet. For bunnet knows neither class nor boundary, is at home on the grouse-moor or the shipyards, is a badge of authority and a symbol of the communard. A bunnet is a joyous thing; it absorbs rain yet does not increase its weight, is an instrument of war, a sun visor, insulation, a rainproof and a beggar's cup. No matter the changes, bunnet never changes and is always recognisable as itself.

Bunnet is zen. It permits no decoration, neither fishing fly nor toorie, is the world's premier sweatband, can carry a newspaper, a fish supper, stones or fruit, presents or commerce, is also a purse and has been an item of ladies' fashion. The bunnet is portable and, folded, can be carried in secret, though bunnet is also a signal.

In spite of many designs and changes, bunnet never changes, is named and recorded here as bunnet. Bunnet was in the beginning, is now and ever more shall be so; named bunnet shall survive; bunnet is eternal. Headwear of the gods and emperors, bunnet is young and old, male and female, an enigma. A bunnet by any other name is still a bunnet.

Bunnet was worn in the Garden of Eden. It has been written, what shall profit a man who hath no bunnet, for man shall be drawn up to Heaven by his bunnet and St Peter's Gates are opened to those whose bunnets are well worn and the end of the world is nigh when women take to wearing bunnets. Firstly the flood, then the bunnet and lastly fire, though bunnet shall signal fire; for as we speak Gabriel is trying on his bunnet to look the part when God shall signal, by the waving of His bunnet, that time has come for the horn to be blown.

Lo, a man had no bunnet. Upon dying he reachest the Gates of St Peter's charge; and Peter saw him a long way off, saying, Hast thou a bunnet? And verily the man spake unto Peter saying, Never didst I have a bunnet, for my mother sayeth it makest me look like unto my father and my wife sayeth it makest me look like unto her father. And Peter knew him not. Later that day a second man reachest the Gates of St Peter's charge; and Peter saw him a long way off, saying, Hast thou a bunnet? And verily the man spake unto Peter, saying, I have a bunnet and have worn the bunnet all the days of my life but the bunnet is not with me, having been lost on the journey from where I was to where I am now. And Peter knew him not. Towards the end of day, a man with a bunnet reachest the Gates of St Peter's charge; and Peter saw him a long way off, running from his charge to meet him, saying, Enter thou to joy with me for thy bunnet hast saved thee. Blessed is he who wears the bunnet and whose bunnet has been worn. Whilst wearing the bunnet thou wast despised and reviled amongst men. This day thou shalt wear thy bunnet with me in paradise.

Darling, I ask you; bury me in my bunnet, so they'll know me.

Sheena Blackhall

I opened my volume of MacDiarmid's poems at random, and decided I'd write on whichever title I saw first – it fell open at

Au Clair de la Lune

The halflin meen's a unicorn
Wha's creamy-flankit an strang
An aa the starnies ben the mucht's
The seed frae oot his whang!

The Lion Rampant

Oh the lion is aff the flag again
*An reengin the countryside...**
Bit fin he wun ower the Muckle Mounth
He didna sikk lang tae bide!

Fur aabody furth o the Doric North
Wis a bitticky antiqueerian
Wi a Ph.D. in a Lallans key
As modern as Shakespearean.

Hid he bin a literary breet
He'd bin shipped tae cauld Siberia
Gin he'd roared oot 'fa' insteid o 'wha'
The purists wad hae hysteria
Oh the academe, wi its bee-bunnet theme
(Weel awa frae the buts an bens)
Howk wards lang deid, tae stap in a screed
Nae ane in a thoosan kens.

"Ochone", cries the lion, "Fit a mineer
Ye've nane o ye cheenged a bit
Wi yer wee cliques there, an yer wee cliques here
Yer aa sae thrawn, an yer aa sae sweir
That nane o ye see fur aa yer steer
Scots is a spikk, nae Haly Writ."

"The Bible's read on the Sabbath day
(Or a twa, three times a year)
Maist ay bi a priest or a dominie
Fa's steepit his harns in lear
Fin I wis young, man, the guid Scots tongue
Roon Buchan, an Mar an Mearns

---

*'The Lion Rampant', Hugh MacDiarmid

Wis alive in the mou (Nae a screive fur a few
A museum piece fur bairns)
Ye'll nae unite, gin ye fleer an flyte
Ower the verra banes o the spikk
Faith, ilkie clan hid its ain tartan
An focht fur its ain peat rikk!
Like Chairman Mao, maun we AA kow-tow
In yer cultural reevolution?
Maun we aa sup brose in the same size dose
An takk lessons in elocution?
Maun we aa weir broon, an a Lallans goun
Maun we aa learn Scots frae a buikie?
If yon's the plan, fur the new Scotsman
He can steek it up his bihoochie!
Maun aa Scots boo tae the Embro ploo?
Can a spurgie cheep like a teuchit?
It's the same auld meen, tho ye spell it müne
Ye're a wee thing weet… We're drookit.
Gin ye canna agree tae differ", (quo he)
"It's back tae ma flag I'm gaun."
An he lowpit awa, mane, virr, an claw
Wi a guid corn-kister sang!

Lydia Robb

A Race Apairt

A pouderin o snaw – the laund ligs lythe
alow the mune. Yer jewel bricht sari leuks
at odds. A dwynin rainbow i the mirk,

ye jouk the shaidaes, turn yer ither chowk.
Pent clarts yon stane-faced biggins. B.N.P.,
a neo-Nazi emblem, Pakis, blecks

gyne hame. Ye mind whit sticks an stanes can dae.
Yer fremmit fuit-prents, broukit i the snaw,
a movin pictur, bleck on white. Ye turn

tae a weill-kent soun. The licht's alowe, the glisk
o reid an gowd, the crack o brackin gless.
Yer mither's tuith chaws words she disnae ken.

Ye pick the bitties up an stert again.
The nicht's a sair affront. Ye byde inby,
syne snib the yett agin the wun o chynge.

• Winner of the first prize and the MacDiarmid Tassie in the Scots Language
Society's annual competition 1992.

THE CEILIDH HOUSE

The High Street wis yince a hub o music, poetry an' talk.
The Ceilidh House pits back that tradeetioun.
Folk nichts – poetry nichts – an aye-bidan come-aa-ye

Cleik yer pals in fur a pint or a dram. Ye'll hae a waarm walcome.

Eldritch neuks and crannies fur smaa foregaitherings
Cellar haa fur middlin-scale occasiouns

The Ceilidh House, 9 Hunter Square, Edinburgh EH1 1QW
Heid Wanger: Cy Laurie
Tel 031-220 1550

Eddie Candlish: The Great Wheel of Whiteinch

Stewart Morrison

1992 Marks the centenary of one of MacDiarmid's lesser-known contemporaries, the poet Eddie Candlish. Rarely referred to and absent from most anthologies, Candlish was a mysterious figure hovering on the outer edge of the Scottish Literary Renaissance of the '20s and '30s. He led a one-man crusade against everything and everyone, particularly MacDiarmid whom he disliked immensely. Candlish despised everything MacDiarmid ever wrote and often took the time to write and tell him so. As far as I can ascertain, MacDiarmid wrote back only the once, in 1935, asking Eddie "Who are you?". In a reply published in the *Glasgow Herald* the following year Candlish retorted "He may not know who I am, but at least I've been to Germany".

It is generally accepted that this hostility was really the result of envy at Grieve's skill as a poet. Candlish countered the "synthetic Scots" of his rival with his own "synoptic Scots". Exactly what he meant by this is still a matter of conjecture, but appears to involve slightly altering words in order to make a line scan or create a rhyme (Candlish felt rhyming was essential in a "real poem" and often went to extraordinary lengths: he rhymes "MacDiarmid" with "fishing permit" in *Ardrossan Exiles*, Stoabie & Blackhead, 1931).

Candlish's poetry cannot be fully appreciated without looking at his background. He was born in Partick, earning a living as a rivetter in the Clyde shipyards; and died, penniless and forgotten, in a sheltered housing complex in nearby Whiteinch. Candlish's early work was markedly political (see *Sonnets on Historical Determinism*, Stoabie & Blackhead, 1923), however he quickly mellowed into the impenetrable Scots lyrics for which he is marginally better known, such as his tour de force, *A Rent Man Looks at Possil* (Stoabie & Blackhead, 1926). Initially the disagreements with his contemporaries, especially MacDiarmid, contributed to Candlish's early notoriety, but they led ultimately to his fleeting fame and a dubious reputation with the critics which quickly petered out altogether. Candlish blamed MacDiarmid personally for his own lack of success, feeling some of his fire had been stolen by "thone postie's boy frae Gallowee".

Eddie Candlish died in 1982 at the age of 90. He published little in his last forty years, bar *My Poetic Life – an Autobiography*, and *Yggdrassil No More*, a verse play concerning Forestry Commission policy in the mid-1950s. During the period 1925-35 we see the elusive genius at the full height of his creative powers, whilst in pitched battle with the literary circles which excluded him. Much of his poetry from this time stems from his struggle for recognition, emerging in themes of isolation, rejection and humiliation (this has also been attributed to his Presbyterian upbringing in Partick). The anger and alienation Candlish laboured under manifests itself most coherently in works like the introspective collection *Clyde Dredger* (Stoabie & Blackhead, 1925) from which the following poem is taken:

A Weary Fankle

A clanjamfrie o' jinglies, yairdwards shiftin'
Through the laichest quither o' sunlicht liftin'.
Hell's empty infants, withooten mither,
Like thochts unbriggit, brocht thegither.

Nae New Age dawn'll ever reach us,
Whit use yer Dantes and yer Nietzches?
The neep-rummle's ower (for whit'wis worth)
Tam's wastelands ploughed for winter birth...

Ahm richt foonert wi' a'thing these days,
Blintert wae ma thocht's roukish haze,
An' camsteerie notions in fits an' starts,
Condemned forever by twa tartan farts.

Aye, noo thone postie's boy frae Gallowee,
A man gei spurious he seems tae me,
Spreid ower thin oan tae much breid,
Like the glabber oan this piece ma Bella's made.

Glossary of Scots words and phrases:

Verse One:			Verse Three:	
clanjamfrie	*noisy gathering*		richt	*right*
jinglies	*small children*		foonert	*in despair, pissed off*
yairdwards	*towards the yard*		wi'a'thing	*with everything*
laichest	*least*		blintert	*blinded, dazzled*
quither	*cold gleam*		roukish	*foggy*
sunlicht	*sunlight*		camsteerie	*unusual, perverse*
withooten	*without a*		Verse Four:	
thochts	*thoughts*		thone	*that*
unbriggit	*incomplete*		frae	*from*
brocht	*brought*		Gallowee	*Galloway*
thegither	*together*		gei	*rather*
Verse Two:			spreid	*spread*
neep-rummle	*turnip harvest*		breid	*bread*
whit'wis	*what it was*		glabber	*sloppy food*
			piece	*sandwich*

Those readers who have not come across Candlish's work before may find some of the references rather obscure or unfamiliar. The following annotation may help in making this difficult poem slightly more accessible.

Line 1, Jinglies: These were children employed in shipyards to retrieve nuts, bolts and tools which had accidentally dropped into inaccessible places, such as a ship's inner hull.

Line 3, Hell: Candlish never really managed to escape his strict Presbyterian upbringing despite becoming an atheist at the age of 18. When he was 62 he wrote "Hell still scares the shite out of me". See, *My Poetic Life*, Candlish Publications, 1955

Line 3, Mither: The poet felt rejected by his mother Agnes, and her stern character haunts his work. She makes a symbolic appearance as Rothesay in *Ardrossan Exiles* (1931). Kenneth Buckley's ground-breaking exploration of Candlish's relationship with his mother, *Oedipus Spurned*, was published by the Scottish Academic Press in 1985.

Line 5, New Age: Eddie Candlish was strongly influenced by Yeats' *A Vision* (London, 1925) and quickly became involved in the New Age movement. Disillusioned, he left in 1928, following a row over his refusal to pay the membership fee.

Line 6, Dante: Candlish greatly admired Dante's *Divine Comedy*, and often recited it at great length whilst at work in the shipyard. It came in for some harsh criticism from a pair of rivetters on the poet's shift, causing him, in a letter to Pittendrigh Macgillivray, to describe the work as "Too long and the use of the rhyming couplet excessive".

Line 6, Neitzche: Candlish began writing to Neitzche in the mid-1920s and kept up the difficult and one-sided correspondence for nearly 60 years. See *The Neitzche Letters vols I-IV*, Scottish Academic Press, 1985.

Line 7, Neep-rummle: Traditionally the wet fortnight following the October turnip harvest. Charitable farmers often permitted the poor and needy to gorge themselves on the damaged turnips left in the fields. See "With a hey and a ho for the bonnie lass o' the neep-rummle" in Ferguson's *Folk Songs of East Dumbartonshire*, Blackie, 1935.

Line 8, Tam: A close friend of Candlish's, Tam Docherty, who worked a farm off Crow Road at Anniesland Cross. Docherty was also an influential critic and minor poet, mostly remembered for his seminal essay, 'Dante, Vico…Candlish, the Great Wheel', which influenced a generation of scholars.

Line 8, Wasteland: See T S Eliot, *The Waste Land*. Candlish recognised the importance of this work in the early 1960s, declaring it to be "a work of great length" (unpublished letter to the *Glasgow Herald*, March 1963).

Line 8, Birth: Rebirth. In September 1939 Candlish wrote to the *Glasgow Herald*, outlining his plan for a Scottish literary renaissance. It failed to materialise due to a lack of interest and Hitler, whom Candlish never forgave.

Line 9, Richt foonert... See "...my weariness with all existence...", F Neitzche, *Thus Spake Zarathustra*, Vol III, 13.

Line 10, Blintered: Probably a reference to Homer.

Line 11, fits and starts: Fitz Bernhamm and Startz Grossman formed a transvestite double act popular in Glasgow working mens' clubs in the 1920s. Candlish contributed to their two-day *gesamkunstwerk* in Berlin, with his only Dadaist piece, 'Yoker Memory Seven'. The event is quite clearly described in Isherwood's *Up for the Weekend*, Jonathan Cape, 1934.

Line 12, Twa tartan farts: Wullie Stoabie and Archie Blackhead, Candlish's publishers throughout the '20s and '30s. They were originally a music hall duo whose act consisted of dressing in loud check suits and was extremely popular for nearly 30 years.

Line 13, Postie's boy: Hugh MacDiarmid's father was a postman, and Candlish resented this as well as MacDiarmid's success as a poet. The lifelong rivalry between the two poets is evident throughout much of Candlish's work where there are many thinly veiled references to MacDiarmid, such as the image of the Renfrew Ferry in the self-searching 'Clyde Dredger'.

Line 14, A man gei ... tae me: See Dryden, 'Abselon and Achitophel', V1, l 3-4:

> A man so various that he seemed to be,
> Not one, but all Mankind's epitome.

Line 16, glabber: A sandwich filling popular with working men in the early part of the century. Consisting of a blend of porridge and dripping, it was applied to the bread whilst still hot, where it set firmly as it cooled, binding both slices of bread together. It was almost entirely tasteless.

Line 16, Bella: Bella McNinch, Candlish's first wife, whose frugality became obsessive. She drowned collecting driftwood near Yoker in 1931.

Stewart Morrison is soon to publish *Hull Scrapes and Refits*, a study of the effects of merchant ship maintenance on the poetry of Eddie Candlish between 1928 and 1931.

A Contemporary Review of
In Memoriam James Joyce

J F Hendry

The professed aim of this work is a vision of world language. It is a deliberate attempt at a unification of knowledge, at the kind of unification of human experience which seemed possible in the days when H G Wells was struggling for a World Encyclopaedia.

The argument is about language as a way of thought; as, in fact, the basis of existence, no less. As Joyce saved us from the spurious in speech, MacDiarmid would save us from the spurious in thought. It is, then, he says, a vision of understanding, not of creation. As Mallarmé said, "to evoke in a deliberate shadow the unmentioned object by allusive words, never direct words, which may be reduced to an equal silence, that means an attempt very near creation". Elsewhere he states that the European mind seizes on one idea at a time, but the Eastern can encompass several at once, here again is the idea that the author is understanding – in a time-sequence – not creating anything – not "cheating" but getting at the real nature of things. As with Fr. Rolfe's fanatical determination in his *Desire and Pursuit of the Whole* there is the same virtuosity of language, the same intense interest in *what is being said*. To be sure, one does read MacDiarmid for what he says, not always how he says it: an exciting thing at a time when mere 'technique' or 'technics', as he points out, is swallowing man. Now and then, nevertheless, we come on passages of the greatest beauty and felicity: orchestrated, as no one now writing could orchestrate them, *in a major key*:

> I think of you Joyce, and of Yeats, and of others who are dead,
> As I walk this autumn and observe
> The birch tremulously pensive in jewels of cairngorm
> The sauch the osier and the crack willow
> Of the beaten gold of Australia
> The sycamore in rich straw gold
> The elm bowered in saffron
> The oaks in flecks of salmon gold
> The beeches huge torches of living orange…

or:

> The gold edging of a bough at sunset, its pantile way
> Forming a double curve, tegula and imbrex in one
> Seems at times a movement on which I might be borne
> happily to infinity…

The accent here is unmistakeably that of the great *Duino Elegies* of Rilke, and as with Rilke too, one admires the sheer virtuosity of the poet.

There are of course other qualities, outstanding among everything the sheer reading involved. Here and there I have checked it personally, where I could: for instance the Chinese moon-symbol, pronounced *Yueh* in Peiping, which as MacDiarmid says is Mandarin; pronounced *Ut* in Canton; *Saran* in Mongolian, in Japanese *Getsu* (not 'Gestu', obviously a misprint in the book). The point here is that the one symbol or ideograph is read in all these countries, though the spoken language is different, a fascinating thought. But then Julian Huxley has told us that all languages have a common ancestral alphabet: if so, it is likely to have been pictorial in nature. And though MacDiarmid does not mention it, the Egyptians had the same symbol for water as the Chinese.

All right, some may say, but why bother as this author does with Athabascan and other out of the way tongues? Well, it has been said that a study of Eskimo, Cherokee and Chinese will tell us more about the origin of man than any amount of anthropological research will reveal. For the poet, the incarnate word, all languages are significant and irreplaceable treasures. For this poet, in a mechanical age, language – fighting a rearguard action against all that is tyrannous and dead – has become a battlefield.

We are, in his words, at the 'marriage of the incompatible into a polycladous tradition, at a summoning of pith and purpose and precision, which is a continuation of MacDiarmid's own work in *Stony Limits* (1934). His concern with language is now deeper: "Language is the instrument for the progressive articulation of the world in spatial and temporal terms".

Words, however, also betray. When they do, liberty is lost.

> das Wort enschlief
> als jene Welt erwachte,

says Karl Kraus of the rise of Hitler; and to MacDiarmid too the race is between the material and its realisation. This is pure Rilke, to whom the world wanted to become invisible. To MacDiarmid indeed sometimes, the material is actually the infernal spiritualisation of the real. But where does it all get us?

> Beyond all that is heteroepic, holophrastic,
> Macaronic, philomathic, psychopetal,
> Jerquing every idioticon,
> Comes this supreme paraleipsis
> Full of potential song as a humming-bird
> Is full of potential motion
> When as we race along with kingfisher brilliance
> Seeking always for that which being known
> Everything else becomes known...
> That which we can only know
> By allowing it to know itself in us
> Since "determinatio est negatio"
> Suddenly "chaos falls silent in the dazzled abyss"
> Cio che lo mio intelletto non comprende
> "Thin thin the pleasant human noises grow
> And faint the city gleams"
> O poet hold thy peace and be content.

Not Eliot, nor Pound, rivals this for brilliance, depth, clarity, humility, poetry or wisdom. In spite of this author's intellect, there is heart. So we are led to the world of words of Part II. Through images, pronunciation to semantics, and meaning. The goal, we are told, is that of pure beauty, but how many lines of startling content are encountered:

> The astronomical universe is not all there is

or

> There lie hidden in language elements that effectively combined, can utterly change the nature of man.

As though in proof, cascades of verbal fireworks are thrown off, dealing with fishing, skiing, fencing, even archery. This spirit does not want to wind itself in its own cocoon. It seeks the "pure phenomenon abiding in the eternal radiance". It fights against all that stands in its way, especially the modern world of "mechanical authoritarianism".

The final section, 'Plaited Like the Generations of Men', with its magnificent opening,

> Come follow me into the realm of music. Here is the gate which separates the earthly from the eternal.

rounds off the whole, by revealing the goal to which we have been striving, that goal where

> ...stars and hearts are one with another

and

> there can be nowhere an end, nowhere a hindrance;

It is a cosmic universe, as personal as that of Rilke, and yet, at the last moment, the 'realist' in himself, of whom the author tells us, has doubts:

> Have I failed in my braid-binding
> At this great crisis
> When the impending task of mankind
> Is to help to bring to a *close* the 'conflict' stage
> Of the present process of the discontinuous
> And to usher in the 'harmony' stage...
> At this moment when braidbinding as never before
> The creation of the seamless garment
> Is the poet's task?

One reader at least says, No, you have not failed. Your braid-binding has been, MacDiarmid, like the gathering of sweetness of another great poet, Rilke, and at a similar point in history. As Rilke remains behind, a lonely and yet significant figure, after the desolation of the last war, when the impending doom has at last become vulgar, so you too will remain, and your braid-binding be a source of delight to generations only now in the process of getting to know one another, throughout the world, Africans and Europeans, Eurasians and Asiatics and Americans of all languages and colours.

J F Hendry, BBC Radio, 1955

"Bought and sold for English gold"

Paul H Scott

In his biography of Hugh MacDiarmid, Alan Bold says that Grieve's nationalist views were pronounced by the time he left Salonika in May 1918. "Grieve was weary of the assumption that the British troops were fighting exclusively for the honour of England. Scotland, he was sure, had a future too." In his attitude, not only to Scottish literature, but to the political status of Scotland, MacDiarmid's views were consistent throughout his life. As he said in a letter to Anthony Ross nearly 50 years later, he could not lend his name to any project which did not accept the *necessity* of Scottish independence. His opposition to the Union and to what he called 'the English ascendancy' was unrelenting.

One of the consequences of this ascendancy, as MacDiarmid said in *Lucky Poet*, was "the fog of ignorance which wraps all Scottish matters and the difficulty of getting to the essential facts behind the incessant pro-English propaganda, and the distortions that have been at work in our midst ever since the Union". One of the most striking and harmful examples of this ignorance and distortion is over the Union itself. For an event which had such drastic, long-lasting consequences, it is astonishing how much misunderstanding and sheer ignorance prevails over the events which led to the Treaty of 1707. How did a country which had defended its independence for hundreds of years with determination and endurance, suddenly surrender with barely a struggle?

Hume Brown, whose *History of Scotland* was for years the standard work, suggested that we had turned our eyes away by "unconscious instinct" from a period which reflected so badly on our national reputation. He was referring of course to the humiliation that members of the Scottish Parliament yielded to bribery and intimidation and sold the independence of their country for paltry sums of money. Much of the evidence that this is indeed what happened became available only long after the event, but the facts were well enough known at the time and they lived in oral tradition. Robert Burns understood. As he wrote:

"We're bought and sold for English gold,
    Such a parcel of rogues in a nation."

So did Sir Walter Scott. In his *Tales of a Grandfather* he expresses his outrage at the whole sordid business in strong language over more than 30 pages: "a total surrender of their independence by false and corrupted statesmen ... despised by the English and detested by their own country".

English historians have tended to focus more on their satisfaction at the outcome than enquire too closely into the methods. Recently the English historian Christopher Hill was honest enough to admit that "Scotland was bribed and swindled into Union with England in 1707". This is true as far as it goes, but how it came about is a complex story.

The loss in 1603 of the royal court and royal patronage was a heavy blow to the prestige and prosperity of Edinburgh, but the political effects were even more serious. Scotland was still nominally independent with its own Parliament, Government and laws, but it now shared a King with England. This mattered a great deal at the time because the Monarch still exercised personally, or through his advisers, most of the executive functions of government. He made foreign policy, peace and war. He made all government appointments, including the officers of state who were the ministers of the Scottish government.

These senior officials were usually members of the Scottish nobility who formed more than a third of the one-chamber Scottish Parliament. Often they were rich in land but poor in money, and government appointments depended on their accepting instructions from London.

The foreign policy carried out in the name of the King was English policy, on which Scotland was not consulted. Very often it was contrary to Scottish interests. English wars with the Low Countries and France, for instance, destroyed traditional Scottish trade. Scotland contributed men and money to these wars, but was forgotten again in the terms of peace. Only very small forces were maintained in Scotland itself and by the end of the 17th century it was virtually without means of defence.

By means of the joint monarchy England had achieved the domination over Scotland which had been her objective since the 13th century. Without the trouble of occupying the country they could prevent its becoming either a military threat or a rival in trade.

In Scotland, however, this semi-dependence, which systematically frustrated Scotland from promoting her own interests, became increasingly intolerable. It was analysed with particular clarity by Andrew Fletcher of Saltoun, so robust a defender of the Scottish case that he has been known ever since as 'the Patriot'. In his pamphlets and speeches in Parliament he described "the miserable condition to which this nation is reduced by a dependence upon the English court" who treated it "more like a conquered province than a free independent people".

Matters came to a head over the Scottish colony at Darien. As King of Scotland, William assented to the Scottish Act which established the trading company. As King of England, he did his best to sabotage it and prevent it from raising capital in England or the Continent. In a great outburst of patriotic fervour, virtually everyone in Scotland with any savings invested them in the company. All this was lost when the colony failed disastrously, partly because the site was ill chosen and partly because of English hostility. These events coincided with a series of poor harvest in Scotland between 1695 and 1699 which led to actual famine.

It was in this unhappy situation that a new parliament was elected in Scotland in 1703, the Parliament which continued in being, meeting for a few months each summer, until it voted for its own dissolution in approving the Treaty of Union in 1707.

When this Parliament first met in May 1703 it immediately turned its attention to the most pressing problem of the time, which was the constitutional position of Scotland. Events in England had presented an opportunity of escape from subordination to the English court. When Queen Anne succeeded to the throne in 1702, all her children had died and she was unlikely to have any others. The English Parliament had solved the succession to their satisfaction by an Act which settled it on Sophia of Hanover and her issue. Not for the first or last time, they had forgotten about Scotland or taken it for granted. Scotland had not been consulted and was in no sense bound by the English Act.

The Queen's letter to the new Scottish Parliament therefore asked for acceptance of the same succession as in the English Act. Parliament did not propose to yield. Fletcher proposed that either Scotland should choose a different successor or, if the same one, then all power should be effectively transferred from the Crown to Parliament itself. The Act of Security which emerged included the substance of Fletcher's proposals. It provided that the Scottish successor to Anne was not to be the same as the English, unless conditions of government had been established which secured Scottish independence "free from English or any foreign influence". Also, men of military age were to be armed and trained.

In face of this resounding declaration of independence, the court and their chief representative in Scotland, the Duke of Queensberry, had lost control. They refused royal assent to the Act and continued their efforts to recruit more support through patronage. Seton of Pitmedden, for example, sold his services for a pension of £100 a year. The longer Parliament lasted, the more the court was able to buy votes in this way.

In the following session of 1704 the court tried again with a new Commissioner, the Marquis of Tweeddale. They failed again and Parliament passed once more the same Act of Security. This time it was given royal assent on the advice of the English treasurer, and effectively first Minister, Godolphin, probably because he was anxious that the Scottish Parliament should vote supply.

The English Parliament reacted with talk of war. There was bound to be Jacobite resistance to the Hanoverian succession and an independent Scotland in alliance with France could become a threat. Both Houses passes the Aliens Act, an ultimatum with sanctions. Unless Scotland accepted the same succession by 25 December 1705, Scots would be treated as aliens in England and made incapable of inheriting property. The import of Scottish cattle, sheep, coal and linen would be prohibited. The Act also authorised the Queen to appoint commissioners to "treat and consult" with Scotland "concerning the union of the two kingdoms".

Union had been discussed many times since 1603, usually on the personal insistence of the Monarch, without much enthusiasm from anyone else. There was no expectation in 1705 that it was any more likely to come to anything than previously. It was also a vague term, capable of many interpretations. Much confusion has been caused by the curious failure of historians to notice that the words, "union", "treaty" and "federal" (a word which the Scots were about to use) were generally used in the early 18th century in different senses from those they have since acquired. Union meant an association of any kind for any common purpose or simply the absence of discord or dissension. Treaty often meant negotiation as distinct from agreement. Federal (from the Latin, meaning treaty as we nowadays understand the word) meant only pertaining to an agreement or treaty. There was therefore not necessarily anything new or alarming about this aspect of the English Act.

In the 1705 session of the Scottish Parliament the Commissioner was the Duke of Argyll. The Queen's message again asked for the settlement of succession and supply but added a recommendation of union as a means of composing the differences between the two nations. For two months Parliament insisted on discussing other matters, including Fletcher's ideas for the limitation of royal power. In August the House was brought to discuss the English proposal for negotiations on union, providing their insulting ultimatum was withdrawn. A clause designed to safeguard independence was defeated by two votes. There was a startling turn of events on 1st September. The Duke of Hamilton, who led the opposition, had assured his followers that there would be no vote that day. After many of them had left the House, he suddenly proposed that the nomination of commissioners should be left to the Queen. The court party seized the opportunity and it was so decided.

This was not the last time that Hamilton deliberately sabotaged the efforts of his own side. Indeed Trevelyan says, not unreasonably, that he was chief instrument of the "almost miraculous" passage of the Union; but Trevelyan does not explain why he behaved with such duplicity. In fact, there is plenty of evidence that he too had been bribed and was consciously playing a double game. For example, James Johnstone, Lord Clerk Register, who was in a good position to know, wrote from London on 13 January 1705: "I have had suspicions, but now I am certain, that Duke Hamilton is tampering by means of Harley with the Lord Treasurer...He must have his debts payed."

Hamilton's action meant that there was now no possibility of genuine negotiation, since both teams would be picked by the English court. Only one man was included on the Scottish side who was not already one of their supporters: George Lockhart of Carnwath, because he was related by marriage to one of the English Whig Lords who hoped to win him over. This attempt failed but it gave Lockhart a ringside seat which he put to good use in writing his *Memoirs*, the fullest and frankest contemporary account of the events which led to the Union.

The so-called negotiations in London lasted from 16 April to 22 July 1706. At first, the Scots made a token stand in favour of a federal arrangement, by which they meant an agreement between the two kingdoms which would preserve the independence and separate Parliaments of both. The English refused to discuss anything but what was now called an "incorporating union", in which the two kingdoms would become one with a single Parliament. From the nature of the Scottish delegation it is not surprising that they capitulated at once. "You see that what we are to treat of is not in our choice", the Scottish Secretary of State, the Earl of Mar, wrote to William Carstares in Edinburgh.

The Treaty which resulted still required the approval of both Parliaments. It purported to abolish both Scotland and England and replace them with a new entity, Great Britain, with a single British Parliament. In fact, the English parliament and everything else in England was to continue undisturbed, apart from the addition of a few Scottish members. Scotland was to have 45 members in the Commons. England which then had five times the population, had 513 and Cornwall alone had 44. The Scottish Lords no longer had a place by right in Parliament, but 16 of them were to be elected to sit in the Lords.

This reduction of Scotland to political impotence was a bitter pill to swallow, sweetened by a number of measures skilfully designed to appeal to the self-interest of the classes represented in the Scottish Parliament. The Scottish legal system, the rights of the Royal Burghs and the hereditary jurisdictions of the landowners were all preserved. The Lords were given all the privileges of English Peers, except an automatic seat in the Lords, but including exemption from imprisonment for debt, which was of more practical use to many of them. Most ingenious of all was the "Equivalent", a sum of £398,085/10/– to compensate Scotland for accepting liability for a share of the English National Debt, but it also simultaneously served a number of other purposes: creative accounting of a high order. The first call on the money was to repay, with interest, the shareholders of the Darien company. Since most members of the Scottish Parliament had been impoverished by the collapse of the company, this was a strong inducement. Then the Equivalent was to be repaid from the imposition of English customs and excise duty on Scotland. As Sir Walter Scott wrote: "In fact, the Parliament of Scotland was bribed with the public money belonging to their own country. In this way, Scotland herself was made to pay the price given to her legislators for the sacrifice of her independence."

The Treaty was received in Scotland with outrage and indignation. In Parliament, with Queensberry again as Commissioner, the debate lasted from 3 October 1706 to 16 January 1707, against a background of continuous public protest. Parishes and burghs all over Scotland petitioned against the Union, as did the Convention of Royal Burghs on behalf of the trading community. Even the leaders of the court party admitted in private correspondence that the great majority of the people were utterly opposed to the Treaty.

The opposition of the Kirk was countered by the Act, considered as an integral part of the Union, which guaranteed the Church of Scotland for all time. A group of Lords who had previously supported Fletcher were won over on the understanding (subsequently ignored) that they would have charge of the distribution of the Equivalent. was London sent up a further £20,000 to buy more votes. In the end, the Treaty was approved. Fletcher is reported to have said that the country was now fit only for the slaves who had sold it.

The episode of the £20,000 was afterwards discovered by George Lockhart, a member of a British Parliamentary enquiry. It was confirmed years later when a letter from the Earls of Glasgow and Seafield came to light. They certified that they could not give details of the disbursement without bringing Parliament into discredit. They end with the request that Queensberry (who had the largest share) should burn the letter after reading it to the Lord Treasurer. Godolphin evidently insisted on keeping it as a receipt because it remained in his family papers until they were sold to the British Museum in 1892.

But the members who voted for the Treaty had another excuse, the threat of invasion. Already in July 1703 Godolphin sent a polite, but unmistakable, threat of military intervention to Seafield. He reminded him that England had greatly increased in wealth and power at a time when Scotland was impoverished and defenceless. The English Government sent troops to the border during the final debate. Years afterwards Sir John Clerk of Penicuik (who had been reluctantly recruited to the Union side by his patron, Queensberry) recorded his view that the main reason for the acceptance of the Treaty was that otherwise the country would have fallen under English domination by right of conquest.

It certainly had little to do with the trade. If anything, such considerations pulled in the opposite direction. Many of the petitions against the Union argued that it would be highly damaging to Scottish trade. They were right. It took Scotland about 40 years before she began to recover by her own exertions from the effects of the Union. The theory that Scotland had bargained away her independence for access to a wider market was invented about 1850 by Hill, Burton and Macaulay, who were trying to find a respectable explanation.

The Treaty of Union was not a bargain of any kind. It was a fake negotiation and an imposition by a strong country on a smaller neighbour when it was particularly weak and vulnerable; a ruthless, calculating application of power to secure the northern border of England and keep Scotland in subjection. It was not accepted by the Scottish people, who made their rejection of it very clear, but by an unrepresentative Parliament which was bribed and intimidated into submission.

Paul H Scott

Tom Leonard

After the nuclear obliteration of Scotland, a fragment of a long poem is found in a lead coffin

Of course as Stalin clearly demonstrated in *Marxism and Problems of Linguistics*:

> ...the significance of the so-called gesture language, in view of its extreme poverty and limitations, is negligible. Properly speaking, this is not a language, and not even a linguistic substitute that could in one way or another replace spoken language, but an auxiliary means of extremely limited possibilities to which man sometimes resorts to emphasise this or that point in his speech. Gesture language and spoken language are just as incomparable as are the primitive wooden hoe and the modern caterpillar tractor with its five-furrow plough or tractor row drill.

This in incontrovertible contradistinction to the terracing rice-pudding-brain whose idea of Scottish Literature consists of readings from Charlie Tully's *Passed to You*:

> If I had a pound for every time I've sent a corner kick swinging into the goalmouth at practice, I'd be a millionaire. When I'm at outside-left, I place the ball in the arc, take a step back and send it over with my right foot. I reverse the procedure if I'm on the right. This is the only proper way to take a flag kick – that is, if you want to put the ball into the danger zone. The ball takes a curve and swings in on goal making it awkward for a goalkeeper to cover it all the way.

(*from* "Scenes from Scottish Literary Life"
first published in *New American Writing*, 1991)

Jeremy Hughes

Anglo-Welsh Reflections at the Eisteddfod

Here Wales crowns her language.

We "Welshmen" without the voice
are pitied for sperm
that came to hew our valleys.

Our gorsedd was dark, wet,
clapping timbers an audience
that didn't let us stand. They crowned us heavily.

Today sheep graze above
blue-scarred men lost in a fall
that claimed a village.

We hadn't lungs
for Cymdeithas yr Iaith*,
nor would it have helped our lot.

Anglo-Wales Welsh forgot.

---

*the Welsh Language Society
Note: the Chair (Gorsedd) and Crown are the traditional
prizes awarded to poets at the National Eisteddfod.

Jim C Wilson

Auchindrain

In the field of the thorntrees,
near the edge of the world,
we tended the beasts
and broke the stones,
before and since the days of Christ.

Our coats were the colours
of mosses, of heathers,
all the hues of the earth.
Sicknesses and darkest storms
did not diminish or defeat us.

We shared the plough, hewn from driftwood;
our cups were made from leather;
we drank the dawn-cold water of life
and sowed the seeds of generations.
The ways of our world seemed endless.

But the cross became too much to bear.
The spirit faltered, faded, died,
and we were scattered far,
throughout the cities, across the plains.
Soon we learned to toil for others.

In the field of the thorntrees
the visitors come;
they wander through our rooms
and through our past; our lifeblood
slows, congealing in the years' slow dusk.

Ellie McDonald

Fugue

Heroes
    in hard hats
        they tyauve awa
           at the fuit o this hill toun
tae bigg a road
      that's howkit out
          o solid rock.
A lang whang
        heizin itsel like a haly curse
owre the roar
      o pneumatic drills.
Auld men
    watch
      wi an air o kennan.
It's niver
    rained
       for weeks
         but still
the waater
     liggs
      in muckle dubs
         aloe the baillie brigs.
Spier
   at the auld men
       whaur the waater's frae.
           They ken.
The workmen
    curse.
      It's no their toun.
Come lowsin time
     there's aye the Ladywell
         an pies an pints.
Sweet waater
    still aloe their feet
whaur
   the livin
     walk
      an the deid are cairriet.
I ken I ken
    there's nae wey back
       for ony o's.
Atween memory
    an daurkness
      the warld gangs heiterin on
as the scent o myrtle
   faas
     on the silence o the stanes.

170

Dear Chris Grieve

A line or twa tae let ye ken hou Scotland fares. Waur nor whan ye left it, that's for shair. 99% o the Scottish nation are fearties an farts still heizin for the murlins affen the Westminster table.

Socialism's deid.

The Arts Cooncil has yased yer book Aesthetics in Scotland for bog paper. Yer idea about "Amateurism being the curse of the Arts" an "striving after the highest possible standard" stinks o élitism. That's even mair o a swear word nou than Socialism.

There wis a hale nicht devoted tae yer birthday on the BBC (Scotland only). Aabody that wis naebody wis there. We're gaein doun intil the daurk MacDiarmid. The Emperor's new claes are aa the rage an the sang is sung bi the deif.

Ellie McDonald

Shugspeer

Jim Brunton

To mark the centenary of his birth we ask what you know about "that exterminator of Scottish rats", "our Sea-green Incorruptible", "most courteous man", "savager of hypocrisy", "splendid propagandist", the model for Hugh Skene in "Poet's Pub", "politically one of the greatest handicaps with which any national movement could have been burdened", "Lucky Poet", Hugh MacDiarmid.

1: Of where did he write:

> Gin scenic beauty had been a' I sook
> I never need ha' left the Muckle Toon.

2: Which three names are on his birth certificate?

3: "Educated at Langholm Academy and Edinburgh University" – what's wrong with this extract from *Scottish Biographies* (1938), the 1971 & 1990 editions of *Encyclopaedia Britannica et alia*?

4: He was allowed to resign from Broughton Junior Training Centre in 1911 and, later that year, dismissed from his first reporting job by the editor of the Edinburgh Evening Dispatch for which same activity?

    (a) stealing books

    (b) being a member of the Independent Labour Party

    (c) plagiarising Scott.

5: Match his description to the Burgh –

(a) boozy little hole	(i) Montrose
(b) booziest place on earth	(ii) Forfar
(c) model of the preference of quality to quantity set here between the hills and sea	(iii) Cupar

6: During WW1, a sergeant in the RAMC, he was invalided home from Thessalonica – "Thistleonica" to him because of the many Scots serving there – suffering from

    (a) malaria

    (b) tuberculosis

    (c) epilepsy.

7: Connected with his earlier writings, who were

    (a) Isobel Guthrie

    (b) Alister K. Laidlaw

    (c) Martin Gillespie?

8: The opening lines of 'A Christmas Carol', published in his first book of verse by Hugh M'Diarmid in 1925:

> His mither sings to the bairnie Christ
> Wi' the tune o Baw lu la law.
> The bonnie wee craturie lauchs in His crib
> An' a' the starnies and He are sib.
> Baw, baw, my loonikie, baw, balloo.

What was the title of the collection?

172

9: "I canna ride awa' like Tam,/ But e'en maun bide juist whaur I am"
– one of the parallels to Burns' masterpiece in which 2685-line tour-de-
force by MacDiarmid?
10: In 1927 he became Secretary of the Scottish Centre of PEN. What does
PEN stand for?
11: At the first public meeting of the National Party of Scotland in 1928
he shared the platform with the following, amongst others. Who wrote
which?
  (a) John MacCormick   (i) autobiography *The Flag in the Wind*
  (b) Compton Mackenzie   (ii) the short story 'Beattock for Moffat'
  (c) R. B. Cunninghame Graham (iii) the novel *Sinister Street*
12: He rated which work by Tom McDonald, published in 1932 under what
pseudonym, as "by far the best and most radical novel of the Hebrides."?
13: Which cities did he describe as
  (a) "Everything is dead except stupidity here."
  (b) "Stagnant and foul with the rigid peace/ Of an all-tolerating frigid soul"
14: He was expelled from which Party in 1934 for "Communist leanings"
and from which other in 1938 for "Nationalist deviationism"?
15: In his first volume of autobiography, *Lucky Poet*, he confessed to the
sin of solipisim, which is
  (a) solecism
  (b) soliloquy
  (c) subjective idealism?
16: Stalinist, republican, scorner of the aristocracy, MacDiarmid – while
living at the grace and favour of the Duke of Hamilton at Dungavel –
accepted in 1950 a King's pension of £150 (later £500) annually, at the
recommendation of which Prime Minster?
17: While contesting Kinross and West Perth in the 1964 General Election,
he called which other Prime Minister "a zombie, a sixteenth-part Scotsman
of the order of oppressive, big landlord hyenas"?
18: Complete the extract from 'To Circumjack Cencrastus':
> I wish I was Harry Lauder,
> Will Fyffe or J.J.Bell,
> – or Lauchlan Maclean Watt
> For the maitter o' that!
> – *** * ****!
19: He expressed the desire to be where –
> When the last trumpet blaws
> An' see the deid come louping owre
> The auld grey wa's.
20: A "consistent" whisky drinker over sixty years, he enjoyed, among
other single malts:
  (a) Laphroaig
  (b) Bruichladdich
  (c) Talisker
  (d) Highland Park
The products of which islands?

21: In 1957 he was granted a Doctorate of Letters by which university?

22: In 1972, on MacDiarmid's 80th birthday his second wife, Valda Trevlyn, wrote 'Haud Forrit!' for him. In the poem she compared him to which American?

   (a) Walt Whitman

   (b) Allen Ginsberg

   (c) Muhammed Ali

23: He died on Saturday 9th September 1978 and was buried in Langholm cemetery where his stone bears which epitaph:

   (a) Haud Forrit!

   (b) A disgrace to the community!

   (c) Dunbar – not Burns!

24: Norman MacCaig said his passing should be observed by what?

25: Who published in 1988 a critical biography *MacDiarmid* with the dedication "For Valda"?

   (a) Alan Bold

   (b) Allan Massie

   (c) Alan Riach

Answers

1: Langholm, Dumfriesshire.

2: Christopher Murray Grieve.

3: In Edinburgh from 1908 to 1911 he attended Broughton Junior Student Centre but never then or thereafter did he study at the University, although he often made the claim.

4: (a) – he went along with the first allegation but vigorously disputed the second which later prevented him being taken on by *The Scotsman*.

5: (a)(iii), (b)(ii), (c)(i).

6: (a) – he called the area "La Belle Terre Sans Merci", full of "running wounds and rotting bones".

7: They were his pseudonyms as were Hugh M'Diarmid and Hugh McDiarmid, and he would use one to pass favourable comment on the work of another.

8: *Sangschaw*.

9: *The Drunk Man Looks at the Thistle*.

10: Poets, Playwrights, Editors, Essayists and Novelists.

11: (a)(i), (b)(iii), (c)(ii).

12: *The Albannach* by Fionn MacColla.

13: (a) Glasgow (b) Edinburgh.

14: The National Party of Scotland; The Communist Party of Great Britain. He rejoined the CP in 1956.

15: (c), also defined as absolute egoism. His chosen name Hugh can mean "divine wisdom"; in ADMLATT he may have had himself in mind – "A greater Christ, a greater Burns may come".

16: Clement Attlee.

17: Sir Alec Douglas Home.

18: "Dae I Hell!" – LMW was The Very Reverend Dr Watt, Minister of Glasgow Cathedral.

19: "Oh to be at Crowdieknowe" – at Waterbeck, 6 miles NE of Annan where his maternal grandfather is buried.

20: (a) & (b) Islay (c) Skye (d) Orkney.

21: Edinburgh.

22: "Head held high, haud forrit MacDiarmid, Like Muhammad Ali – you're the greatest."

23: None of these – he had chosen (b) but from ADMLATT there are engraved the lines: "I'll hae nae hauf-way hoose, but aye be whaur/ Extremes meet – it's the only way I ken/ To dodge the curst conceit o'being richt/ That damns the majority o' men."

24: "Two Minutes Pandemonium".

25: (a).

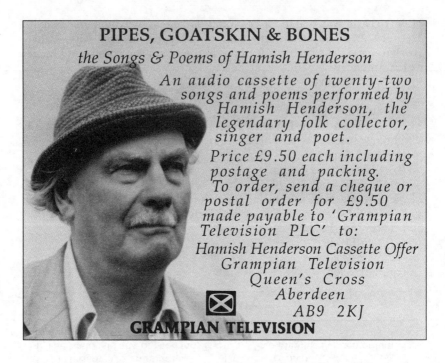

The Immoral Memory

Iain Crichton Smith

Ladies and Gentlemen,

We are gathered here tonight to pay tribute to Hugh MacDiarmid, a true son of Scotia, a lad who was born in Langholm, as you might say.

I thought long and hard about what I might say tonight as the poetry of the bard is very difficult, and I cannot say that I understand it, so I thought I would make a few remarks about the Man, whose like we shall not see again.

I saw Hugh MacDiarmid once. He was in Milne's Bar and I was at that time working for the Prudential Assurance Co. He was standing with some other bards partaking of the barley bree, and I thought at the time 'That is Hugh MacDiarmid' for I had seen a photograph of him in the papers when he was making an attack on the banking system. He had the true look of the bard about him though he looked healthy enough. He was laughing and joking and I heard the word 'whodumdeid' a few times. I thought of introducing myself to him but decided against it. I suppose it was awe of the great poet who at that time didn't have the reputation he has since had with poetries like *A Drunk Man Looks at the Thistle*. Indeed he is now known the length and breadth of Scotland from Dumfries to Stornoway. I remember that he had a piercing gaze and his eyes rested on me for a moment and then passed on. I often wonder what would have happened if he had spoken to me. Would he have advised me to leave the Prudential Assurance Co, which I did shortly after that. Maybe his eagle eye had something to do with it.

Many people have said that MacDiarmid would take a good drink, but I would say he was a convivial drinker, a man you could take into your house and have a deep discussion with: and of course he was an expert on the Lallans and read the dictionary from end to end. So he was not a great drinker: he was a moderate drinker, one who indulged in the grape to help his inspiration but was not dependent on it to excess. My reading of him was that he was not an extreme man, and he loved to smoke his pipe quietly in his study. I believe that he was a Bogey Roll man.

Another libel has been put upon him that he was not a Christian. I may say that if you go through all his poetries you will find the word 'God' and 'Christ' many times. Especially in that poetry *A Drunk Man Looks at the Thistle*. I will quote:—

> A greater Christ, a greater Burns may come.
> The maist they'll dae is to gie bigger pegs
> to folly and conceit to hang their rubbish on...

and we all know those kind of people who talk about poets without having read their poetries and without knowing anything about them. The audience here is not like that though. At another time he joins God and the lassies together when he says,

> I've been startled whiles to find
> when Jean has been in bed with me
> a kind of Christianity.

For MacDiarmid was fond of the lassies though in a moderate way. All in all he was a sober man, with a great love for his pipe, a man like ourselves in many ways. Many of us though we are not great poets have a little drink now and again and many of us have an eye for the lassies. It is true that he did not go to church but that was because in my opinion there was no church in his area that would suit him.

Another thing that I have heard is that he was against the Chinese, because in his poetry *A Drunk Man Looks at the Thistle* he writes:

> You canna gang to a Burns supper even
> wi oot some wizened scrunt of a Knocknee
> Chinese turns roon to say, Him haggis velly goot
> and ten to wan the piper is a Cockney.

I think that our bard is being jovial here, as a bard is allowed to be. And we all know that the Chinese put an 'l' where an 'r' should be. And he only put in the word 'Knocknee' to find a rhyme for 'Cockney'. The poet is not making aspersion on the Chinese 'r's, but he is pointing out that a Chinaman may be as Scottish as anyone else. And indeed he was a seer as well as a poet for there are many Chinese now serving in Chinese restaurants and some of them speaking Scots. Indeed I heard one of them saying the other day, "It's gleat weathel we are having now". And I have bought haggis in a Chinese restaurant myself.

My own feeling is that the great bard was one of the people, a simple man who indulged in his simple pleasures, especially his bogey roll, of which he was very fond. There is a story that I have heard that he refused 'Three Nuns' insisting that Bogey Roll was better for his inspiration. We might ask ourselves how big an influence tobacconists have had on great poetries but that will be for another occasion. We are told that he studied a great deal as many of us do. We're told indeed that he read 10,000 books when he was young and that was a lot of books but we must remember that that was at a time when life was slower than it is now, and there was no television. He didn't go so far as to have a profession, but he could have become a teacher if he had wanted to, though I'm not sure that he had a certificate. Indeed with his simple mind and his love of books he would have adorned the profession. We can imagine him as a Primary Headmaster in Dumfries, but that was not to be. We can imagine him struggling manfully with Standard Grades and withal having something to say about tests for primary school children, and school boards. But as I have said, nothing like that happened, alas.

I have said already that Hugh MacDiarmid was a true Scotsman. All one has to do is read the vocabulary he used, for example the word 'doup' which means 'backside', 'cullage' which means 'genitals' and 'fower' which means 'four'. Not many of you would have known that 'plat o chairn' means 'cow dung' but you can all see how expressive such words are and how they spring from the soil of Scotia.

It is a deep task to delve into the life of this great man who, as I have said, is very like ourselves. He always wore a kilt and he had a passion for learning because he didn't have a profession. He had, unlike us, plenty of time on his hands for his poetries and indeed he visited America and China and was a soldier in his youth, fighting for king and country with might and main. We wonder what he would have thought of the merging of the Scottish Regiments. I am sure he would have disapproved.

A Christian, then, if there had been a good church in his neighbourhood, a moderate drinker, and a lover of the lassies, the great poet is a man we can identify with. MacDiarmid says:–

> I'm not the kind of poet
> that opens a sale of work.

I think when he says that he was being humble. Many would have been proud of asking him to open a sale of work and he would have made a good job of it too. He was certainly capable of making an excellent speech and mixing with ordinary people. He would have had a few couthy things to say. But in his statement he was showing the traditional humility of the Scotsman.

Finally, what did this great poet think of our other great poet Rabbie? He admired him and Burns's Suppers as we can see from the following:–

> Thought may demit
> its function fit
> while till to thee. O Burns,
> the punctual stomach of thy people turns.
> Most folks agree
> that poetry
> is of no earthly use
> save thine–which yields at least this annual excuse.
> Other cults die:
> but who'll deny
> that you your mob in thrall
> will keep, O Poet Intestinal.

This is a fine tribute from one great poet to another and if Burns was alive today he would pay his tribute to Hugh MacDiarmid.

I will therefore close by giving you this toast. Ladies and Gentlemen, *Hugh MacDiarmid.*

Iain Crichton Smith

Hayden Murphy

Feather and Stone
IM *Christopher Murray Grieve*

Eel nouns, crowned
Teeth, capped on Riding
Day with sombre headdress.

Handed over the grave,
Blown needle thin,
Are tree-drawn wind
Flayed words
Into memory.

         Feather

Testimony of tribe.
Scribe, chieftain
Of rock-hewn terms
Of agreement. Water
Gently marking
Divides.

      Red

Woven into black
Meeting blue.
Flat on the palm
Against the palm
Handing over the grave
A leaf grained feather.

         Stone

Earthed. Against
Grey skin, the watching
Sky, a white veiled
Rose is worn. Stubborn
As black.

      Plain,

Pale, brave.

Mole verbs, tapped
Tongue, horse-drawn
Freeman crowned.

Bloomsday, 16th June 1992,
Dumfries

Hugh Bryden

Howard Purdie

The Time To Say Goodbye

When the birds no longer sing
    in the Borders,
when every hill has been laid waste
    from top to toe with Sitka,
and through the long, dark tunnels
    blows a hot, stale wind
like in the London Underground –
    will that be the time to say goodbye?

When the singers no longer sing
    in the Borders,
and, in the little pubs
    all over the countryside,
the musicians no longer play,
    and the poets fall silent
because they lack the courage of conviction –
    will that be the time to say goodbye?

When the white settlers have taken over
    in the Borders,
when every valley has been insulted
    by a cobweb castle or a carbuncle;
when the roads are commandeered
    by pseudo-lairds in vintage cars,
and the hotels are alive with the sound of Muzak –
    will that be the time to say goodbye?

When the sun burns like a molten ball of money
    over the Borders,
when the Tweed becomes a trickle
    and the merse a desert;
when acid rain has eaten lochan, burn and river,
    and St Mary's Loch shrinks to a stagnant pond
in the midst of a concrete jungle –
    will that be the time to say goodbye?

When all these things have happened
    in the Borders,
when the spirit has burned out of us
    like oil in an old lamp,
when Burns, and Scott, and Hogg, and MacDiarmid
    no longer turn in their graves,
but meekly accept the death of Scottish Culture –
    that will be the time to say goodbye.

MacDiarmid with Wendy Wood and Hamish Henderson   *Photo: William Kellock*

MacDiarmid in the company of Norman MacCaig, Sydney Goodsir Smith, Sorley
MacLean and Alastair Fowler, May 1972   *Glasgow Herald*

At Langholm, September 13, 1992

1: Hamish Henderson

Nothing was more characteristic of the great Chris Grieve than to flyte; and I was honoured to be his opponent on more than one occasion. In the book *The Age of MacDiarmid*, edited by P H Scott & A C Davies, and reprinted recently, there's an imaginary dialogue between Roy Campbell and Hugh MacDiarmid. At the end of this dialogue, which takes place (needless to say) in Heaven, they both have a drink of excellent malt whisky, in the best bar in Heaven. (This must surely be the bar the blessed damozel leaned out from!)

At the very end, after a number of curious and not-so-curious exchanges, Chris takes a glass of excellent malt and says to Roy Campbell "In this I bury all unkindness." Now of all the most unlikely imaginary dialogues in world history, that must take the biscuit! For I cannot imagine exchanging a drink or two with Chris Grieve beyond that Gulf, in that great bar of Heaven, and expect him to say something like that about me!

I first met him not long after coming out of the army, and it was a privilege, naturally, for a bloke who had loved his poetry for a long time, to meet this being of bright genius, who descended on the Muckle Toon o' Langholm 100 years ago. He's not only a world poet, a poet of huge significance everywhere, but he's also a strongly *local* poet. He loved Langholm, and said that Langholm was his touchstone in all things creative. I first saw a poem by Chris Grieve – you've just heard it read by Tom Fleming – "Mars is braw in crammasy"; it was included by John Buchan in an anthology called *The Northern Muse*. I was at school in England at the time, and opening this book and seeing in a collection of poems this astounding poem, which was quite unlike anything else in the anthology, I wondered who this C M Grieve was – it was signed not "Hugh MacDiarmid" but "C M Grieve". So after a little while I ferreted out that Hugh MacDiarmid and C M Grieve were one man, and eventually I succeeded in picking up copies of *Sangschaw*, *Penny Wheep*, and above all, *A Drunk Man Looks at the Thistle*, which changed my life. Lots of people have said this, and I just add it to the other expressions of appreciation of that amazing goliardic book. I carried it with me, incidentally, throughout the war, took it out to Africa, and had it with me in the desert, and through Libya and Tunisia, and into Italy. The only other poetry I had with me all the way was *17 Poems for Sixpence*, a wee bookie containing work by Robert Garioch and Somhairle MacLean. These were my poetic companions throughout the campaign – and not bad company, you must admit!

But earlier on, when I returned as a teenager to Scotland from school, after reading this poem in *The Northern Muse*, I found to my astonishment that contemporaries of mine, teenagers like me, kent naethin aboot him! The very existence of MacDiarmid was unknown to them. Now, you know what's happened to him in the meantime, and this amazing transformation in the cultural life of the country is above all due to the magnificent, single-minded spadework of Hugh MacDiarmid himself. He did what he once said might happen in a little poem called 'Glasgow 1960' when a great crowd making for Ibrox is not going to see a football match, but is going to hear an intellectual debate, or a Turkish poet's "abstruse new song". Anyway, Chris made it – he did it.

As I say, I was astonished that none of my contemporaries, aged around 15-16, knew about MacDiarmid, and when eventually I read the *Festschrift* published in 1962 for Chris's 70th birthday by K.D.Duval and Sydney Goodsir Smith, there was a contribution by Maurice Lindsay in which, with admirable candour, he admitted he had not heard of MacDiarmid's existence until he was already an officer in the army. He'd been through a Glasgow education and he'd come across *A Drunk Man Looks at the Thistle* in a second-hand bookshop. That excellent, candid statement throws into high relief the achievement of MacDiarmid in the intervening years. Nowadays it is different, and I know from occasionally judging competitions like the one we've just heard the results of, that MacDiarmid is actually a popular poet among young folk now – an amazing development.

Now to go back to these flytings. MacDiarmid thought, wrongly in my opinion, that the folk song revival was a kind of resumption of the kailyard. He thought that the people interested in the old ballads, and some of the magnificent bothy songs which reflect the life of the north-east farm servants, excellent folk poetry; that in some way all this was connected with the sort of petit-bourgeois Victorian poems that you associate with the kailyard. How wrong can you get? Now, I put it to you that this was a great error on Chris Grieve's part. In fact he should have welcomed the folk song revival. (Why should I renege now on my position of then?) Nevertheless, as I say, I give all credit to him for being what he called "the catfish in the aquarium" – this tremendous stimulus to intellectual life in Scotland. And may I add, not exactly in the tone of John Wain's imaginary dialogue, with a glass of malt whisky exchanged in a bar, that eventually, near the end of his life, he actually told me he liked one of my own songs! And as far as the flytings are concerned, I think it should be pointed out that one of the characteristics of Chris Grieve was the old Border Riever spirit he shared with countless ancestors. He *had* to have flytings. It was in his nature. I just happened to be the fall guy in all this at one particular point in his history. Anyway we went at each other hammer and tongs, and I personally don't regret it: I don't think if we ever exchange that glass of malt whisky in the best bar in Heaven, that we will ever do anything else than resume the flyting.

Who are the characters in European or world history that resemble Chris Grieve the most? People have compared him to many poets, but

I'm going to suggest a person that might not come first and foremost into your mind. It is the Bedford tinker John Bunyan, author of the *Pilgrim's Progress*. He was a man who also enjoyed his own rammies. He was a remorseless fighter, was John Bunyan, in his own way, for what he thought was the right; and in one of his famous songs he says

> There's no discouragement
> Shall make him once relent
> His first avowed intent
> To be a pilgrim.

Well, MacDiarmid took his pilgrimage into the Communist Party of Great Britain. And many folk may consider that he made a wrong political choice. But I would put it to you that in view of his temperament, and in view of his own indomitable nature – "aye gaun whaur extremes meet" – there was nowhere that he could land up except in a Stalinist Communist party. Now this, needless to say (in my opinion), didn't do Scotland any good. I belong, as you might say, to the Dubcek wing in all this; and consequently that's another reason why I would have to have flytings with him. If I concentrate on these antagonistic things, incidentally, it's because I feel it's part and parcel of the whole nature of Chris Grieve, and in fact I would almost like to say that without this particular vein he wouldn't have been the man he was.

So may I, at the very end, quote one of the poems he made out of Scottish folk poetry – this folk poetry he claimed to despise. It is 'Empty Vessel'. He went, as we all know, to Jamieson's dictionary and found some of these amazing words. At one time he said "it is out of words that you create poetry" and of course so it is, but the words in Jamieson's dictionary led him on inevitably to the folk poetry, out of which these words had come. Out of David Herd's great collection, for example. And it was in Herd's collection that he found a poem, which is a roch randy poem, called 'Jenny Nettles'. This is the opening of the second verse:

> I met her on the kairney
> Jennie Nettles, Jennie Nettles,
> singing to her bairnie
> Robin Rattles Bastard...

"Unpromising material" was George Bruce's rather tight-lipped comment in the 1962 *Festschrift* I have already mentioned. But out of it MacDiarmid made this truly magical poem 'Empty Vessel' which many of you probably know by heart:

> I met ayont the cairney
> A lass wi' tousie hair
> Singin' til a bairnie
> That was nae langer there.
>
> Wunds wi' warlds to swing
> Dinna sing sae sweet.
> The licht that bends owre a'thing
> Is less ta'en up wi't.

Langholm byspale, we salute you!

184

2: Sorley MacLean

I did not alway agree with Hugh MacDiarmid. I remember on Whalsay arguing about his position about Douglas' Social Credit; and arguing that if Douglas' Social Credit could solve man's economic ills, what was the need for Socialist convictions? I think his position was that social revolution was a necessity, in a psychological or spiritual sense, and that what you might call the evil, of what you might call the ethos of the bourgeoisie must be destroyed, be got rid of somehow.

Nor did I agree with him about folk poetry, or rather, what a brilliant Skyeman James Ross has called sub-literary poetry – 'sub' not being a derogatory prefix at all. It was Ross who first used that phrase, as far as I remember. I also think that if I had been against Hugh MacDiarmid personally, I would have had the same regard for his poetry. I think Yeats was a very great poet, but I loathed his politics and still do. His elitism was a very social elitism, unlike MacDiarmid's.

I once or twice referred to MacDiarmid as the greatest poet in Europe. That doesn't mean that I ever set myself up as a judge of the poetry of Europe. For one thing I couldn't set myself up as a fit judge of the poetry written even in Wales or Ireland because I don't know Welsh at all; I don't know Irish Gaelic well enough to be a judge of the poetry. And there is no other European language I know well enough to be a judge of its poetry. Therefore, to say that MacDiarmid was the best poet of his time in Europe means only that I could not, and cannot yet, imagine a better poet than the poet of *Sangschaw, Penny Wheep, A Drunk Man looks at the Thistle*, and many more things that were written by MacDiarmid. So my ridiculous statement is not so ridiculous as it seems.

No poet or artist can be judged except by thinking of his best poetry or art. And that is as true of MacDiarmid as of others. There is enough of his best in MacDiarmid to be astounding. A great number of his lyrics are to the ear and to the mind, and even to neuro-physical perception, the words of a man sending back messages from a forward observation post on the frontiers of consciousness. They are words that can set a human situation against the great universe with resonances and rhythms for which the first Scots word I can think of is uncanny and the English word 'magical'. (MacDiarmid himself once referred to those lyrics as chocolate boxes, and Norman exclaimed "What chocolate boxes!") His messages are such that the high frequency of his sensitivities are transformed in language to what I and a great number more recognise as truth and profundity, the kind of truth that Matthew Arnold called 'high seriousness'. And often that high seriousness is, as it were, implicit and understood without being explicitly said.

It is not only in the soaring, irradiating, sometimes coldly passionate lyric that Hugh MacDiarmid was supreme, and as original as any art can be. I cannot imagine any other long poem as original and as great as his *A Drunk Man Looks at the Thistle*. In it the great Symbolist movement of

European literature has a breadth, variety, and an inevitable organic unity in diversity that makes other long Symbolist poems seem factitious, laboured and contrived. I am sure that there is nothing like it anywhere else; that it is the last word in originality, and in its whole effect, supreme!

MacDiarmid had a sensitivity that was beyond words, and with that a courage and spiritual ambition that made him live a life of material poverty in order to have no trammels on his visionary spirituality. I don't care that he made mistakes this time or that time: he was the kind of man who was at once a philosophical materialist and a moral idealist of idealists, and to me at any rate that is the most admirable of men. He once said "A Scottish poet maun assume/ the burden of his people's doom." And the burden of one nation's doom is the burden of the doom of all peoples; and of that Grieve was mostly, if not always, aware, for he had the accidental inconsistency inevitable in one who sought to be "whaur extremes meet". I consider those inconsistencies accidental, not at all essential. It seems to me that they were the byproduct of his spiritual ambition, one result of which was the attempt to do the impossible in poetry. I do think that some of his longer poems fail because they attempt to do the impossible; but such spiritual ambition is a glorious thing, and MacDiarmid's failures are glorious failures.

Matthew Arnold said of Byron:

> When Byron's eyes were closed in death
> We bowed our heads and held our breath.
> He taught us little, but our souls
> Had felt him like the thunder's roll.

Of MacDiarmid I would say that "our souls had felt him like the thunder roll" and that he taught my generation, and I dare say many of this generation too, not a little, but mountains of things about the human spirit.

3: Edwin Morgan

I think anniversaries have their benefits – they ask us to look before and after, to see what the particular person came out of, what he or she admired or rejected, and what it all led to, or was hoped it would lead to, in the end.

But before I say a word or two about that, let's remind ourselves that there's a part of MacDiarmid which would be detached almost completely from such things. Although in public and in books he had a soapbox, or a number of soapboxes, to give messages from, in private conversation he often gave the impression, I found, that the life of the imagination was more important than changing the world socially or politically. And what could be more imaginative than thinking about the *next* world instead of this one? He does this in one poem, 'Esplumeoir', not with any nonsense about St Peter at the gates of heaven, rather he pictures eternity in a very strange, very appealing way, as a sort of upmarket 1920s American speakeasy:

> A sma' demure white biggin;
> Wi' shutters and a canopy.
> The canopy's royal blue
> And it says *Eternity*
> In discreet soap-glass letters
> On ilka-side. Under the canopy
> You walk up and the front door
> Is a' mirror wi' a cool strip
> O' fluorescent light on top.
> You push the pearl button,
> And listen to the delicate chimes
> And adjust your tie in the mirror
> And fix your hat – but the guy
> Ahint the bullet-proof mirror
> Sees a' that too,
> Only you canna see him…

This guy turns out to be a big black doorman with white hair called Tutti-Frutti Forgle, and he gives you the once-over, and if your credentials seem right, lets you in. The poem ends:

> Aince past Tutti, you check your hat
> In a quiet soft-lit anteroom,
> Syne the haill place is yours.

That's not the MacDiarmid people often talk about, but it's just as real as the other MacDiarmids, and it serves to remind us that he delighted in using pure imagination, the play of imagination, and that's one of the things we enjoy in him.

To return to our before-and-after anniversary theme, MacDiarmid when he was young looked back to his immediate predecessors without much love or enthusiasm, but with one exception, and that was John Davidson, not a major Scottish poet but a significant minor one. When Davidson committed suicide off Penzance in 1909, probably by wading out to sea and shooting himself in the head, MacDiarmid wrote later that it was `as if the bottom had fallen out of my world'. He was seventeen at the time, with that adolescent sensitivity which looks for heroes, and it's reminiscent of Tennyson who at the same age rushed out and carved on a rock *Byron is Dead* – to Tennyson, Byron's sudden death seemed the end of an era. But to MacDiarmid, once he got over the shock and began his own writing, it was more like the *beginning* of an era. He wrote a short poem about it ('Of John Davidson'):

> I remember one death in my boyhood
> That next to my father's, and darker, endures;
> Not Queen Victoria's, but Davidson, yours,
> And something in me has always stood
> Since then looking down the sandslope
> On your small black shape by the edge of the sea,
> – A bullet-hole through a great scene's beauty,
> God through the wrong end of a telescope.

But why Davidson? This was a rebel poet, an outsider, someone with unpopular opinions, a materialist who wanted to put man and not God at the centre of things ("God through the…"), and that appealed to MacDiarmid; but he was also a great believer in the present and the future rather than the past, a poet of modern times who wrote about trains and docks and city streets and the Crystal Palace, and who speculated on the futures that science and technology might bring. It was this straining towards the future that dazzled MacDiarmid, and he made it one of his own main themes. "What use to let a sunrise fade/ To ha'e anither like't the morn,/ Or let a generation pass/ That ane nae better may succeed?" (*A Drunk Man Looks at the Thistle*, 1236).

Nowadays the future tends to get a bad press. The present seems desperate enough, and the so-called New World Order, if that is the future, is a mess. So how do we see MacDiarmid's futurism now? What will be the fate of one of his most striking short poems, only four lines but once read never forgotten: 'The Skeleton of the Future' (subtitle 'At Lenin's Tomb') –

> Red granite and black diorite, with the blue
> Of the labradorite crystals gleaming like precious stones
> In the light reflected from the snow; and behind them
> The eternal lightning of Lenin's bones.

It's all perfectly real – the actual mausoleum in Red Square in Moscow where Lenin's body was preserved – but of course it's also deeply symbolic – red for revolution, black for mourning, ice-blue for the hard but glittering doctrine of revolution. And down inside the tomb, in the cold and the dark, guarded by soldiers, there's the brightly lit glass case where you can certainly imagine Lenin's bones shining under his flesh. But now today what? With the fall of communism and the probability that Lenin's body will be removed and quietly buried beside his mother's in St Petersburg, has the eternal lightning gone out? Have we seen the future, and it *didn't* work? MacDiarmid would probably get very angry with these questions, but I think once he had composed himself he would say something like this: `Poetry has its own truth and can cast seeds of hope or aspiration (as Shelley believed) into futures that are still unseen. If one social system has failed or collapsed, it doesn't mean that we have to give up the ideal of a more *just* society as distinct from a more *free* society. Who knows, in any case, whether Lenin's ideas are dead? Seventy years is not a long time in human history.' And so on. Then he would refill his pipe and give it a few good emphatic puffs, daring anyone to demolish his argument.

If there is something undemolishable about MacDiarmid it's the strange fact that however wrong or apparently wrong he is, he leaves us with an amazing sense of *potential*, something that keeps thought going, keeps a feeling for the future going, despite all the bloody setbacks we've seen in recent times especially.

I would like to end with a quotation which has a rather exotic provenance that I think would appeal to MacDiarmid, who liked far-fetched comparisons. Moses Znaimer, a man from Tajikistan who is now a mighty force in the world of Canadian television, said recently at a conference, "Any sissy can make programmes. I make channels." MacDiarmid, like Moses, made channels, extraordinary channels which we are still sailing and exploring, and will do for a long time to come.

4: Norman MacCaig

I was once in a position like this before, introducing MacDiarmid to a group of people who I knew were very familiar with his work; most of them knew him. I didn't know what to call him – Christopher Murray Grieve, Hugh MacDiarmid, Hugh, Dr Grieve, Chris? Well, I'm in the same situation now and when I speak I call him Chris.

I'll quote some of the things he said to me. He stayed with me when he was in Edinburgh, and I chummed him to get his bus home to Biggar. It started to drizzle. He carried a beret in his pocket in case it started to rain. Now that man had the thickest crop of hair you saw in your life. Every hair had hair growing from it. He groped for his beret and said, "Ach, I've left my beret at home" and I said "It's not you that needs the beret, it's me!", to which he said "Good subsoil, Norman."

He used to write against Scots. He said it was paddling up a backwater of literature, and that the future of poetry depended on writing in English. It didn't surprise me – he contradicted every single thing he ever said. He told me when he was Montrose he came to three decisions: "One, I'm a communist. Two, I'm a Scottish nationalist" – he was flung out of each because he was in the other – "and three, I was going to be a great Scottish poet." Now poets are very rational people. None of this heads-in-the-clouds stuff, no rolling eyeballs. They are very practical-minded people. How can you become a great Scottish poet? "Think of the English and do the opposite." The English write in English so he decided to write in Scots. A practical man again, he got Jamieson's Dictionary, though he was still signing everything 'Christopher Murray Grieve'. Now Christopher Murray Grieve dived in one end, and Hugh MacDiarmid splashed ashore at the other, sprinkling the ground around him with those wonderful lyrics which were fifty times better than anything he'd written before.

He continually surprised me. I thought I knew him; I didn't really. For example, for years he roared away about the necessity for a poetry that dealt with the advances of politics, history, geography *et cetera*. Once – odd coincidence of the planets – we emerged from a pub. Two men, one of whom knew Chris, joined us and came up to my house with Chris, and we started talking about Burns, whom Christopher sometimes liked to call 'Mr R Burns' (I think he was a wee bit jealous). One said, "what do you think is the best line of verse Burns ever wrote?" I expected of course a political poem, or a satirical poem; and he said "The best line Burns ever wrote was 'Ye are na Mary Morison'." Not very striking. But put it in its context, as I'm sure you'll know – I'll quote the second verse:

> Yestreen when to the trembling string
>   The dance gaed through the lighted ha',
> To thee my fancy took its wing,
>   I sat, but neither heard, nor saw:
> Though this was fair, and that wa braw,
>   And yon the toast of a' the town,
> I sigh'd and said amang them a',
>   'Ye are na Mary Morison.'

How can a man load these ordinary words with such feeling? That kind of lyric MacDiarmid couldn't write. Not even Chris could write it, never mind Dr Grieve. He couldn't stop thinking, and in his lyrics (and nobody loves them more than I do) he reminds me of the great English painter who was once asked by one of those idiotic women who are used for such stories, "What do you mix your paints with, Mr Turner?" and he said, "Brains, madam." That's what MacDiarmid does in his lyrics. Quite different from Burns – absolutely wonderful, but different. I used to say MacDiarmid was the greater poet. That was when I was young and silly. I used to say that he was the greater poet because he covered areas of experience that Burns never set foot in – and I'll bet you Burns would be the first to agree with that.

On the other hand, this obstreperous, obstropulous man, was very much more self-aware than you would think. Consider the famous sentence he wrote in a letter to George Bruce when George worked at the BBC. Chris was uncontrollable. When you asked him for a piece to last 30 minutes you got a piece that lasts 45. Once this happened and George sent it back asking him to cut it. And in his reply he offered this splendid sentence: "My job as I see it has never been to lay a tit's egg, but to erupt like a volcano, emitting not only flame, but a lot of rubbish." That famous sentence he uttered once in *A Drunk Man* "I'll hae nae haufway hoose, but aye be whaur/ Extremes meet..." is a famous remark, one with a lot of truth in it. And what about these other lines in that poem which are very different but which strike me as just as extraordinary:

> For I've nae faith in ocht I can explain
> And stert whaur the philosophers leave aff.

When he switched over from writing in Scots to English, his fans couldn't understand why. His usual answer was that "I find that the aggrandized use of Scots which I've been writing in is not capable of dealing with advanced technology, psychology *et cetera*." But once, in my house we were just talking about this and that. He stood up from the sofa where he was sitting, took two steps to the fire and turned round. He was silent for about a minute. Referring to the long poems, from *In Memoriam James Joyce* onwards which he avowedly claims to be the best things he ever wrote, "Now Norman," he said, "do you know why I've been writing all that rubbish for the last forty years?" I said, "well what do you think, Chris?" and he replied "I lost my sense of rhythm" meaning verbal rhythms. They are, of course, absolutely magnificent in *Sangschaw, Penny Wheep, A Drunk Man* and some others. But he lost

190

it, and I said "Well I noticed that. It happened about 1934," and he agreed. There is a story, which is true, that in London he fell off the top of a bus, landing on his head (which was the safest place for him to fall) and he actually was unconscious. I reminded him of this, and I said I've heard things about various parts of the brain controlling different powers, one of them being, for example, rhythm – rhythm in walking *et cetera*. That was far too simple for him. He went on and on and on, referring to his divorce from his first wife – a rigged divorce: he had agreed to a divorce as long as he got continuous relations with his children. Well, she reneged on this, and he was forbidden to see the children, and he was terribly shattered. When I suggested that the knock on the head was the cause of him losing his sense of rhythm, he started talking about this, anima complexes, other things. He couldn't take just a simple knock on the head as an excuse.

He of course contradicted himself all the time. He like to quote a sentence from a poem by Walt Whitman: "Do I contradict myself? Very well, I contradict myself. I am large, I contain multitudes." There is truth in that about MacDiarmid.

(One wee point. When you think of Chris, a name that doesn't spring to mind is Socrates. But Socrates all these two or three thousand years ago, looked at Attica, his country, and the people dozing in the shadow of a tree to keep out of the sun, and he said that he considered himself to be a cleg, that went and bit them and sent them galloping all over the field. Now Chris flattered himself he did that to the Scottish people – deliberately trying to kick them out of their stodgy apathy.)

When I got to know him I tried to catch him out with esoteric Scots words. Never once did I succeed. One time I said, "Do you know the Scots word 'sly'? Not the English meaning of it." He said "yes," so I said, "What does it mean, then?" He spattered out a length of Latin, a language of which he knew not a lot. He thumped me with this and I said, "No, no, no. Have another thump. What's the meaning of 'sly'?" He said that it was the green scum that forms on a pool, and he had given me the scientific name for it. Well, I couldn't deny it of course, and I told him "I've only seen that word in a particular poem of his, where he has the last verse talking about men fishing in the river here:

Their queer stane faces and hoo green they got
Just like Rebecca wi' her shawl o' sly.

I didn't know the word 'sly' and I looked up the bible Rebecca. No mention of shawls. I said "who is Rebecca?" and he said "I don't know – she just fitted the metre!"

Reviews

On a Raised Bookshelf

The Age of MacDiarmid, ed P H Scott &
A C Davis, Mainstream, £7.99; *Mac-
Diarmid in Shetland,* Brian Smith &
Ruth McQuillan, Shetland Library, £7.95;
Hugh MacDiarmid – Selected Poetry,
ed Alan Riach & Michael Grieve; *Hugh
MacDiarmid – Selected Prose,* ed Alan
Riach, both Carcanet, £18.95

In choosing to reprint *The Age of Mac-
Diarmid* in a paperback form essentially
unchanged from the hardback publication of
1980 the editors and publishers have missed
an opportunity to reintroduce and reinvigor-
ate a dated text. As a result they have made
the republication an event of merely historical, rather than of critical occasion. The book
cries out for a new introduction: as it is we
have Paul Scott's introduction proclaiming
"We are less than two years away from Mac-
Diarmid's death on 9th September 1978."

Some of the individual essays still afford a
certain pleasure; Stephen Maxwell, hesitant
and pragmatic about MacDiarmid's influence
on Scottish politics, Kenneth Buthlay's
revealing essay on allusion in the later work,
and Neal Ascherson's prescient comments on
MacDiarmid sitting at the centre of the Communist Party's contradictory attitude to
nationality and nationalism. Mostly though,
given that many of the writers here took a
consciously provisional approach, and given
that one third of the book is devoted to Mac-
Diarmid and politics, publishing them again
without at least a reminder of the context of a
1980 publication is a disservice to the contrib-
utor as well as to the reader, bearing in mind
the growth in Scottish cultural production, the
rise of a group of authors writing out of post-
industrial Glasgow, the twin developments of
a strengthening cultural scene and a political
nationalist movement that has fluctuated in
strength, whilst often trying to distance itself
from the growth in cultural self-confidence.
All these topics are directly relevant to Mac-
Diarmid's cultural and political agenda, and
the original contributors should have been
given the opportunity to comment on them.

Proving that the history of the '30s can
often seem less old-fashioned than that of the
early '80s the publication of *MacDiarmid in
Shetland* is a positive move; perhaps even
part of a regional repossession of MacDiarmid's work. The book contains two essays,
one biographical by Brian Smith, the other,
by Ruth McQuillan, critical; a photographic
section; the text of *On A Raised Beach,* and a
selection of other poems composed on Shetland. Of the two essays, Brian Smith's
humane biographical study is in many ways
the more rewarding, particularly in its details
of the physical and material pressures which
accelerated Grieve towards his major breakdown. Smith underlines the pressures of
work, of short deadlines, of publishing disap-
pointments as Routledge first insisted he cut
Red Scotland then decided not to publish it,
and the pressures of physical ill-health exac-
erbated by living in a home which the Shetlanders described as 'a hovel'. This argues
neatly against seeing Grieve's collapse as a
sudden, unprecedented psychic crisis. Smith
also writes amusingly of the Shetlanders'
reaction to Grieve's work, particularly his
voracious acquisition of Shetland phrases:

An ee day Wilfred called da men ta come for
der denner or somethin, an he gies a great
roar; "Scaramadoo!" an Grieves [*sic*] shot
his head oot aa bed an glowered at Wilfred,
all excited and said "What word was that?!
What word was that?!" He tocht dis wis a
right wird at we used, but hit wis just a lok o
dirt at Wilfred wis made up.

Ruth McQuillan is strong on this area too,
pointing out, in an ingenious piece of criticism, two occasions ('With the Herring Fish-
ers' and 'Off the Course of Fiedeland') where
MacDiarmid may have misheard the speech
of the fishermen, and used his creative mis-
hearings in poems where they became bound
up in his own poetic meaning. More often
though, her critical observations are both
breathless and woolly. She does however reit-
erate a valuable point on the difficulty of

dividing MacDiarmid's work chronologically, and the tendency of the themes of his major poems to ebb into poems written and published later on. *MacDiarmid in Shetland* is a valuable and stimulating piece of work.

The *Selected Prose* edited by Alan Riach and the *Selected Poetry* edited by Riach and Michael Grieve are part of Carcanet's Mac-Diarmid 2000 project, and the selected prose is particularly welcome. Published here are early reviews by Christopher Grieve in which, often using the occasion of a review of another author, he advances his literary aesthetic and cultural programmes; also there is pleasing play between his various personae. In part these pieces play a stimulating game, affording wonderful material for literary critics to analyse what Kenneth Buthlay has called the 'author function' in MacDiarmid. They also of course represent a pragmatic and imaginative marshalling of available resources, Grieve striving to follow Wordsworth's advice about the need for radical poetry to first create the audience by which it will be appreciated, and better, doing it himself; Grieve as the midwife to allow the birth of MacDiarmid is a pleasing image. Pleasing too is the reprinting of the author's notes to *In Memoriam James Joyce*: MacDiarmid's later work, like Joyce's contains and analyses his own lyric beginnings; in knowing the previous work it moves beyond it, and in analysing it, it lays bare the bones of that poetic polity and the present one; the reiteration of that idea, of MacDiarmid's later work not only possessing a huge range of material, from science, from other cultures, but also possessing itself (like the curly snake eating its own tail) is well made by this collection. Also included are notes as various as Grieve's election literature for his contest with Alec Douglas Home and the humorous prose of 'The Dour Drinkers of Glasgow'.

An interesting appendix to the *Selected Poetry* addresses the issue of MacDiarmid's borrowing from diverse sources, offering a short reading list for those tempted to look further back, or further in, in search of seeds; a further appendix gives sources for the poem 'Perfect' which of course started, on its publication, much of this discussion in the first place. This is fruitful ground for critics; modern literary theory is less likely to talk about 'plagiarism' than it is, drawing the term from contemporary music, to think about 'sampling'. That concept has become part of the consumerist perception of culture, and has, in the process, thoroughly disrupted many popular notions of authorship and, since they often mean the same thing, ownership. It would be fitting if the next wave of critical attempts on MacDiarmid sought to apply this thinking; if post-modernism disrupts the implied unity of the authorial voice then how much more open to that idea should we be in a poet who was the persona voice of a jobbing journalist, a persona which was both symptom and further cause of psychic disruption in Christopher Grieve. That approach cries out for an application to the bundle of characteristics and postures which was MacDiarmid. After all MacDiarmid disrupted notions of authorship simply by being MacDiarmid, or rather by being MacDiarmid and Grieve; the 'author function', was shared, or divided. Alan Riach has elsewhere argued that *On a Raised Beach* can be read as a critique of the idea of unity; in another sense the complex of attitudes that was MacDiarmid was a critique of unity, as was his conception of Scotland.

Perhaps there is still too much weight of acquaintance and proximity in the critical response to MacDiarmid. Biography, the theoretical root of both of the critical books reviewed here, is a stolid basis for analysis of his work. In the sense that MacDiarmid contained and stabilised his contradictory views within his personality, his biographical identity may deny the fissiparous identity of the poetry. For all new readers now, as for most during his lifetime, the acquaintance is a textual and not a personal one; it is this acquaintance, with its playing between the Grieve personae, with its poet deliberately disrupting poetic unities and aestheticising new ones, which may be the most fruitful basis for the next stage of MacDiarmid criticism. That criticism should use as many different approaches and theories as possible, even if that means blind alleys and chasing wild geese. MacDiarmid's declaration of being 'whaur extremes meet' is also testimony to the power of being creatively wrong.

David Stenhouse

Tearing Up The Bracken

Scottish Highlanders: A People and their Place, James Hunter, £14.99; *The Claim of Crofting: The Scottish Highlands and Islands 1930-1990*, James Hunter, £14.99, both Mainstream; *Scottish Voices 1745-1960*, T. C. Smout & Sydney Wood, £6.99; *A Search for Scotland*, R.F.Mackenzie, £4.99, both Fontana.

With recent moves by crofters in Assynt to buy and manage the North Lochinver estate co-operatively, things in the north seem to be stirring. If we can get out of the historic snare of landlordism it will be nothing short of a miracle. These two books by James Hunter are a great contribution to the liberation. *The Claim of Crofting* makes a historical and political case for crofting, which as he points out is an alien and oppressive creation. History is a strange thing. That "dealing" with the Highlands, as successive governments have tried to do, should come back and haunt these same governments would seem ludicrous, but it is certainly now the case.

I found *Scottish Highlanders* a very moving book – I guess that's because I'm a Caithnessian. The thing I like, and which annoys me confoundedly about James Hunter, is that he never seems to come to any conclusions, he just lets the evidence build up so that there can only be one conclusion. Of course it is his, and his skill is that by the end of the book it is ours. I admire that a lot.

Looking at the history of the Highlands there can only be one conclusion as to the use and ownership of land. Hunter's case is unanswerable, except by the Assynt crofters. Nothing positive has happened in the Highlands except what the people themselves have made. Land raids and the Crofters Union are the result of a collective will to resist and survive. There was and is no other option.

As much as *The Claim of Crofting* is a chronicle of destruction and how to survive it, Hunter's other book, *The Scottish Highlanders*, is a reaffirmation of a search and a finding. There is as much inscape, in this book, as there is landscape. For example Skye features in both James Hunter's books as it does in the annals of the Crofting Act of 1886 and its con-

current history. Yet, if I have a criticism of *The Claim of Crofting* it is this: I wonder if Hunter's position on the board of Highlands & Islands Enterprise has modified his views a little. It is certainly the case that *The Claim of Crofting* is red-hot at the beginning but when we move through time, up until the formation of the Highlands & Islands Development Board and its transmogrification into the HIE, things get, shall we say, diplomatic.

This is important for this reason: the HIE is shortly to disappear; and whatever half-baked notions of social conscience the HIDB had will go with it. In the Highlands & Islands of the 1990s we will have 10 Local Enterprise Companies. These LECs are unaccountable quangos serving the interests of the moneyed class, of hoteliers, rich farmers and various and dubious entrepreneurs. £millions have been filched from the taxpayer in order to spend it on the board members of these LECs and make them even richer. This is the price the Highlands will pay for free enterprise. This is John Major's Highlands, corrupt and pitiful; and it is alien. James Hunter's two books offer an alternative to this state capitalist corruption. But something in Assynt stirs. If the North Lochinver Crofters Trust is successful then we can break landlordism. If they fail we remain in the dark ages. I just wish Hunter would stop being so soft on the current breed of bureaucratic piranhas. His arguments are strong. Both these books are essential reading for anyone who wants to know anything about the Highlands. History is in the blood. History, in Assynt, is tomorrow.

One thing is certain: the Highlands are *not* about tourism. The north is about people living on and from the land, with a little help from the greedy sea. This relationship is ancient and profound and cannot be tampered with. Tourism is a cancer and it destroys what it brings people to see. I fear desperately for the north, as does Hunter. His two books are more eloquent than anything I can say. Read them, I beg you, read them.

Highlands people are the basis of success if the Highlands are to survive as a working society and these same people, along with others the breadth of the land, are the genius behind *Scottish Voices 1745-1960*, put together by T.C. Smout and Sydney Wood.

The voices in this book are brilliant. There is a wonderful and graphic description of a ship in the Aberdeenshire village of Whiterashes. Also, in 'A Comfortable Life' (What's that, cries a voice from Lochinver) there is a fascinating description of the preparation of a meal in a townhouse in Edinburgh *circa* 1840. It made me very hungry.

These things are valuable; but what I object to is the political assumptions behind this book. Chapter 3 begins: "Increasing wealth and confidence, after Culloden, that peace had at last arrived in Scotland, encouraged the well-to-do to provide themselves with spacious new homes." Tell that to Highlanders who found themselves on a leaky, cholera-infested bucket halfway across the Atlantic. Space? There was plenty behind *them*. Peace did not "arrive" in the Highlands, it came on the end of a bayonet. But I still recommend this book simply for the "voices", even though there is a lot of twaddle in between. Fortunately academics, by quoting people in their place of work and in their time, cannot rewrite history, much as they may like to.

The beginning of R.F. Mackenzie's book, *A Search for Scotland*, is quite the most heartfelt description of Aberdeenshire I have read. Behind all these words there is a huge love. Outwith the Borders, which is also very vivid, the rest of the book is a bit sketchy. But what does come out of this book is a very uplifting pedagogy. Mackenzie's Aberdeenshire is a place of light and wonder; it is a delight to read. I have a feeling he discovered Scotland very early on in his life. Perhaps that is the curse of the Scottish writer, we never know where we are until we've left.

These books have one thing, love, in common. To see Scotland now in her sad place in Europe is not to recognise her. But crying isn't enough, and this brings me back to North Lochinver. The Assynt Crofters are offering us a glint through the mirk. Grief is like bracken. It can be weeded. It takes a lot of work and even more purpose. We have to put our grief and our anger behind us. We have to make this country work, we have to make her free. Read these four good books, and then perhaps we can start to pull the bracken out by the roots. It's hard. It is very hard.

George Gunn

Poetry From Galliard and Akros

Shorter Scottish Poems, ed Ruth McQuillan, £6.95; *Twenty of the Best - A Galliard Anthology of Contemporary Scottish Poetry*, ed Duncan Glen, £5.95; *August Morning on Tweed - Selected poems*, Deric Bolton, £7.95; *Dundee Doldrums*, W N Herbert, £4.95; *Selected Poems*, Duncan Glen, Akros £6.95.

Shorter Scottish Poems edited by Ruth McQuillan contains poems and songs from the 14th to 20th century. Poems range from Mark Alexander Boyd's sonnet 'Fra bank to bank...' to one of Sorley MacLean's, to Eimhir, 'Camhanaich' or 'Dawn'. Songs from 'The Flowers of the Forest' to 'Freedom Come All Ye'. Each work is paired with a page of analysis which examines rhyme schemes, scansion, meaning and context. Despite this didactic burden the text is both informed and funny, illuminating and enthusiastic. Both scholars and teachers will discover, in this slim volume, a refreshing primer. One might, as a poet first rather than a technician, quibble about selection. Soutar's 'The Gowk' instead of 'The Tryst' for example. But I guess the poems, 53 in all, have been chosen as the best vehicles for dissection rather than appreciation. MacDiarmid is represented by the 'Emis Stane', but given the quality of his lyric, where technique and meaning are so effortlessly married, a wheen mair from *Sangschaw* or *Penny Wheep* could easily and justifiably have been included.

One of Duncan Glen's selection criteria for Galliard's *Anthology of Contemporary Scottish Poetry* is that the works do not appear in Robin Bell's recent anthology *The Best of Scottish Poetry*. Readers may recall the stuishie roosed by Bell when in the introduction to his volume he lamented not the lack of Lallans, saying, "...Lallans, begotten of Jamieson's dictionary with its tabular juxtapositions of words from different centuries and regions, was always too artificial to be an effective means of communication with the average reader". Glen counter-attacks: "That good poetry can be written in any language, and by any mixture of language spare, baroque or in between is surely so obvious that it should not require restating. And the intention here is to confirm the excellent variety in style, form and vocabulary which Scottish writers have achieved in full measure, in spite of efforts made in some quarters to have them draw in their horns, or cast another glance south..." So we have the Skye and South Uist Gaelic of Maoilis Caimbeul and Meg Bateman. The Dundonian of Fitt, Herbert and Ellie McDonald. Alexander Hutchison's Buchan. The Glesca of McIlvanney and Leonard. And the so-called standard English of Abbot, Rose and Turnbull amongst others. "Scotland small?" At least not linguistically. But the lover of tetrameters and iambics might look hard for satisfaction in this volume. Perhaps we are not as stylistically various as the editor would have us think?

In *August Morning on Tweed - Selected Poems by Deric Bolton,* nature is a recurrent theme. 'August Night' paints a Samuel Palmer nightscape. The short staccato lines create an almost hypnotic quality which leads from the sensual experience of nature to the abandonment of self, and then to oneness with the world. Again in 'June Wood at Sunset' the author evokes the magical quality of a midsummer night's dream with a lyrical hymn to nature. 'When I was young in Perthshire' portrays an acute sense of youthful identification with the landscape. Elsewhere he explores themes of human relationships, class and society. 'A girl in blue' is a sharp cameo of a latterday Betjeman heroine, or rather her overpowering south east English accent. Here the author's humanity is tinted with humour in his description of "that tiny, very noisy very London transistor of a girl in blue". In 'A Memory of 1935: the Piccadilly Tube' he skilfully delineates love, memory and a feeling of loss in an evocative glimpse of an incident on the underground, drawing the reader into the scene with a few well-chosen word-pictures. This is another recurrent theme which contrasts with the permanent and fundamental qualities of nature. The ambitious 'Outside Saughton Prison' speaks of original sin – the inevitable artificiality of man's society. Here he tackles the contradiction between universal human aspirations which by their very existence, diminish the possibilities of achievement.

At last: *Selected Poems* by Duncan Glen, instead of hunting around in anthologies and magazines. These are mostly poems of recollection. The poet trying to reassemble the prospect of himself in the past by writing a form of diary. For me the photograph on the back says it all. The poet, a long thin man, his back to the camera, a dark foreground to the bright garden he seems sadly to survey through the window of his study. We do not know for sure, we do not see his eyes.

These appear to be simple poems with an easy, elegant language and rhythm; but they permeate like Lanarkshire drizzle, speaking of a dead father, a lost youth and love for his wife. Glen has problems trying to make a unity of Scotland. In 'The Hert of Scotland' he has travelled the length of the land, knows the facts about each region, but feels he has never really known the land and its people. In 'The Gullion' there is a distortion, like a sheet of old glass, between the perceptions of youth and those of maturity. "Time's gane oot and we haw snibbed the door" he says in another poem. One night, in 'The Hert of the City' he is advised by four unfortunates – one with a bleeding head – below Glasgow's Highlandman's Umbrella, "ye shouldnae be here by yersel". Thank God this poet is.

Dundee Doldrums by W N Herbert is a series of 22 pieces of automatic writing occasioned as the author explains, by experience of the places the poems describe. In this case 22 places in Dundee – not that this presents any problems to those unfamiliar with the city, for as the poet says "These Doldrums ur fraw ivry town in Scoatlan - Inglann tae, or onywherr". The universal through the backdoor of the particular, in other words. They are forged in an alloy (R Bell tak heed) of urban speech remembered from childhood, and some unashamed dictionary-trawling when necessary. There seems nothing wrong in trying to reassemble an adult tongue whose roots were torn up in childhood. Let us judge the flower by the sound it makes. And sound indeed is the primary concern of these poems. It is perhaps both their strength and their weakness. Meaning, as the author himself admits, falls between Garioch's urban poetry and an aggressive Tom Leonard persona.

John Murray

Just Another Cultured Year in Dublin

O commemorate me with no hero courageous
Tomb - just a canal-bank seat for the passer by.

The poet Patrick Kavanagh died in Dublin, November 1967. On the following St Patrick's day 18 people moved in somewhat stately fashion from McDaid's pub to a concrete seat at the edge of the Grand Canal on the south side of the city. The poet had got his wish. Poets, publicans, politicians, artists, their offspring trying to drown a three-legged dog, artisans and trade-unionists made up the original motley. Short speeches were made; drinking was resumed.

Since then this liquid pilgrimage has become a cultural part of every year for a select few. Necessity fuelling invention for the dry moments during the extended closing hours on the national holiday.

This was the paradoxical essence of Dublin during its designated year as European City of Culture. Incorporation rather than innovation marked the signposted moments. On March 17th 1991 the poet Macdara Woods faced up to the Culture question when he spoke at Kavanagh's seat. He quoted the artist Patrick Collins who, asked to respond to an incoming "foreign" exhibition, exploded: "What do we need with more Culture? Haven't we too much Culture? Too much Culture of our own! Isn't that what's wrong with us? Too much Culture!"

Dublin's Year as "European Capital of Culture" started in March and ended in November (a Pavarotti concert apart). Taoiseach Charles Haughey opened the eight-month year with a coded message of political ecumenism. He recalled how Belfast poet Louis MacNeice had "vividly conveyed a long and turbulent history which gave us the city we know today":

> Fort of the Dane,
> Garrison of the Saxon,
> Augustan capital
> Of a Gaelic nation
> Appropriating all
> The alien brought.

Several days later this hidden agenda of cross-border fertilisation went public. President Mary Robinson handed over the £4,000 Christopher Ewart-Biggs Memorial Award to the Directors of Belfast's *Blackstaff Press*, who, said the President, "have been producing books, often under the most difficult of circumstances, which have genuinely added to a greater understanding between the peoples of Ireland and Britain."

Incorporating cultures for change became central to the unwritten text for the year. The appointment of Garry Hynes as new Artistic Director at the Abbey Theatre was typical of the new breath of change. She is the first female appointed to this position. A traditional "Culchie", Hynes was, like the new President, reared in the west of Ireland. In 1975 she helped to set up Galway's *Druid Theatre Company*, which in a few years rocked the Irish theatrical establishment and shook the cultural dictatorship of the capital. Her sparse, bare, skeletal production of O'Casey's *The Plough and the Stars* was followed by a magnificent *Hedda Gabler*, directed by Deborah Warner and starring Fiona Shaw. These productions ensure that the Abbey, though mugged by the near commercial past can still plan for a feisty future.

1991 marked the 75th anniversary of the 1916 Easter Rising. The government announced that there would be "a short and dignified ceremony involving a reading of the Proclamation (of Independence) and the hoisting of the National Flag". It was fashionably revisionist in its brevity. A lack of political nerve pervaded the non-event; a far cry from the parades, pageants and political opportunism that marked the 50th anniversary commemoration in 1966.

There was pageant in the nearby GPO on Easter Sunday 1991, however. "The politicians had reckoned without the poets" said publican Tom Smith, who combines pulling pints with being the "token layman" on the Directorship of *Poetry Ireland*. This is an organisation of glorious intent if occasional disarray, more of which later. Smith joined the throng that assembled when the politicians had finished their sanitised tributes. Then, poets and writers occupied for six hours the space inside the GPO that had seen the most concentrated fighting in 1916. Based on the idea that many of the leaders had been poets, organiser John Stephenson invited over 80 writers to speak from two podiums set up inside the building. Dubliners came in to buy their commemorative stamps and stayed to listen. In the background, artist Robert Ballagh had screens set up with film footage of the original fighting flickering across. Writers came from the North – Michael Longley, Seamus Deane, Gerald Dawe among others – and the South: Brendan Kennelly, Eilean Ni Chuilleanain and Pearse Hutchinson led a large non-Dublin contingent. All read from their own work and in some cases the words of the Insurrectionists. Both Irish languages were heard from writers of both genders. The 90-year-old novelist and poet Francis Stuart, who remembered celebrating the original event found it "a rewarding, indeed redeeming occasion where and when words revealed resonances historians and politicians ignore at their peril".

Also among the throng was Theo Dorgan, poet and Director of *Poetry Ireland/Eigse Eireann* (funded by both Belfast and Dublin Arts Councils, and active throughout the 32-county island organising readings and publishing the quarterly *Poetry Ireland Review*. In a basement in Dublin's Upper Mount St. it also maintains the 6,000 volume library of the late Austin Clarke, bought on behalf of the nation). In 1989 Dorgan and Gene Lambert of *Clashganna* (a community based group dedicated to the provision of resources and facilities for the disabled and their families) had produced a limited edition of illustrated poems by Paul Durcan.

From that was born the idea of *The Great Book of Ireland*. Poets and composers were invited to write directly onto its vellum page; an artist was invited to respond. The idea "mushroomed". It was to be "a dialogue between the communities of poets and artists on the island". Michael Longley slipped in an "appreciative marginalia" to celebrate the election of Mary Robinson as first woman President of the Republic in the south. A south where, as Brendan Kennelly says, "there is a conflicting oneness" among writers. It eventually incorporated the work of 140 poets, 8 composers and 120 artists. Kennelly talks of this participation as "making whole the physical and imaginative element in every poet; making a mark."

"The *Great Book* is a priceless and unexpected artefact". The words are those of Lewis Clohessy, Chief Executive of *Dublin 91*. He was necessarily modest about his aims for the abbreviated year. £4.7M is petty cash compared to the sums allowed to Glasgow and Madrid. He was, however, delighted to "appropriate" an additional £4M from the regional section of the EC for "the refurbishment of the Temple Bar Area of the city". What was once a narrow lane, darkened by permanently delayed buses, is to become "a vibrant left-bank riverside village of studios, galleries and rejuvenated bars and cafes". This projected scheme, still to see fruition never mind conclusion, held Clohessy's "pride of place in the year's proposed achievements; it will last, endure, excite and create a centre of cultural tourism for generations to come." In the face of such optimism and enthusiasm, criticism seemed churlish.

***

Unfortunately at this juncture one must pause to sound a note of caution, to counteract the optimism, break through the cosmetic façade draped over the city during the artificially designated year.

Though born a Dubliner and having spent most of my formative years there I have since the '60s lived in number of other cities and within other cultures. I recognise the truth but question the present-day relevance of Daniel Corkery's maxim that Irish literature in order to be considered truly indigenous must deal with the problematic themes of land, religion and nationalism. To some this means Big House and Small Hovel novels, pietistic verse announcing lapsed faiths or prejudice-enhancing polemic, or dramas full of bog, verbal fog and dirges. Now, I believe, it should mean an examination of urban and rural conjunctions rather than contradictions and a questioning of social certainties. It could be a time for the introduction of secular verity and its sacred virtue of commonsense. I would like to see and hear the removal of religious imperatives all over the island and as a professional man of literature I feel this can be the business of writers.

Within Dublin over the last ten years there has been a movement towards such integration. But there is a confusion that this will require rejection of the past as some outdated and obsolete heritage that imprisons us. Heritage is not tradition. And it is on tradition that we must build: a country for "new thinking" where Gael, Planter and Dissenter can be one in a Republic of minds.

There have been signals that such ambition is more than idealistic nonsense; unfortunately it has been most in evidence in a Dublin that is disintegrating both geographically and aesthetically. A city of dispersed communities. The sprawling suburbs and the neglected city squares are evidence of social defeat.

This is the city I walked and drove through over many visits in 1991. A dead city of bleak nights. Outside the cosy companionship of pub and theatre there was a desolation that made me blink. The run-down, dreary night-spots were evidence of a new "don't care" philosophy. On O'Connell St. the mock-modern artefact celebrating Joyce and "Anna Liffey" was a playground for rent-boys and glue-mouthed dew-eyed girls. It was dispiriting.

I read with interest but fearful empathy Ferdia Mac Anna's essay on modern Dublin and Dublin writers, 'The Dublin Renaissance' (*The Irish Review*, no. 10) hearing echoes of reflected pessimism and despair. His essay gives a vivid account of the new voices who record the vacuum in the city. He believes they have had to battle against a literary heritage. Put simplistically he believes "Joyce had hijacked the city" preventing future literary exploration. I feel that this is to confuse heritage and tradition again. Patrick Kavanagh said something similar thirty years earlier: "Who killed James Joyce?/ I, said the commentator,/ I killed James Joyce/ for my graduation." Mac Anna writes: "*Ulysses* put Dublin into a literary black hole run by deconstructionists and professors for the benefit of High Art students who would one day themselves go on to become deconstructionist." I feel Kavanagh and Mac Anna both in their separate generations distort to suit their particular theses. I followed Mac Anna's argument in the context of *Dublin 91,* hoping to find some light at the end of his discursive tunnel.

It glimmered, but not without shifting a few idiosyncratic roof-falls. He feels that my generation, which left for exiled careers elsewhere or stayed to write in other words and images, were fearful of the Dublin remaining after the excavations of the Joycemen. He goes on to extol those who did stay to stare in the cracked mirror. He praises those who do go on to etch out their visions with sharp shards of "Dirty Dublin Poetic Realism".

The new voices are poets Paula Meehan and Michael O'Loughlin. Novelists such as Roddy Doyle and Dermot Bolger. Playwrights such as Mannix Flynn and Paul Mercier, particularly the latter with his theatre company The Passion Machine. All are fortunate to be coaxed, cajoled and positively criticised by journalists such as Colm Toibin, John Waters and Fintan O'Toole. Personally I find much of the new work grim, unrelenting and less than persuasive but must recognise these authors' unfettered and explosive evocation of new place, new thinking and stark reality. In deference to space, examples from two of these writers must suffice.

In Roddy Doyle's novel *The Commitments* (1986), now a marvellous film, the soul-music fanatic and band leader Jimmy Rabbit initiates a new vision:

The Irish are the niggers of Europe, lads.
They nearly gasped: it was so true.
An' Dubliners are the niggers of Ireland. The Culchies have fuckin everything. An' northside Dubliners are the niggers of Dublin – Say it loud, "I'm black and I'm proud."

Michael O'Loughlin in his poem 'Stalingrad' takes up the spirit of a common alienation:

I was born to the stink of whiskey and failure
And the scattered corpse of the real.
This is my childhood and country
The cynical knowing smile
Plastered onto ignorance
Ideals untarnished and deadly
Because never translated into action
And everywhere
The sick glorification of failure.

***

June 16th 1904 is not only the day that a great horse called Throwaway won the Gold Cup, it is also the day Stephen Dedalus stepped out of *Portrait of the Artist as a Young Man* and met a wandering Jew, Leopold Bloom. Bloomsday is the birthday of the 20th century novel. *Dublin 91* absorbed it into an International Writers Conference. The theme was *Europe and its Legacy.* The platform was a mix of East Europeans, English novelists and Irish poets. Irish- and English-speaking colonialists battled with the translators. Too often stimulating ideas became bogged down in detail. A glorious exception was the poet Paul Durcan: "I am a Dubliner/ For whom Ithaca/ Is Dublin Bay at twilight as I tightened my seatbelt. ...May I, A Dubliner, live always in exile/ In the village of Ringsend between the Drain and the Gut:/ May I lack always a conistent vision of the universe/ When I am saying my poems;/ May I remain always inarticulate/ When I am composing my poems;/ May I belong always to the oral tradition/ Who is a woman keeping her man on his toes:/ She permits him to speak solely from memory."

The European locale of the themes and a local variation came across loud and clear from Dr Brendan Kennelly who, wearing his academic hat, declared "European literature is an extension of the consciousness of the average Irish person". This reader/writer made sense of the Maker's words and heard Italian Ecos among the puns and pensioned monuments when personal moments intruded and the sense of pilgrimage returned. As Joycean scholar Senator David Norris said "All Dubliners are swaddled by Culture."

Behind all of this was the absent figure of another. One Samuel Beckett, reported missing in Paris, 23rd December 1989. He was ever-present in the Autumn of Dublin 1991. The Gate Theatre staged all 19 of his plays. This was a move full of moves of unparalleled bravery. One October Sunday Ireland were playing Australia in the quarter-final of the Rugby World Cup. Outside Landsdowne Road two buses waited for the final whistle. Marked "Beckett". In the centre of the city actor David Kelly delayed his final performance of *Krapp's Last Tape* until all – bewildered and baffled Beckett aficionados, exhausted but enervated theatre-goers and sweaty but elated rugby fans – had settled in:

Perhaps my best years are gone. When there was a chance of happiness. But I wouldn't want them back. Not with the fire in me now. No, I wouldn't want them back.

And we all in the audience knew this was a moment that could never be repeated, never forgotten, ever after.

Almost side by side the usual Theatre Festival unfolded. There was one moment of unique serendipity and serene intellectual pleasure. Novelist John McGahern's much maligned first play, *The Power of Darkness*, was ploughing uneven furrows through the emotional clichés of stage Irish mannerisms. Two landlocked male antagonists are tied to each other by a length of rope. One wants to hang himself. The other to secure himself to a source of income. The unstated echo of interdependence between Lucky and Pozzo in *Waiting for Godot* was not lost on Dubliners in the audience. With total disregard for spied strangers or the script-tied actors, they buzzed with self-congratulatory recognition.

The newly-opened Writers' Museum at 18 Parnell Square and next-door Irish Writer's Centre was the venue at the end of November for Charles Haughey's launch of the 3 Vol, 4,044 pp *Field Day Anthology of Irish Writing*, his last act both as host for Culture year and as Taoiseach. Seamus Deane's anthology originated in Derry. Its failure to represent Irish Womanhood led to a furious debate that has become a faction-making dispute. There are 21 Editors, all male. Among the 31 Contemporary Poets only three are female. But, as with Blackstaff's award in March this Anthology has fuelled positive contact between North and South, urban and rural, Gael and gauleiter. There was, despite the strident arguments and male bias, a reassuring and continuous urge to communicate . The hidden agenda for change was still relevant. It gave related substance to the cosmetic culture that glittered only in tourist-trade journals. It was an important (if largely unreported) aspect of the year as a whole; it will be the Year's cultural legacy for the future.

***

I re-entered my native city throughout the year and re-emerged renewed. That had nothing to do with the imposed cultural events or the superimposed Culture. It had everything to do with igniting the memory, examining the scars, touching the wounds, and still emerging battered but whole, fusing optimism to light future memories. As a physical exile I mentally returned home. From there I report on just another year in cultured Dublin.

Hayden Murphy

Pamphleteer

In the light of the Government winning a mandate from the English electorate to keep Scotland in the Union, Alasdair Gray's *Why Scots Should Rule Scotland,* (Canongate, £3.00) seems less like an active political intervention and more like another stone on the cairn of Scottish political history:

Publisher: (looking over author's shoulder) Are you not being too historical? Why should modern Scots think their mediaeval history matters today?

Author: Because our Scottish MPs are in the same state as the Scots barons when they had sworn allegiance to the English king.

But even when writing in the "dry, historical way" he planned, Gray is able to make his theme interesting and accessible, keeping it surprisingly free of party bias.

Gray examines the status of Scottish culture as distinct from the English tradition, arguing that "a poor government need not stop a small independent country having a rich culture, and that a wealthy government does not always help the culture of a large one."

The one suspect piece of historiography in Gray's account deals with the Reformation. The Reformation in Scotland was a night in which all cows – Catholic, Protestant or otherwise – were black, and so it is rather disingenuous to ask John Knox alone to foot the bill for that part of our heritage. The concept of a "small god in our brain who may sometimes sound like John Knox or a local schoolteacher" makes for excellent fiction, but is of doubtful historical provenance.

Knox's *History*, with its passionate struggle between logic and conviction, can be counted as a model for Gray's pamphlet: the author's voices include "dry" history, personal reminiscence and excited declamations which are clipped in mid-flight by his publisher's desperate appeals that he cut the rhetoric and have a cup of tea. As well as enlivening the narrative, Gray's device of having his publisher interrupt and challenge his views helps break up the horror of the historical content as Scotland stumbles from one disaster to another. Gray manages to fit a fair selection into a short space: from Edward the Hammer to the Darien scheme and the Act of Union,

through the Clearances down to the Labour Party's sellout of socialism and collusion with the government in frustrating national democracy.

Gray argues that though "a new Scottish parliament will be squabblesome and disunited... it will offer hope for the future". Unfortunately, as the recent election has shown, Gray's vision of a land "where Scots mainly live by making and growing and doing things for each other" will be frustrated as long as the soul of Scottish justice is tied to the dying animal of British imperialism.

The tone of much recent English poetry has been one of revulsion from the cultural atrophy of modern society and a longing for a fictional wholeness. Such is the theme of Dave Sowerby's collection *Red Hat and No Drawers* (National Poetry Foundation (NPF), £4.50). 'Monumental Arrogance' is a heartfelt cry against the claims of modernity which Sowerby rejects as "...foulness, waste,/ built as a monument/ to our arrogant technology". Cut adrift from the decencies of the past the poet is confronted by an angry, uncertain England, exclaiming "I see the future and it hurts!"

Elizabeth Bewick's *Heartease* (Peterloo Poets, £5.95) is in much the same vein; in 'Sunday Train'

an excessively English Sunday moves beyond our reach, and we are moved to talk about the pattern of the past

Such intuitions contrast strongly with the domestic familiarity of 'Buttons' or 'Kitchen Cantata' which demonstrate Bewick's feeling for the "small memorabilia of the heart".

Michael Laskey's *Thinking of Happiness* (Peterloo Poets, £5.95) finds similar inspiration in the quiet rhythms of domesticity. From anniversaries to bereavements his observations are tender and insightful; 'Herring', an elegy for his father, is the strongest piece.

Norman Griggs' best work (*Sharp-eyed and Wary*, NPF, £4.50), is his ironic commentary on the glibness of bourgeois decency:

But now that anarchy is half-installed we gaze across the ruins and discover we have nothing to put in their place.

The dirty-postcard-in-verse 'A Traveller's Tale'" similarly ends with the splendid motto

"Remember such indignities/don't happen in Southend".

Angrier, more assured, is Bill Littlewood's *Of Silver Spiders* (NPF, £4.50). He continues the theme of decline and "the tardiness/of current aspirations"; 'Late Century credo' declares the death of England: "Sod your tomorrows;/ England is finished/ the cancer of greed's/ knocked the old bugger out!"

In a similar vein, Cliff Forshaw's 'Land of Hope and Glory' (*Esau's Children,* NPF, £4.50), questions "the bitter cost/of Dunkirk spirit in foreign ports" and ends

now that the sun's already set – thank God! – upon an empire coloured pink,
we'll sing the blues and kiss the market's rod, and seek out psychic balm in drink.

In Tony Roberts' *Flowers of the Hudson Bay* (Peterloo Poets, £5.95) it is refreshing to see a modern poet have a powerful and *true* relationship with the past. Roberts' past encompasses the Classical Age, Shakespearean England and the American Civil War. There is an equally wide range of voice, from the humour of 'Spirit of Place' to the tender pathos of 'Call': "Let's bury deep in books/ our separation, praying/ the truths that we find there/ will help to heal the wounds." This is a very strong collection from a poet who promises much in the future.

Out from Beneath the Boot (Neruda Press, £2.95) is an impressive and entertaining collection of verse in Scots and English by largely unpublished writers. The strength of editor Bobby Christie's selection lies in its variety; covering flu, sex, unemployment and old age. Two poems stand out; Johnny Duffy's 'Multicultural Education' and Brendan Cleary's magnificent study of ageing cynicism 'Peter Pan on Acid'.

Kay Bourne's *Now and Again* (Stockbridge Press) covers familiar territory: the violence of industrial progress, the absurdity of contemporary life and so on, yet she finds time to satirise the crass romanticism of the outsider's view of the North of England; 'Return to the North – Oldham' and 'The Inhabitants of Manchester' pile cliché upon cliché; "chimneys, bricks and smoke", brass bands etc. Such a strategy deconstructs the Victorian fantasy of England so many modern poets have been keen to articulate.

The anthology of gay poetry *Take any Train* (The Oscars Press, £4.95) bears out editor Peter Daniels' commitment to "negotiate the shared experience, the common ground that goes with these texts". Intelligent, technically accomplished verse is here the rule rather than the exception and the publishers can feel confident that this collection stands examination as good and important poetry. Christopher Whyte's sensitive translations from Gaelic deserve special mention; 'Hope' (*'An Dochas'*) stands out as an expression of desire denied, directed as much at the forces of Capital as at those of homophobic repression.

In *Anither Music,* (Vennel Press, £4.99) W N Herbert makes a determined and intelligent attempt to expand the limits of Scots poetry. 'Mappamundi' is a humorous "poetic map o thi warld" satirising the closed parochiality of contemporary English literature. Herbert's Scots has an energy and flair reminiscent of Garioch. 'A Chasm' is typical of his sensitive and powerful verse:

That art's anithir airt frae life's
a thocht Eh canna thole –
yi say yi hate me sae, ma luv,
Eh've a callus til ma sowel.

John Dixon's *Scots Baronial* (Polygon, £5.95) tries a wide, sometimes overambitious variety of verse-form. While most of his work is original and challenging, he is most accomplished in his landscape poems, among which the most outstanding are 'Loch Treig' and 'Looking Back on the Kilsyth Hills'.

George Doyle's *A Song for Mr Fixit* (Merlin Books, £4.95) is a frighteningly complex and absorbing tale of terrorism in 70s Ulster. By detailing the planning and accidents which make up a fictional IRA operation Doyle highlights the contradictions and absurdity of the political situation in Ulster, and is able to capture the feeling of unreality an outsider confronts on the streets of Belfast. In his assured handling of a realistically complex plot, and his ability to create sympathetic and believable characters, Doyle raises a number of issues questioning the received histories of both Loyalist and Republican, and highlights the incongruity of a British army occupying a land that all sides acknowledge is not truly British.

Jack Gibson

Theatre Roundup

The big question uppermost in everybody's mind during the recent Edinburgh Festival was how Brian McMaster's very radical programme would work out. In particular, how would the brave and bold move to feature major retrospectives of two highly regarded playwrights, Howard Granville Barker and Jewish-Scot CP Taylor, serve as the cornerstone to the drama part of the Festival.

The critical drubbing received by the CP Taylor plays especially will be, unfortunately, what sticks in most people's minds. *Schippel* was regarded as a satisfying production, well performed by Greenwich Theatre Company, which coped with the subtleties of the play and the music which forms an integral part of it. *Walter* was overproduced by the Dundee Rep, and lost in the cavernous St Bride's, an inimical setting to such an intimate and affectionate play. *The Black and White Minstrels* was poorly served by King's Head Theatre Club, Islington, with a ridiculously overfussy set, naturalism gone mad, which turned this sexual comedy into an inferior *Upstairs Downstairs* without the class politics. Dated though this play is, there are genuine issues here, and none of them came through without being sent up or trivialised by the production.

Alan Lyddiard, previously of Tag and now with the Northern Stage, gave us a very creditable production of *And a Nightingale Sang,* Denise Welsh as the crippled Helen played with notable sincerity and simplicity. David Whitaker as her father, ivory-tinkler George, livened up the production with all those songs you've loved. But I found the play quite unbearably sentimental, and in the end couldn't resist the crack that it seemed to me a cross between the Broons and When The Bo-at Cooms In. However good the production and the actors, there's only so much you can do with such material.

Byre Theatre, St Andrews, doesn't ususaly get a crack of the Official Festival whip, but they put on one of CPT's children's plays, *Operation Elvis,* an incredibly moving little piece about an 11 year old lad who has delusion of being the big EP himself and is severely estranged from his family and in his school environment. His only friend is a tramp who has a way with the pigeons. Until, that is, he meets a spastic girl, and an unusual and crucial relationship develops between these two which enables both to find their individual identities and realise their potential. Trouble was, though, that the Byre production couldn't engage actors who would look credible on the international stage. Maggie Kinloch, rightly in terms of her own operations, mounted a production which could subsequently tour round her TIE outlets in Fife schools, but there are irreconcileable tensions in these two separate agendas.

Most controversial of all, and most severely rubbished by the critics, was Fifth Estate's *The Ballachulish Beat,* which I thoroughly enjoyed. Considering that it predates 7:84's *Cheviot* by about 5 years, this black political fairy-story was much ahead of its time. That it was never produced in the sixties could be easily attributed to the lack of facilities in the corporate body of Scottish Theatre at the time, and the lack of a developed rock music scene, both of which of course now we have. The play was wrongly dismissed as agit-prop, when in reality it is anti-agit-prop, and quite subtly so. The script had never gone through the endless revising that CPT's plays received in the process of production and revival, and needed severer cutting than perhaps Allan Sharpe dared to do. I was incensed, since it is an important play in Scottish historical terms; and also playing to the wrong audience. People were making a snobbish point by walking out: a middle-class rightly offended by the radical politics of the play (although one of the play's main targets is the worst kind of socialist agitators' phoney left-ism). The tragedy is that it is a play which, mounted in the right way and in the right places, should be roundly enjoyed by a wide range of the Scottish theatrical audience. Since it looks unlikely now that this will happen, let me make a plea for someone to revive it, with Dave McNiven's wonderful music - perhaps in Mayfest - or on a tour of community centres and certain reps, like Dundee. Paul Ambrose Wright's set, and indeed the production as a whole, was inventive and fun, and if it hadn't laboured under such a panning, could have risen further still.

The problem was that the plays weren't put

in their proper setting in relation to the broader corpus of CPT's work: unfortunately, not enough of his first-rate work such as *Bread and Butter* was being performed.

But there was one undoubted success: the Tron's production of *Good*. Someone advised me to go to it, urging that I'd never be likely again to see a better production. This advice proved to be accurate. Halder, the central character, was superbly delivered by Conrad Asquith, who showed unnervingly sympathetically how good people are drawn into evil in the most natural way imaginable. The design, of having a series of doors round the back of the stage, representing the different mental compartments of Halder's mind, was stunningly effective; as musicians, Halder's senile mother (played with utter and disturbing accuracy by Edith Macarthur). Michael Boyd's production beautifully caught the subtle movements of the play, and maintained the difficult juxtaposition of humour and tragedy right to the end of the play, bringing out the essential ambivalences. I think this was my Festival Highlight.

There is a great deal in McMaster's retrospectives which is to be applauded. Interestingly, the Granville-Barker plays received similar, but not so severe, critical scepticism. But how good to be able to see seven plays by a Scottish playwright, and the opportunities to discuss the work with experts. How good too to bring such a range of Scottish companies into the body of the kirk, but there is a need for more expert guidance in the selection and administration of the plays, and in making a clearer critical statement in advance as to how these plays relate to the playwright's work as a whole. I certainly had the feeling that the Scottish critics in particular were making their pronouncements with one eye over their shoulder, anxious to be saying things that would earn them respect on the international scene. I rather agreed with Tom McGrath during the Festival Symposium on CPT that the problem had been a critical failure, rather than essentially a failure of the dramas to come up to the mark. How tragic it would be if after this festival people were afraid to utter the words: CP Taylor.

We were of course glad that McMaster paid at least lip service to the MacDiarmid centenary by featuring Tom Fleming's reading of *A Drunk Man Looks at the Thistle*. Apart from this, his first festival deliberately marginalised poetry, one casualty of which was the Saltire Society's programmes, which normally pack St Cecilia's, but this year via the Fringe attracted only a handful. Harp concerts were also affected. Whatever else you may say of Frank Dunlop, one of many welcome and, indeed, courageous innovations he allowed was the presence of Scottish literature at the heart of the official programme. I hope this will change next year as McMaster, having established himself as a radical and innovative director, reappraises his strategy.

Briefly on the Fringe: congratulations to Edwin Morgan's tremendously successful adaptation of *Cyrano de Bergerac* by Communicado, mounted at the Traverse. Using just about every dialect and register of Scots invented, and some that haven't yet, Morgan's richly inventive language was happily matched by the energy and innovation of the production, with a startlingly good performance in the title role. Raymond Ross's new play, *The Haunting of Billy Marshall* at the Netherbow was another instance of Scots being put to original but powerful use in this story of the last hours of Billy, the Gypsy King. And the Tron's hit production of *The Guid Sisters* by Michel Tremblay notched up yet more evidence for the dramatic potential of the mither tongue.

One play which didn't get enough recognition was Clyde Unity's new John Binnie play, *A Little Older*. It covers familiar territory for this company: relationships between homosexual and heterosexual, but did so most movingly here in the story of the painful recovery of Isla, a minister's daughter with more than a passing similarity to a certain Kate the shrew, who is seriously injured in a car accident. Produced and performed incredibly simply, this remained one of the best moments of this year's Fringe. But, finally, on the Fringes of the Fringe, down in the Vaults of Leith, the Scottish Malt Whisky Society was providing the real McCoy in terms both of drink and of song and story in what must be probably the most relaxing way to spend an evening at the Edinburgh Festival Fringe. *Joy Hendry*

Catalogue

Akhter Ahsen's *New Surrealism: the liberation of Images in Consciousness* (Brandon House, $25) cries out for a firm editorial hand. In this MacDiarmid centenary, such a book, challenging in both the depth and breadth of its multidisciplinary vision, a welcome push to "make it new", as "the famous American poet Ezra Pound" demanded, should not be sending one to sleep. Dr Ahsen, psychologist, literary critic, poet entertains, irritates, dazzles and bores in turn. With a sense of humour being a *sine qua non* of surrealism, one wonders, arriving at J H Matthews' 'Lead Commentary on "New Surrealist Manifesto"' which opens by referring to Marinetti, Tzara and Breton's manifestos of 1918/24/29 and then goes straight to Ahsen's, should we be smiling or not?

Kahlil Gibran: his life & world (Canongate, £17.50) essays a definitive biography of the remarkable Lebanese-American author of *The Prophet*, New York avant-gardiste, written by cousin Kahlil Gibran and his wife Jean. Distributed by Nick Hern Books (£7.99) is *The Presence of the Actor* by Joseph Chaikin, champion of American actor-oriented theatre much reminiscent of Peter Brook.

Roaming the world, from Open Letters come *Servants of the Buddha* by Anna Grimshaw (£9.99) is an anthropologist's account of a winter spent among nuns at a Himalayan convent; and *Women and War in South Africa* (£10.99) by Jacklyn Cock, a sociological study based on interview. This is an important book because it ramifies far beyond the locale, bringing together attitudes of "liberal democracy" and third world freedom fighters: the issues surrounding women in combat are profound, not just for women.

Talking of Rome, a selection of Literary Companions from John Murray (£16.95 hb; £11.95 pb). That Francis King's on *Florence* opens with 'Part 1: Visitors' sums the place up, in modern cultural terms. Other titles: *Rome* by John Varriano, *Venice* by Ian Littlewood, and *India* by Bruce Palling. In similar vein, their *Cities of Spain* by David Gilmour (£17.95). But *why*?

Back home, Charles J Smith's *Morningside*, (John Donald, £9.95) includes a before-and-after photo of the Plaza, now Safeway, where a lamppost has remained miraculously unchanged all these years. Morningside, not so much a place as an attitude, maybe has its antonym in Leith, which features extensively, along with the Old Town, in *Thomas Begbie's Edinburgh* (John Donald, £32), a magnificent large-format photo-portrait of mid-Victorian times edited by David Patterson and Joe Rock. The empty streets seem eerily silent, matched to a minimal commentary which lets the pictures to do their job. John T Reid embarked from the selfsame mid-Victorian Leith to write/draw *Art Rambles in the Highlands & Islands* which inspired Mairi Hedderwick's *Highland Journey* (Canongate, £14.95), interspersing JTR's material with the author's own text and colour sketches.

Roughly equidistant from Lewis are Rona to the north, and St Kilda to the west. Charles Maclean's *The Story of St Kilda: island on the edge of the world* is now a Canongate Classic (£5.95) while Michael Robson's *Rona, the Distant Isle* (Acair, £?) tells the story of community precariously established on, and ultimately forced from, this forbidding frontier. Other Canongate Classics: Eric Linklater's *Private Angelo* (£5.95) and *Divided Loyalties* by Janet Teissier du Cros (£6.95): both WWII books, Linklater's novel from his experiences in Italy, and du Cros' account of life in France under the Vichy régime.

I don't know who Cecil Cragg is: his Merlin publication *Roamings* (£8.95) has no biographical note but an apt title. Some attempt to give this collection of critical essays and blusters the kind of order that invites the reader along – aka professional production values – would improve it no end.

Good point to mention *How to Start and Run a Writing & Editing Business* by Herman Holtz (John Wiley, £9.95), a real service-industry guide for the post-industrial age. Refreshing, if nothing else, for being full of American energy. Andrew Crofts' *How to Make Money from Freelance Writing* (Piatkus Books, £12.95) plows a similar furrow, feels a little more practical being UK based, but I prefer Holtz's zest. Also from Wiley (£8.95) comes Paul Dickson's *Word Treasury*. Somewhere between a sub-Bierce *Devil's Dictionary*, thesaurus and dictionary, such notions as "Astrologaster: A lying or deceitful astrologer" are entertaining; the lack of etymology means one risks making a fool of oneself if you use one of these words unwisely.

At the Stirling Writers Weekend earlier in the year Iain Crichton Smith called for novelists to tackle centres of power in modern Scottish fiction. Willing writers might like to consult *The Scottish Government Yearbook 1992* (the first) ed Lindsay Paterson & David McCrone. Published by the Unit for the Study of Government in Scotland, Edinburgh University: perhaps dated already in parts, it includes reports on progress at the Scottish Constitutional Convention. Same willing writers might like to find *Lord Advocate's Diary 1961-66* by Gordon Stott (AUP, £12.95) in their Xmas stocking.

John Nyren Buchanan's manuscript *Crown and Covenant: a Study in Conflict* was discovered in an Edinburgh Printer's in 1976. If not as entertaining as Hogg's *Justified Sinner*, the resulting *Marginal Scotland* (Peter Lang, £?) is an exhaustive study of the Covenanters and their historical context. *Enlightened Scotland* is a 'study and selection of Scottish Philosophical prose from the 18th and early 19th centuries' by Philip Flynn (Scottish Academic Press, £22.50) covering the mind, morals, creativity & aesthetic taste, and society; hopefully a prelude to wider availability of the original texts. In Peter Lang's *Scottish Studies* series comes *Die Schottische Renaissance*, a German-language study of Scottish literature and politics in the 20th century by Susanne Hagemann covering such topics as the background to the renaissance, nationalism, language, thematic undercurrents and so on. Priscilla Bawcutt's *Dunbar the Makar* (Clarendon Press, £50) is a welcome new study focussing on how the poems are *made*.

Mario Vargas Llosa's *In Praise of the Stepmother* (Faber, £4.99) is now available in a beautiful paperback edition; the pages almost pink with the glow of sensuality. From Dedalus in their *Europe 1992* series, which aims to publish translations from all of the eight (official) EEC languages, comes *Architect of Ruins* by Herbert Rosendorfer and *The Black Cauldron* by Faroese writer William Heinesen. Dedalus's previous Meyrink editions are recommendation enough. Tariq Ali's novel *Shadows of the Pomegranate Tree* (Chatto, £14.99) is set in 16th century Spain, dealing with the defeat of the Moors.

Children's books, and 3 Canongate Kelpies: *Alf's Secret War* by Donald Lightwood – are modern 11-yr-olds interested in WWII backdrops? *The Adventures of Endill Swift* by Stuart McDonald (age 9-90) is set in the biggest school in the world, original and funny; *The Green Gang* by Aileen Hunter (age 9+) begins with a school conservation project finding a poisoned buzzard. From Hamish Hamilton comes *So Far From Skye* by Judith O'Neill, set initially in 1852 Skye, and following a family forced to emigrate to Australia, much like O'Neill's ancestors. Duncan Williamson's *Tales of the Seal People* (Canongate, £5.95), West Coast folk tales, will suit children and adults alike.

Three plays from Nick Hern Books, all valuable in different ways: David Edgar's *The Strange Case of Dr Jekyll & Mr Hyde* represents London theatre at its best; *Angels in America* an important new American writer in Tony Kushner. The value of Stephen Sondheim/John Weidman's *Assassins* is that it gives one the opportunity to study a dog.

Carcanet celebrate the centenary of Edna St Vincent Millay with *Selected Poems* (£7.95); an American original, follower of no school. In similar vein, more tangible, less elusive, *First Awakenings: the early poems* by Laura Riding (£14.95). *Thomas Hood: Selected Poems*, ed Joy Flint (£6.95) resurrects a minor poet from the late Romantic/early Victorian period. Still with Carcanet, and much more pertinent, is a collection of recent Octavio Paz essays, *The Other Voice: poetry and the fin-te siècle* (£12.95), reflections on poetry in the modern age.

A couple of limited editions to end with: *Settled Terms: poems 1965-89* by David Summers (Montpelier Press): mellow, toothsome. Finally, Angela Molnos' *Waiting in Wonder* (Circle Press) is the poetry of one forced to leave Hungary by war and subsequent peace, who travelled extensively, became a psychologist, wrote in several languages, but discovered the key to herself in her native language only recently. The result is that these elegant, refined poems are presented here with translations *into* Hungarian. An interesting and unusual collection.

Notes on Contributors

Donald Adamson taught English abroad; now lives in Galloway, writing and editing EFL books. Winner, 1985 Radio Clyde Poetry Prize.
David Angus, b 1925, best known for verse & prose in *The Scots Magazine*; also appeared in *TheLand Out There* and *New Makars*.
Mary Angus, winner of the MacDiarmid Centenary Prize, b Glasgow 1944, now lives in Hong Kong.
Donatella Bisutti lives in Milan. Has won many prizes for her poetry. Those translated here are from *Penetrali* (Boetti & C, 1989).
Sheena Blackhall: North-East poet, short story writer, folk singer and illustrator. Poetry collection *Back o Bennachie* due out in 1993.
Alan Bold's definitive MacDiarmid biography, which won the 1989 McVitie's Prize, is now available as a Paladin paperback.
George Mackay Brown's first novel for 8 years, *Vinland*, is published by John Murray.
George Bruce: b Fraserburgh 1909. BBC producer (1946-70), poet and critic.
Jim Brunton: retired Health Council Secretary. A third-generation Socialist & republican, he writes quiz books with Brian Pendreigh.
Angus Calder: Staff Tutor in Arts at the Open University in Scotland.
Deirdre Chapman: Journalist and writer, lives in Glasgow; married to Michael Grieve.
David Craig: Professor at Lancaster Univ. Recent books *On the Crofters' Trail* (Cape); *The Grasshopper's Burden*, (Littlewood Arc).
Robert Crawford lectures at St Andrews; co-editor, *Verse*. Recent books *Developing English Literature* (OUP) and *Talkies* (Chatto).
Theo Dorgan: Poet, arts administrator, broadcaster, director, Poetry Ireland; Most recent collection *The Ordinary House of Love*.
Robert Maxwell Duncan: b Glasgow 1946, now a TV producer in Newcastle.
Menna Elfyn: former university lecturer, now a full-time poet & playwright. Winner of numerous awards including Welsh Arts Council prize for volume of the year, 1990/91.
Donald C Farquhar lives in Dunblane and works for the Hydro Electric Board.
Rab Fulton: Young Glaswegian poet insisting on his own language.
Jack Gibson lives & works in Kilmarnock; currently thesising on contemporary Scottish fiction at Stirling University.

Valerie Gillies, poet, is presently writer in residence for Midlothian & East Lothian DCs
Sam Gilliland, co-organiser, Scottish International Poetry Competition, is currently translating the poetry of Mario de Sa-Carneiro.
John Glenday was the 1990/1 Scottish Canadian Exchange Fellow.
Stanley Roger Green: b Edinburgh; travelled widely. Books include *A Suburb of Belsen*, *Advice to Travellers*, *Whither O Ship*.
Andrew Greig's first novel, *Electric Brae* has just been published by Canongate. *The Heretical Buddha*, a new collection of poems, due from Bloodaxe in 1993.
Michael Grieve, son of CM, sometime journalist, editor, TV producer, vice-chairman, SNP; has contributed to various books on Scotland and Scotch.
George Gunn, Writer in Residence, Banff & Buchan. His play *Songs of the Grey Coast* is touring the Highlands (Oct-Nov 1992), published (with *Gold of Kildonan*) by *Chapman*.
Hamish Henderson: Honorary Fellow, the School of Scottish Studies, Edinburgh University, where he has worked since its foundation.
J F Hendry (1912-1986) poet, scholar, professor of Russian, founder member, New Apocalypse movement.
W N Herbert: author, *To Circumjack Cencrastus* (OUP 1992) and several vols of poetry. Co-editor *Gairfish*.
John Herdman is a novelist and critic. *Imelda and Other Stories* due from Polygon in 1993.
Brent Hodgson: Born NZ 1945. Awarded SCOTVEC Diploma in Dairy Technology 1986, Johm Coppick Prize 1986, Scottish National Milk and Health Association Medal 1986.
Tom Hubbard, writer & lecturer; librarian, Scottish Poetry Library, co-instigator, Poetry Theatre Scotland. Published in *four Fife Poets* (1988), *The New Makars* (1991).
Jeremy Hughes: poetry & stories in *Verse, Poetry Ireland, Outposts, Planet* and *others*.
Pearse Hutchinson b Glasgow 1927 of Irish parents, now in lives in Dublin. Latest book *The Soul that Kissed the Body* (Gallery, 1990)
Robert Alan Jamieson: currently working on second collection of poetry, fourth novel & Faroese translation thanks to SAC bursary. Most recent novel/poem *A Day at the Office* (Polygon, 1991).

Billy Kay: writer & broadcaster. His play *Lucky Strike* broadcast recently won 1992 Sloan Prize for new writing in Scots.

T S Law: b. 1916 Newarthill; now versifying time away in Auctherarder.

Gordon Legge: currently writer in residence at the Royal Edinburgh Hospital.

Tom Leonard: Leading poet and exponent of Glaswegian idiom.

Frederic Lindsay: novelist and scriptwriter. Latest novel, *After the Stranger Came* (Andre Deutsch, 1992).

Ellie McDonald: First person to take *Chapman* magazine on the GR65

Ian McDonough is a member of the Central Writers' Group; 'Poems & Pints' regular.

Carl MacDougall reviews fiction for the *Herald*, edited *The Devil & The Giro* (Canongate Classics). 2nd novel *The Lights Below* due from Secker & Warburg 1993.

Lorn Macintyre: freelance writer and NUJ member.

Douglas MacKay resides in Glasgow. Poet and co-founder of *PolyPhony* magazine.

Hugh McMillan teaches in Dumfries. 2 collections of poetry, inc *Tramontana* (Dog & Bone)

Aonghas Macneacail, the distinguished Gaelic poet, is among the writers on STV's new Gaelic soap opera.

Ruaraidh MacThomais (Derick Thomson) has edited *Gairm* since 1952. latest collection *Smeur an Dochais/Bramble of Hope* 1992.

Alexander Moffat is head of painting at the Glasgow School of Art.

Edwin Morgan's recent books include *Nothing Not Giving Messages* & *Collected Poems* (1990); *Hold Hands Among the Atoms* (1991).

Stewart Morrison, 29, born in Ayr, studied in Northern Ireland, now lives in Edinburgh.

Hayden Murphy: poet and arts journalist b Dublin 1945.

John Murray, a Borderer, teaches landscape architecture at Edinburgh College of Art.

Thom Nairn edits Cencrastus, is Writer in Residence at Ross & Cromarty.

Timothy Neat: currently completing a film, *Walk Me Home* (with John Berger). A book on the symbolism of C R Mackintosh will be published by Canongate in 1993.

William Neill has recently published excerpts of *The Odyssey* in a Scots translation (Saltire Society, 1992) and *Straight Lines* (Blackstaff).

Tom Pow is 1992/3 Scottish/Canadian Fellow, based at the University of Alberta, Edmonton.

Howard Purdie: Playwright, poet and Border Riever.

Lydia Robb: Winner of first prize & McLellan Tassie for prose, SLS competition 1987. Poetry & prose in various anthologies.

James Robertson works in a Glasgow bookshop. First collection of stories, *Close*, 1991.

Paul Scott, former diplomat, writer on Scottish literature, history & politics. Latest book *Andrew Fletcher and the Treaty of Union* (John Donald).

Tom Scott: Expect to see his *Collected Shorter Poems* in a joint *Chapman/Agenda* publication early next year.

Iain Crichton Smith's *Collected Poems* (Carcanet) and novel *An Honourable Death* (Macmillan) are the most recent of his many writings in Gaelic and English.

David Stenhouse: ex-BBC producer now working on PhD at Edinburgh University.

Ian Stephen: coastguard officer, storyteller, photographer. Author, *Malin Hebrides Minches* (Dangaroo); *Varying States of Grace* (Polygon)

Patrick Toal: currently studying English & Philosophy at Glasgow University.

George Todd: Member of the Clyde Group, now resident in Malaga Province.

Gael Turnbull may occasionally be seen picking up litter around Edinburgh.

Raymond Vettese: Preses of the Scots Language Society, his collection *The Richt Noise* is now available on a Scotsoun cassette.

Roderick Watson: poet & critic, Reader in literature, Stirling Univesrity; writes on modernism in the arts, MacDiarmid & other modern Scottish poets.

Jim C Wilson's collection of poetry *Cellos in Hell* will soon be published by *Chapman*. Stirling District Writer in Residence 1989-91.

Jack Withers, Glaswegian, loves to go a-wandering. Poet-performer no longer on the tools.

Douglas Young: poet and dramatist, translated Gaelic and Greek into Scots.

Malcolm Youngson: "tramping through Europe" for experience. Takes a deep interest in Scottish affairs and literature but this is the first article he has had published.